W9-AXN-589

STUDIES IN THOMISTIC THEOLOGY

STUDIES IN THOMISTIC THEOLOGY

Thomas R. Russman
General Editor

STUDIES IN THOMISTIC THEOLOGY

Editor
Paul Lockey

Associate Editors
Paul Hahn
Janusz Ihnatowicz
John Sommerfeldt

Center for Thomistic Studies
University of St. Thomas
Houston, Texas 77006
1995

Copyright © 1996 by
The Center for Thomistic Studies

All rights reserved. No part of this book may be
used or reproduced in any manner whatsoever without
written permission, except in the case of brief quotations
embodied in critical articles or reviews.
For more information write to
The Center for Thomistic Studies, 3800 Montrose Blvd.,
Houston, Texas, 77006.

Manufactured in the United States of America

Library of Congress Cataloging-in-Publication-Data

Studies in Thomistic theology / editor, Paul Lockey : associate
    editors, Paul Hahn, Janusz Ihnatowicz, John Sommerfeldt.
            p.   cm.
    ISBN 0-268-01755-7 (alk. paper). — ISBN 0-268-01756-5 (pbk. :
alk. paper)
    1. Thomas, Aquinas, Saint, 1225?–1274. 2. Theology, Doctrinal—
History—Middle Ages, 600–1500. 3. Philosophy, Medieval.
I. Lockey, Paul. II. Hahn, Paul, 1949– . III. Ihnatowicz, Janusz
A. (Janusz Artur), 1929– . IV. Sommerfeldt, John R.
BT26.S78   1996   95-51417
230'.2'091—dc20   CIP

CONTENTS

INTRODUCTION

INTRODUCTION

Paul E. Lockey
The University of St. Thomas

Studies in the Theology of St. Thomas Aquinas is composed of articles which gravitate to one of two questions central to the volume: "Who is God and how is it that we speak of God?" and "Who are human beings and how is it that we speak of them and their destiny?" It might be said that these two questions are fundamental to human experience. Certainly, they are the fundamental questions in the sweeping domain of Thomistic theology and philosophy. Hence, each article here seeks to address a particular issue in one of these two areas of theological and philosophical concern. Whatever question addressed, each author brings to the discussion his or her own insights into the issue of Thomism at hand. They are insights that have as their horizon not only a text or texts and the topic, but also the willingness to bridge the different horizons of philosophy and theology.

No theology can be argued successfully outside the parameters of philosophy, even if one of the textual horizons of theology is "revealed" scripture. Philosophy, in a strict sense, often tends to be suspicious of such scripture that claims as its source divine revelation. Without the parameter of philosophical discipline, theology is mere opinion with an unconvincing appeal to "revelation." Each article seeks to discover some theological insights within the wider parameters of revealed scripture or doctrine within the wider parameters of revealed scripture or doctrine while utilizing the definitive parameters of philosophy. Indeed, authors chosen were those who concentrated on the utilization of rational exegetical methodology rather than the more speculative or dogmatic methodologies specific to a particular religious opinion. Given these parameters of the book, it seemed wise to begin this volume with articles on thomistic methodology.

In his "Toward Understanding Aquinas' Theological Method: The Early Twelfth-Century Experience," Romanus Cessario, O.P., states that his aim is to provide what he considers critical background information for the study of Aquinas' theological methodology, as distinct from his philosophical methodology. Cessario organizes his material within the view that the "new" scholastic methods of demonstration and syllogism and the more dialectical characteristic of twelfth-century theology were primary to Thomas in his reading of Scripture, Church doctrine and dogmatics, and controversial theological opinion. We are taken on the grand tour of eleventh- and twelfth-century theological Europe, from the rise of sentential literature to the development of the *Summa* and its attendant theological enterprises.

Mark Jordan, in his "Aquinas' Middle Thoughts on Theology as 'Science,'" asks whether or not the discovery of the *reportatio* of Thomas' second or Roman commentary on the *Sentences* teaches us anything "new." In particular, he focuses on the sequence of Thomas' own texts leading up to the *Summa* and asks whether or not the new text alters debates regarding the meaning of Thomas's other texts leading to the *Summa*? The structural and sequential implications of Jordan's article coupled with the sequential tour of Cessario's article enhance the landscape for critical readers of Thomas, especially regarding the *Summa theologiae*.

Forming a bridge from methodology to ontology is William Dunphy's *Maimonides, Aquinas, and Theologism*, an investigation of the medieval necessity of constructing a philosophical world view that did not compromise the traditional Jewish-Christian-Islamic faith in a personal God with the Aristotelian concept of an unmoved mover. As Dunphy correctly notes, it was Etienne Gilson who first called this medieval need to reconcile religious faith and Greek reasons "theologism." Dunphy considers two "theologisms," then presents the subsequent responses of Maimonides and Aquians. His reiteration of "Bad philosophy never makes good theology" is an apt caution for contemporary investigations of Thomas' theological efforts as well as contemporary efforts to theologize from Thomas' theology.

In his *The Theological Character of St. Thomas' Five Ways*, Mark Johnson proposes that Thomas's ways are not only rationally probable proofs for the existence of God. Rather, the five ways have a logic internal to the arguments themselves which point the personal God of Abraham rather than the rational god of Athens. The integral logic delineated in Johnson's article rests upon the context of both the teaching and the genre of the literature from which Thomas drew the nominal definition of God.

Thérèse-Anne Druart in her *Averroes on God's Knowledge of Being Qua Being* considers the question of God's knowledge as equivocal to human knowledge, along with the attendant issues of God's knowledge as particular and universal, and his knowledge of being qua being as knowledge at all. Druart insightfully uses a dual comparison between Averroes and Thomas alongside contemporary commentators in discussing the equivocacy of divine and human knowledge and its attendant issues in order to place herself in a position to draw out the distinction between knowledge of being qua being as neither universal nor particular and knowledge of being qua being as superseding any distinction between particular and universal.

Kevin White, *Aquinas on the Immediacy of the Union of Soul and Body*, discusses Thomas's view of the immediacy of the union of soul and body, while clarifying similarities and differences between Thomas's own position and those found in his sources, as well as other more philosophically adversarial views. White gives a comprehensive background to the question of "intermediaries between body and soul," particularly regarding Thomas's commentary on Lombard. He outlines Thomas's development from early investigations to his position in the *Summa contra gentiles* of the "union of body-soul," as "the soul as form of the body." Continuing, the reader is shown the further broadening and developing notions of Thomas' ideas in his more mature works, such as in *Quaestio disputata de spiritualibus creaturis*. An important turn in Thomas's consideration of the body-soul union vis-a-vis the whole individual rather than the soul alone. Hence, his consequential position in the *Summa theologiae* and in *Sentencia libri de anima*, where he maintains his most mature position on the question of the immediacy of the soul to the body as the form of the body, is that the body-soul union is an immediate union without intermediaries. White's contribution is a rigorous reading of texts dealing with the soul-body union. It is a union necessary for the human person to be theologically a whole person, as many modern pseudo-neoplatonic views of anthropology over emphasize the distinction between soul and body to such an extent as to endanger the physical aspects of the resurrected body and its experience of the beatific vision.

In Pamela Reeve's "Exploring a Metaphor Theologically: Thomas Aquinas on the Beatific Vision", we move from White's anthropological theme to that of eschatology. Reeve turns an eye to the visual metaphors Aquinas uses to characterize the beatific vision. She further examines Aquinas's theory of human knowledge in light of the beatific vision as intellectual.

Reeve maintains that Thomas moves the tradition discussion from the more sensorial notion of "seeing" to the more noetic notion of "knowing," by which the beatific vision is known more "immediately," that is, not by means of something else. The essence of what is known of God is joined to the intellect without intermediary or intermediaries. Because of the materiality of their essence, material things cannot be "seen" immediately. God, however, is immaterial, and thus necessitates a different form of knowledge.

Reeve contrasts ordinary human knowledge to the beatific vision, elucidating Aquinas's view that the beatific vision is not knowledge about God, as creation might be known, but is knowledge of God. This unitive knowledge is caused by a divine mode of the intellect itself, making the rational creature "deiform." The natural intellect undergoes a change in its condition so as to know immateriality. Yet, the transformation is not so radical as to render the natural knower a totally different thing. As Reeve explains Aquinas, this presence of divine essence does not destroy human nature or cause its assimilation into God, because the "deiform" is caused by God becoming the accidental and not the substantial form of the intellect.

For Aquinas, the intellect is enabled by God to "see," as it were, the divine essence by its elevation according to a supernatural disposition. By the elevation of the mind by a supernatural disposition, Thomas seeks to avoid claiming a true change of the human intellect into something of a difference in kind. Beatitude does not destroy but perfects the nature of a thing. By analogy, Reeve illustrates "how the human intellect can acquire a form that is proper to a higher nature." She concludes with Thomas's thoughts that though metaphors are appropriate to an understanding, one must not set one's sights on merely the material realm.

Following Reeve's inquiry into Thomas's understanding of beatific epistemology, William Dunphy in "Maimonides and Aquinas on Faith, Reason, and Beatitude" likewise examines beatific epistemology from a different interrogative angle: What is the condition for knowledge of God in the beatific vision? Dunphy echoes Reeve's claim that Thomas advocates an elevation of the basic nature of the human intellect to "see" God by the divine addition of grace. Dunphy, however, asks what is the condition in which one is gifted with the beatific vision by comparing Maimonides and Aquinas on the issue.

Maimonides in his *Guide for the Perplexed* suggests a hierarchy of the knowledge of God in the beatific vision. It is a knowledge tiered and ascended according to one's pursuits in speculative metaphysics. The lowest stage is for those who obey the law but do not probe its depths. The highest stage is for those who not obey only the law, understand its reasoning, including by way of logic, and investigate cosmological philosophy, but who pursue also the speculative questions of ontology.

Aquinas, on the other hand, as understood primarily in his *Summa contra gentiles*, maintains that God grants the beatific vision to whomever He wishes, since the nature of man prevents self-attainment of knowledge of God's essence. Thus, it might seem that the two positions are irreconcilable.

Dunphy suggests that while there are differences between Maimonides's self-attained ascension to the vision of God and Aquinas's populist position of grace, regardless of intellectual insight, presenting the vision of God, the similarity is more striking. Both reject humanistic philosophy as a means to attain the beatific vision. Indeed, the point of coincidence regarding the two is the necessity of revelation, though Aquinas understands it in Christian terms whereas Maimonides speaks of it in Jewish terms. The apparent distance between Aquinas and Maimonides is bridged by the common road whereon the journey to God involves not only virtue, morality, and philosophy, but most importantly, the revelation by God of his will.

The beatific vision and the contemplation of God therein by the human intellect form the horizon on which David Gallagher meditates on the differences between Thomistic moral thought and Abelardian intentionalism. Gallagher in his "Aquinas, Abelard, and the Ethics of Intention" considers the aspects of intention, consent, and choice of the "internal forum" and the acts or deeds of the "external forum," revealing in what way Thomas avoided the Abelardian position.

For Abelard, sin in no way lies in the deed or the performance of the deed. Rather, sin lies in the consent (intention) of the will to the deed. Nothing of the body alone is able to cause sin in the soul. Thus, if all acts were committed without consent of the will, there would be no vile deeds. Abelard contends that since all we can judge are external acts, then we cannot truly judge sin, because no one but God can look into the heart of a person and know whether or not that person truly consented to act and, hence, to what degree a sin was committed.

Thomas, on the other hand, defines a properly human act, or moral act, as an act arising from reason and will. An act is done within the person's control, both interiorly and exteriorly. In contrast to Abelard, Thomas distinguishes the parts of a human act without separating willing and acting.

Exteriorly, a human act is either natural or moral--natural insofar as the material external act constitutes a certain kind of action-moral insofar as the material, external act carries out a chosen act of the will. Abelard, alternatively, seeks to relegate all moral acts to the realm of natural acts, separating the will's intent from the exterior act altogether, as might be done on the occasion of ignorance.

Thomas does not stop with the unitive aspect of the interior will and exterior act, but proceeds to define an exterior act as in itself good, bad, or indifferent, and whether or not it tends toward human fulfillment. For Thomas, the interior will's choice of a specific act draws its morality from the morality of the exterior act as understood by reason and not as actually performed. In contrast to Abelard's position, Thomas maintains that the exterior act does indeed specify, not efficiently cause, the interior will's act by its object insofar as reason is able to understand it.

Not only does Thomas distinguish the levels of morality of the exterior act but also with regard to the interior act of the will. Such a distinction does not divide the interior act into end and choice, but rather points out that every chosen exterior act, in its objective sense, has an end, a goal. An indifferent act done for an evil end makes it evil, as does the same act done for a good end make it good. An act is good if all its significant elements are good or at least good in addition to indifferent. But, an act is evil if just one element of the act is evil. Thomas's position on the moral integrity of an act, both in its interior and external aspects, seems to near the Abelardian position. Thomas, however, parts company with Abelard by further distinguishing the order of intention from the order of execution, the order of wanting from the order of attaining what is wanted. The choice of the will truly is a choice only when it is perfected (completed) in the achievement of the willed exterior action. Thomas corresponds to Abelard in the order of intention but parts with Abelard in the order of execution. Insofar as the executed exterior act completes the interior act of the will, it is said to be more perfect than an interior act of the will which is not executed exteriorly.

Gallagher maintains that Thomas's defeat of Abelard's ethics of intention rests not only on Thomas's contribution of distinctions within interior and exterior acts, but also on the bedrock of Thomas's thought. Foundational for Thomas's position is his understanding of the unitive composition of body and soul, including the relationship of exterior and interior acts as matter and form; the perfection of human nature as not only the perfection of the will but of the whole of what constitutes a human person as an end; and finally, the perfection of the intellect, achieved through the contemplation of the divine essence. Gallagher provides the reader Thomas's intended clarification and proposition for the place of the moral life in the contemplation of the beatific vision.

Given the articles in this volume, it might seem that a wider girth has been provided for what is meant by "theology" than is the norm today. Perhaps some of the articles appear to move more in the direction of philosophy than theology. This movement is a reflection of Thomas's own method of waging his theological enterprise by philosophical means while informed by Scripture and the Roman Catholic theological tradition of his day. Thomas's concern in the *Summa theologiae* is not so much with a strict interpretative demarcation betwixt theology and philosophy as it was to bring together the theological and philosophical enterprises, which for Thomas were seen more interdependently than independently.

Professor Mark Jordan once said that the *Summa* could be understood as a movement "from God" "back to God," *exitus-reditus*. Such an observation is not unique to him, as is well known. But, when a contemporary thomistic philosopher of his stature knows that Thomas's execution of his work was to demonstrate the reasonability of Revelation vis-a-vis philosophical elements and arguments, not independently of their theological context but rather interdependently with them, it is clear to all who would stand on the shoulders of the Thomistic giants who precede them that the philosophical and theological elements and arguments of Thomas's *Summa* may be distinguished but never effectively unbound.

Thomas waged many of his arguments toward an end known to him by Revelation but not directly and immediately derived from Revelation. The arguments often seem to be waged within the parameters of philosophical reason. Nonetheless, Thomas as he writes never forgets who he is, a priest of the Roman Catholic Church. He holds steadfastly to the Scripturally derived Tradition, while expanding the horizon of the thirteenth century's philosophical theology by seeking the truth wherever it might be found, be it in Jewish, Islamic, or Greek scholarship as well as the long line of Christian authorities. Thomas sees his enterprise as consistent with that of the Catholic fathers before him: Wherever the truth is to be found, it is from God, it points to God, and it is in accord with the reasons of God's mind, of which we might know but of which we can never know fully. For Thomas, Reason, the Logos of the Universe, delineates according to the nature of God's Mind what is fully revealed in the Scriptures and developed within the Tradition of the Church. Thomas, like many before him, believes that reason, waged alone, can discover much, but never fully reveal what God and God alone must reveal to humankind, according to the belief and practice of the Church, who alone, is bestowed with the fullness of God in the Holy Spirit. Wherever he finds the truth, Thomas believes that its one and only source is the Divine Truth Himself, from whom all truth comes and to whom all truth points.

METHODOLOGY

TOWARD UNDERSTANDING AQUINAS' THEOLOGICAL METHOD: THE EARLY TWELFTH-CENTURY EXPERIENCE

Romanus Cessario, O. P.
The Catholic University of America

This essay aims to provide some important background information for a study of Aquinas' theological methodology precisely as he understood it when, in September of 1252, he assumed his baccalaureate task of commenting upon Peter Lombard's *Sentences*. The so-called "second entry" of Aristotle comprised the discovery and use of his *Prior* and *Posterior Analytics,* the *Topics,* and the *Sophistical Refutations.* This "new logic" provided the medieval schoolmen with studies of the syllogism and methods of demonstration, of probable reasoning, and of the places or *loci* of reasoning. In short, these philosophical advances constituted the basis for a theory of knowledge and demonstration. And we know that by the latter part of the twelfth century, as a direct result of this "second entry," theology, especially as developed by the summists, became more and more

dialectical in method. But the earlier part of the
twelfth century witnessed a different kind of
theological activity, one that mainly sought to organize
in a fitting and intelligent way the vast amount of
theological materials which, by that time, had became
available in the Latin West. E. Synan describes these
sententioners as "seeking to employ in orderly fashion
the views (*sententiae*) of Church Fathers in order to
read Scripture with greater understanding, above all by
reconciling apparent contradictions among authorities
through a discreet use of rationality."[1]

Because it can serve as a criterion for
discriminating what belongs to Aquinas and what, in
his role as "commentator," he carries over as
"tradition," background concerning the *Sentences* of
Peter Lombard and earlier examples of twelfth-century
sentential literature can help us appreciate Aquinas'
uniqueness in his own writings (*scripta*) on Lombard's
Sentences. Thus, the question: what problems and
solutions does the "tradition" bring to bear on Aquinas
as *magister sententiarum,* and what problems and solutions are uniquely his own? While contemporary
research amply illustrates the rich variety of theological
writings that belongs to this period, it is safe to say
that the influence of the "tradition" seems to derive
from two principal sources. In the first instance, there
is the *Sentences* itself, which focuses and summarizes
the whole theological experience of the twelfth century.
Peter Lombard (c.1100-1160), however, inherited his
theological genre from other sententioners that wrote
during the early Scholastic period. And so one must
also consider the documents that either immediately
precede or are contemporary with the Master's
Sentences. These twelfth-century efforts at theological

systematization offer an informative view as to how certain early medieval authors of textbook theology devised varied methodological schemes so that they might order large quantities of theological materials gleaned from biblical and patristic texts.

S. Brown dates the early scholastic period from 1080 to 1230; during this time, he maintains, "the term 'school of theology' indicates a group of central thinkers who were surrounded by a number of authors sharing some distinctive traits or ideas."[2] The major section of this paper examines a representative selection of texts from twelfth-century authors who either surrounded or were influenced by such central figures of the period as Abelard and Hugh of St. Victor. I contend that the collectors of *sententiae* well represent the kind of systematic instruction that the majority of twelfth-century students of theology actually received, whether in monastic settings or at cathedral schools.[3] As an essay in historical theology, the present study takes up, then, the recent suggestion of Marcia Colish, namely, that we need to take a fresh look at how theology was done in the early twelfth century.[4] But it is also inspired by the work of Jean Leclercq, who encourages us to uncover the variety of approaches to systematization that writers developed before the work of Peter Lombard achieved a certain hegemony in theological education. In particular, Leclercq writes:

> Applied to the twelfth century, the modern category of "systematic" helps us to discern, in the teachings of the various authors, certain organizing principles, and we notice that these principles vary in keeping with the personal option of each author until Peter Lombard's *Sentences* introduced some

sort of practical order which, little by little, became
the general rule.[5]

While the authors that I have chosen for this study
favor different "organizing principles," I suggest that
their efforts at compiling books of *sententie* all point
nonetheless to a perennial question for the Christian
theologian, namely, how can one articulate properly the
intrinsic relationship that exists between divine Truth
and its revelation in human history, especially as the
latter is recorded in the biblical narratives?

As a general premise, this study assumes that
clarifying earlier moments in the genesis of Aquinas'
theological science promotes a deeper understanding of
its later stages. But in order to understand Aquinas'
earliest efforts at theological systematization, we need
to know something about the dominant theological
culture in which Aquinas began his Parisian teaching
under Master Elias Brunet. For an intelligent reading
of the articles in which St. Thomas probes the
Lombard's Prologue and of Aquinas' own inaugural
lecture in the office of *magister* (the *opusculum, Rigans
montes de superioribus suis,* usually prefixed as a
prologue to his *Scriptum super libros Sententiarum*)
requires an informed view of the sentential literature
that antecedes and shapes Peter the Lombard's
celebrated textbook of theology. While the principal
interest of this study appears historical in character,
within and in interplay with this objective, there lies
one that is deeper and more important. As is the case
with any process, we can suppose a genetic link
between early stages and later development, i.e.,
between these early sententioners and the development
of Aquinas' self-understanding as a theologian; and so

this study aims to provide some first steps towards gaining a better grasp of Aquinas' notion of what constitutes theological science.

1. The Twelfth-Century Problematic[6]

In the rich and vigorous renascence of culture and life that marked the twelfth century, one feature stands out as especially characteristic: the drive toward systematic appreciation and toward systematic excellence in performance. This drive can be verified across the full range of human endeavor in this century. For example, there was the awakening of an appreciation of nature as a cosmos, an *universitas*--and no longer as simply a juxtaposition of elements; this systematic intuition of nature was turned back upon the human person and bore as its fruit a new project of self-interpretation (Chenu, *Théologie,* 19-51). The same century saw the rise of the Gothic style in architecture. Just how systematically necessary were the various components of this style (e.g., the flying buttress) remains a matter of argument for historians of architecture;[7] however, as mirrors of how a person of the twelfth-century construed him or herself, the cathedrals of Chartres and Notre-Dame de Paris and the church of St. Denis are nonpareil stone witnesses to an interest in the systematic organization and articulation of elements. More formally speaking, it is worth noting that the first systematic works of philosophy in the West since Boethius were produced in the first half of this century, for example, the *Liber de sex principiis* (once thought to be the work of Gilbert of Poiters) or the *Heptateuchon* of Thierry of Chartres. The same thrust toward systematic appreciation motivated Gratian's rationale of canon law, the *Decretum*, and Peter Comestor's organization of history in his *Historia scolastica*.[8] Finally, this thrust was a prominent feature of twelfth-century theological endeavor, as represented in the rise of the sentential literature.

Sentential literature does not arise in the twelfth century by spontaneous generation; the precedents are several and of sufficient weight to be of authoritative influence. Scholars note three stages and classes in the earlier development of sentential literature.[9] Firstly, there was the sentential collection that arose when a reader jotted down, in no particular order, sayings from a Father that he was reading; an example of this class would be the *Liber sententiarum ex Augustino delibatarum* ascribed to Prosper of Aquitaine (*PL* 51.425-496). The second class consists in a *caetena* of patristic *sententiae,* now arranged according to the order of the books of Scripture and intended as a commentary thereon; an example would be the *Liber de expositione veteris et novi testamenti de diversis libris sancti Gregorii concinnatus,* complied about the year 600 by Paterius, the putative secretary to Gregory the Great.[10] The third class grouped excerpts from the Fathers and ecclesiastical writers under doctrinal headings and arranged these in some semblance of logical order; as examples one might cite the *Sententiarum libri tres* of Isidore of Seville (d. 636; *PL* 83.537-738) and the *Sententiarum libri quinque* of Taio of Saragossa (d. ca. 651; *PL* 80.727-990). This project, carried on largely, if not exclusively, by clerics, continued in the early decades of the twelfth century, but with the important difference that the *sententiae* of contemporary masters, the so-called *magistralia,* were added to patristic *auctoritates*. This difference is illustrated in the *Liber Pancrisis* of the School of Laon and in the *Elucidarium* of Honorius Augustodunensis.[11]

Parallel to the development of sentential literature, there is a deepening of and a shift in the meaning of *sententia* in which five moments can be discerned. In the first instance, *sententia* was only the expression of a thought or formula of an opinion which was garnered from reading an author (*defloratio,* a practice that extends back into Hellenistic antiquity); it was not so much the actual opinion of an author (*sententia animi*) as an impersonal proposition in which a given opinion was expressed (*sententia verborum*). *Sententia* thus understood was deepened in a second moment, when it was subjected to grammatical-rhetorical analysis, for example, by Isidore of Seville. Following the anonymous Latin text *Ad Herennium* and Quintilian's *Institutio oratoria,* Isidore distinguished the pithy, impersonal *sententia,* whose gnomic validity was not tied down to a given occasion of utterance, from the *chria* or saying necessitated by the exigencies of a particular moment or situation. A third understanding of *sententia* came to be superimposed upon these first two, one that is less grammatical and more exegetical/hermeneutical. It arose from Hugh of St. Victor's distinctions among *littera, sensus,* and *sententia* in his *Didascalion*. According to Hugh, *littera* referred to purely syntactic intelligibilities, those of words and their combinations; *sensus* referred to the surface semantics of a text; and *sententia* referred to that deeper level of intended meaning in a text. This exegetical usage quickly passed into hermeneutical usage in the twelfth century, according to which *sententia* came to mean the solid analysis of a problem supported by *rationes*. This meaning is exemplified in John of Salisbury: "There is, however, . . . reasoned argument, that is, whatever is adduced or can be adduced to establish an opinion or collaborate a *sententia;* for much opinion slips away from the truth, but *sententia* always approaches it."[12]   The fourth stage in the development of the meaning of *sententia* builds upon the third and is occasioned by the atmosphere and practice of the schools, particularly the *disputatio*. The *determinatio* which a *magister* gave to a *disputatio* was expressed in a *sententia,* that is, a scientific conclusion founded on *rationes*.   Finally, under the influence of Aristotelian methodology and through Avicenna particularly, *sententia* came to mean a proposition accepted with complete and definitive certitude, the result of scientific reasoning.[13]   This self-understanding of the theologian's task leavened all the "schools" of twelfth-century theology: that of Anselm of Laon; that of Abelard and of St. Victor at Paris; and finally the amalgam of schools that arose after 1140, the year when ecclesiastical intervention urged teachers of theology away from a narrow adherence to the less felicitous proclivities of Abelardian dialectics.

2. Twelve Twelfth-Century Texts

Firstly there is the *Sententie divine pagine*.[14] The methodology of the *Sententie divine pagine* is unsophisticated; systematization is limited to grouping questions which arose not from any systematic oral teaching, but from a "magisterial" *lectio* of selected biblical texts. In both the *Sententie divine pagine* and the *Sententie Anselmi*,[15] an initial brief consideration of God is quickly succeeded by a more extensive exploration of creation theology; in this latter, the author(s) followed the text and order of Genesis 1-3, although they made room for an investigation about the natures and properties of men and angels. This creation-centered movement terminates in a treatment of Adam's fall into sin and his damnation. In accord with the sheerly historical order of the texts favored here, a movement of *regeneratio* and *reparatio* is also traced along a three-fold axis: the era of natural law; the era of the written law; and the era of the dispensation of grace.[16] Though in an admittedly rudimentary way, the text clearly, if inchoately, recognizes the distinction between what can be gained from commentary on the biblical narrative and what can result from reflection on matters of systematic interest.

    Secondly, we have the *Sententie Atrebatenses*.[17] This collection has the common features of any such work that follows the persuasion of Laon. It differs from the *Sententie divine pagine* and the *Sententie Anselmi*, however, in the greater succinctness with which it treats its material. There is a significant difference in the arrangement of certain sections, for the author places his treatment of Christ and the New Law and of the theological virtues before a consideration of the natural and written laws. Lottin has argued that these *Sentences* from an Arras manuscript are prior to the *Sententie divine pagine* and to the *Sententie Anselmi*, that they are the *fons* for these two latter works and that they come closest of all the literature of the "School of Laon" to Anselmian authorship.[18] If this thesis is accepted, the

rectification of the plan of the *reparatio* represents a
clear methodological advance by the authors of the two
subsequent works.

Thirdly, there is the work of Master Hermann.[19]
Here we encounter a sentential work that already bears
the stamp of Abelard, one of that body of literature that
arose in the decade of the 1130's; according to the
current view, this work should be dated after 1139. It
was originally regarded as a work of Abelard and was
published as such in its first modern edition as
Petri Abelardi Epitome Theologiae Christianae.[20]
H. Denifle first cast suspicion on this attribution, a
caution that was adopted by M. Grabmann as well; it
remained for H. Ostlender to formulate the argument
on internal grounds and to attribute it to a certain
"Hermannus" who would be a pupil of Abelard.[21]
The work has a particular affinity to the second
redaction of Abelard's *Theologia "Scholarium"* (of
which its first eleven chapters are excerpts) and to the
postulated *Liber Sententiarum*. The controversial
opinions of Abelard appear in all the principal subjects;
the author even preserves alternations in Abelard's
positions due to criticism. Thus, the text presents a
wide range of problems and detailed solutions, an
advance over works of the same provenance, e. g.,
Sententie Florianenses.

In its organizational grasp of its objects, this
work subscribes to the *Theologia "Scholarium"* in
reducing the content of Christian doctrine to the quasi-
scientific categories *"fides--caritas--sacramentum,"* a
movement as characteristic of the logical party of
twelfth-century theology as the scheme *opus
conditionis--opus restaurationis* was to the biblical-
historical party of St. Victor. Within this overall

scheme, there is introduced Abelard's twofold discrimination of the objects of faith, corresponding to immanent and economic Godhead: God in his unity of essence and Trinity of persons and the *beneficia Dei*. After treating God, the author proceeds to discuss the Incarnation as the *"summum et maximum beneficiorum"*;[22] the Christological treatment focuses on both the redemption and on the person of Christ. It is to Hermann's credit that his systematic insight is capable of bringing the sacramental system under the objects of faith as *beneficia* closely related to his Christological exposition.

Fourthly, there is the *Sententie Parisienses* I.[23] This work bears the imprint of direct Abelardian influence, and perhaps even that of the now lost *Liber Sententiarum*; Ostlender dates the *Sententie Parisienses* between 1125 and 1138. Although its treatment of Abelard's doctrine is much too succinct, it does present a systematic structure and a logical order, again along the *"fides--caritas--sacramentum"* line: "There are three things that are necessary for our salvation: faith, the sacraments, and charity."[24] The inversion of *sacramentum* and *caritas* in this and other works of this school represents a deviation from Abelard's own order and probably derives from the *Liber Sententiarum* (thus, Ostlender), a work composed by someone other than Abelard. It is worth noting that procedural school terms have found their way into this text, e. g., *quaeritur, solutio, opponitur*, and *responsio*. A keen dialectical spirit suffuses this work: *sententiae* from Scripture or the Fathers are incorporated into rapid, rather sketchy, arguments which are themselves generally integrated into the overall systematic vision. A treatment of God is followed by a treatment of the

beneficia, the Incarnation being the *primum beneficium*.
The Christological treatment is lacking a soteriology,
but, as is the case with the work of Master Hermann,
the sacraments are fully incorporated as objects of
faith. The section on *caritas* provides an occasion for
the development of and proposed solutions to moral
problems.

Fifthly, there is the *Sententie Florianenses*.[25]
The last of these works which is exclusively
Abelardian in spirit, these *Sententie* from a manuscript
of Sankt Florian seem to depend on Abelard's
Theologia "Scholarium" and on the lost *Liber
Sententiarum*. They are dated in the 1130's, viz.,
before Walter of Mortagne, one of Abelard's finest
critics and a student of Anselm of Laon and Alberic of
Rheims, wrote to him. They exhibit both a slavish
service of the most controversial of Abelard's positions
and at the same time a disservice in that the
argumentation is so truncated and unpolished as to
make these positions seem all the more shocking. One
concludes from this that they antedate the caution that
resulted in Abelard's school from Walter of Mortagne's
letter, and that they probably were never intended for
public use. The *Sententie Florianenses* exhibit the
usual Abelardian organizational schema: "Tria sunt in
quibus summa nostre salutis consistit: fides, caritas,
sacramentum." But the author's slavish loyalty to the
fides--caritas--sacramentum schema prohibits him from
appreciating the sacraments in their relation to the
objects of faith, either those related to the immanent
Godhead or those that belong to the economic Trinity.
Thus in these *sententie*, only the incarnation and
redemption are treated under the rubric *beneficia*. In
the other respects, however, the *Sententie Florianenses*

conform to the usual plan: they represent the duality of the objects of faith, namely, *theologia* and the *beneficia Dei,* and place the treatment of Christology following upon a discussion *de Deo.*

Sixthly, there is the unusually influential *Summa Sententiarum.*[26] No other work of the sentential literature of the first half of the twelfth century has generated a comparable profusion of historiography: this is understandable in view of the crucial role that this work plays in the subsequent evolution of the "sentences" in the latter portion of the twelfth century. Three questions have been the focus of debate: authorship, date, and doctrinal orientation. Since the original attribution of this work to Hugh of St. Victor has been superseded, authorship has been fixed on Hugh of Mortagne,[27] Odo of Soissons, Odo of St. Victor, Hildebert of Lavardin, and Otto of Lucca.[28] The doctrinal orientation of this work, i.e., its relation to the several twelfth-century theological schools, has been much controverted. Although Hugonian authorship can no longer be upheld, this work is clearly situated in the line of Hugh's *De sacramentis christianae fidei.* R. Baron has attempted to make the *Summa* depend on an earlier redaction of Hugh's *De sacramentis,* one in which there was a certain appreciation for the Abelardian method and doctrine and which would thus antedate the conservative reaction caused by the intervention of William of St. Thierry in 1138/1139 to which the present form of the *De sacramentis* bears witness.[29] But D. Luscombe underlines the hypothetical nature of such a reconstruction.[30] This work is also related to the "School of Laon": Anselm at Laon, William of Champeaux at Paris, and the *Sententie Anselmi.*[31]

The more important doctrinal orientation that can be noted in this work is its relation to the school of Abelard--a strange feature seemingly for a Victorine work and one that is decisive for the whole subsequent project of twelfth-century theologizing.[32] While there is some justice in such an opinion and, in particular, when one considers the influence that the *Summa* had on the subsequent literature (where such a "fusion" does in fact occur), this assertion needs qualification. Luscombe presents a thorough resumé of the parallelisms between the *Summa* and the works of Abelard and his early school, suggesting that there are other (Anselmian or Victorine) alternatives for the derivations of certain doctrinal positions.[33] At the same time, he is most emphatic in rejecting any methodological dependence of the *Summa* on Abelard; such an assertion was a misreading of a purely material arrangement which began with P. Claeys-Boúúaert in 1909 and has been perpetuated in the bulk of subsequent scholarship. If the *Summa Sententiarum* represents such a fusion, it is a tentative and highly critical phase in this development. Those, moreover, who advocate a thoroughgoing Abelardianism in this work must account for the fact that, in terms of methodology, the author expresses a "conservative" horror of such innovations in his Preface:

> In his First Letter, Peter says, "Always be prepared to make a defense to anyone who calls you to account for [the faith and] the hope that is in you, yet do it with gentleness and reverence" (I Pt 3: 15). Therefore, following the injunction of the Apostle, observing gentleness in speech, reverence in assertions, "avoiding profane and vain babblings" (I Tim 6: 20), we do not wish to enter

> any area precipitously. For it is better not to speak ...
> much, than to define contraries. Wherever we can,
> let us follow in the footsteps of the authorities; but
> when no sure authority exists, we strive mightily to
> assent to those who are close to the authorities; and
> not presuming on their meaning, the scriptures are
> interpreted from piety.[34]

Although *fides*, *caritas*, and *sacramentum* are of
necessity material components of the *Summa*, they
enjoy no formal, determinative role in the
organizational structure (as in the typical Abelardian
arrangement). Rather, the author falls back on the
more congenial Hugonian principle of *opus
conditionis--opus restaurationis*. Indeed, his overall
methodology is biblical-historical, rather than logical
in the Abelardian sense. At the same time, in his
organization of the first part of the *Summa*, the author
does have recourse to Abelard's twofold division of
the objects of faith: "There are two things in which
faith especially consists: the mystery of divinity and
the sacrament of the incarnation."[35] There is,
therefore, an undeniable Abelardian influence on the
organization of some of the material of the *Summa*,
but this influence in no wise extends to the overall
systematization. While this qualified sense of
"fusion" may be allowed, the *Summa* demonstrates a
clear advance toward defining theological categories
beyond those suggested by the texts of the Scriptures
themselves.[36]

Seventhly, there is the atypical *Ysagoge in
Theologiam*.[37] Luscombe has argued that this work
derives from an otherwise unknown Odo of the
twelfth-century, that it is to be dated before the

1140's, and that it has an affinity to, if not origin in, England.[38] Among the unusual features of this work, mention can be made of its Greek title, its auspicious use of *sophia* to signify theology and *philosophus* to refer to Aristotle, and especially its citation of the Bible in both Hebrew and Latin. The work appears to be a rather sophisticated apologetic addressed to the Jews or a manual for such a purpose.[39]

Doctrinally, the work belongs to the same movement of Victorine Abelardianism as the *Summa Sententiarum,* to which it is principally linked in dependence. Nonetheless, it reproduces three of the Abelardian propositions condemned at Sens in 1140: (1) that there is a similarity between what Christians mean when they refer to the Holy Spirit as the divine goodness and the spirit of God and what the pagan philosophers mean by the divine goodness and the world-soul; (2) that Christ did not redeem the world from the devil by his sacrificial death; and (3) that actions, being extrinsic to the will, are morally indifferent and cannot be meritorious. What is most striking about this work is precisely its methodology, which is neither Victorine nor Abelardian. It can only be called "logical." Indeed, in his Prologue the author notes his debt to the *artes* and in particular to logic, the pre-eminent *ars* and scientific tool. Although his use of logic is largely limited to the dialectical moves that forge a definition, it is important to appreciate the fact that the author understands his theological methodology as built upon logical methodology. This becomes evident when, after the author has sketched the three orders of the real which constitute the material object of theology (the divine, angelic, and human natures), he seeks to present a rationale for this division in a fashion that is remarkably "Peripatetic." Thus, in the order of natures, the divine has priority, while the inverse is true in the order of discovery, of cognition, and of teaching.

The author of the *Ysagoge* has the perception to seize upon the intrinsic intelligibilities of these natures as they are revealed to our minds and to construct his work accordingly, i.e., according to a logic of discovery.[40] At the same time, he is sensitive to the historical character of Christian faith and so chooses to structure individual elements of his work along the familiar biblical-historical lines, as for instance his discussion of the human creature: "But for the [study of the] human person, one should consider the first creation, then the fall, and lastly the restoration."[41] In this way, the author of the *Ysagoge* succeeds to a remarkable degree in superimposing logical upon historical movement in his theologizing. No comparable achievement exists which can be traced to the influence of this work; it remained for Thomas Aquinas, a century later, to attempt such a synthesis with keener perception and finer tools.

Finally, the question must arise: what led Odo to this brilliant, if isolated, achievement? Any answer must be hypothetical, of course. Although it is more refreshing to believe that this Odo achieved a rare "insight" to which he was "converted," it is perhaps safer to assume that the apologetic intent of this work was in great measure responsible for the logical, rather than biblical-historical, systematization.[42]

Eighthly, there is the *Sententie Parisienses II.*[43] This is an anonymous work which dates from the middle or late 1130's. The author intended to present a true *summa humane salutis*, that is, a comprehensive survey of theological doctrine in a systematic manner. To this end, he adopts the usual Abelardian organizational scheme: *fides--caritas--sacramentum*. In this Abelardian mood, the author displays a sharp dialectical acuity, with a great emphasis on definitions and terminological precisions; this same dialectical methodology is turned to the examination of the *sententiae* of the *auctoritates*. This strand of his work stands principally under the shadow of Abelard's *Sic et Non* and the *Theologia "Scholarium"* (with the possibility of recourse to the *Liber Sententiarum*). To this dialectical spirit is added the historical dimension in a methodological structure similar to that of the *Summa Sententiarum*, which is the other source of this work. Here, however, the synthesis is effected in an entirely original fashion. For instance, there is a dialectical investigation of "faith," that moves toward framing a definition, but which is succeeded by a historical analysis of the development in the knowledge of the faith through the major aeons of history. As with other works that illustrate Abelard's theology, this *Sententie* shows a marked connection with the school of St. Victor. Like many works by the students of Abelard, the *Sententie Parisienses II* comes from the pen of an author who consciously wishes to juxtapose and evaluate the two traditions.

Ninthly, there is the work once ascribed to Roland Bandinelli.[44] The *Sententie* of Rolandus were published in the year 1150 or shortly afterwards; however, scholarly opinion no longer identifies the author of this text with Roland Bandinelli (later Pope Alexander III).[45] Although the "other Roland" was probably a contemporary of Peter Lombard as well, the methodology of his *Sententie* belongs to a more primitive tradition, namely, the prevailing Victorine Abelardianism. Thus, he reproduces the traditional Abelardian organizational scheme into the arrangement of his own work: "There are three things that make up the salvation of humankind, namely, faith, the sacraments, and charity."[46] At the same time, after discussing God, the author introduces into his treatment of faith (*fides*) the historical leitmotif characteristic of the Victorines: the angels and the creation, the fall and restoration of man.

The *Sententie* of Rolandus of Bologna do represent an advance in that they offer a more exhaustive and thorough doctrinal treatment than do any of the other purported disciples of Abelard; his exposition is more formal and more completely rounded out. The skill of the dialectician shines out everywhere. Rolandus divides each subject into its parts and then carefully and systematically discusses each in turn. In treating each matter, he employs a stylized version of the school *quaestio* procedure: first, the *auctoritates* for a given position are introduced and their *rationes* for such a solution presented; then, the same method expounds the contrary *auctoritates*; the ultimate solution achieves, where possible, a conciliation of the differences or at least some criterion for rejecting some and accepting others. Luscombe emphasizes the impact that Gratian's exhaustive methodology in canon law had on the formation of these *Sententie*; and there is reason to suppose that Rolandus, also a Bolognese master, was familiar with Gratian just like the noted canonist-pope.[47]

Tenthly, there is the *Sententie* of Master Omnebene (or Ognibene).[48] The author of a collection of Sentences bearing this attribution has been identified with still another *magister* at Bologna, who was a colleague of Roland Bandinelli. It is supposed that Omnebene composed this work in the 1150's; he also produced an abbreviation of Gratian's *Decretum*. His association to Roland continued during the latter's pontificate and led to his appointment as bishop of Verona in 1157, in which position he was a valuable ally of Pope Alexander. He is said to have died in 1185.[49]

Luscombe opines that the *Sententie* of Omnebene is related to and dependent upon the *Sententie* of Rolandus. He develops a doctrinal stance and methodology quite similar to Rolandus' version of the prevailing Victorine Abelardianism--except that his doctrinal loyalty to Abelard is much more pronounced. His acceptance of certain controverted and condemned propositions of Abelard, in particular, those dealing with the mysteries of the Trinity and of Christ, is not motivated by the recklessness of the author of the *Sententie Florianenses*. Rather, it is a well thought out and intentional affiliation. Like Rolandus, this author adopts the usual threefold schema *fides--sacramentum--caritas* and then enlarges this logical organization with a biblical-historical methodology based on the twofold objects of faith. Omnibene evidences little originality (except in his willingness to subscribe to Abelard's errors) and seemingly had negligible influence on subsequent methodological developments.

Eleventhly, there are the works of Robert Pullen (d. 1146).[50] According to the brief resumé offered by J. de Ghellinck,[51] Robert Pullen (or le Poule), the archdeacon of Rochester (1139), was a professor at Oxford and a key figure in its early organization. He then passed to a "professorship" at Paris in 1142, where he was acquainted with John of Salisbury. He became the first English cardinal in 1144 and rose to be chancellor of the Roman See (1144/1145), dying in late 1146. His friendship with St. Bernard attests the purity of his doctrine, as the testimony of his contemporaries agrees on his learning and virtue. On Landgraf's account, the *terminus a quo* for the *Sententiarum Libri VIII* is 1138, and opinions incline to the early 1140's. There is a certain reasonableness to Ghellinck's suggestion that the *Sententiarum Libri VIII* was completed prior to Pullen's sojourn at Paris; for the character of this work is entirely foreign to the achievements of systematization current in the Paris schools of the late 1130's and early 1140's.

The organizational plan can be termed biblical-historical, but is much less in control in Pullen's work than in Parisian works contemporary with this. The *Sententiarum* begins with the treatment *De Deo* and passes thence to creation and man's fall; then something like the *opus restaurationis* is traced: first, redemption in the Old Testament and, then, in Christ and the sacraments. The final subject to which Pullen turns is eschatology. It is fair to say, however, that no methodological scheme can tame this unruly, repetitious, digressive and generally confused work. Colish further observes: "The biggest schematic difficulty in Robert's *Sentences* is a redundancy reflecting his uncertainty as to where to place certain topics."[52] Dialectic is applied to a prolix number of problems, but the dialectician cannot see beyond any given problem to a unified whole toward which he is moving. Because he was a student of Robert of Melun, Abelard's successor at the School of Arts in Paris, certain links to Abelard show themselves, however poorly, in Pullen's work.

Twelfthly, there is the *Sententie* of Robert of Melun.[53] Robert of Melun (d. 1167) was part of that wide-ranging interchange of ideas between England and the Continent in the twelfth-century. He taught the *trivium* at Mont-Ste.-Geneviève with great success as a dialectician and was an auditor, if not a pupil, of Abelard. He began teaching theology at Melun in 1142 and proceeded thence to Paris. John of Salisbury in his *Historia Pontificalis* reports that Robert was the comrade of Peter Lombard in his successful prosecution of Gilbert of Poitiers at Rheims in 1148, although John of Cornwall reports that Robert later joined with Maurice de Sully in a similar attempt to have the errors of the Lombard condemned.[54] During this period of his teaching he produced the comprehensive *Questiones de divina pagina* (1145-1157) and the *Questiones de epistolis Pauli* (1145-1157), as well as his masterwork, the *Sententie* (dating from the middle or late 1150's). In 1163 he was named bishop of Hereford and consecrated by his patron Thomas Becket. He had the misfortune, however, of being disloyal to Becket in his solicitude for the King's favor, although his position changed toward the end of that tragic dispute.

It is clear that Robert was a contemporary of Peter Lombard and that his *Sententie* (1152-1160) may even postdate Lombard's work. While there is a notable self-consciousness of methodology evidenced in his work, Robert of Melun witnesses a stage of development in the sentential literature which is prior to the Lombard's achievement. In fact, Robert represents another fruit on the grafted tree of Victorine Abelardianism; he speaks of two contemporary masters (and their respective methodologies) that he proposes to follow: "[They] are two outstanding ones, who in matters to be investigated and explained by reason regarding both the sacraments of faith [Hugh of St. Victor] as well as faith itself and charity [Abelard]."[55] Robert, moreover, seems to indicate that he attended the lectures of both.[56] Another doctrinal orientation-- this time a negative one--deserves mention, that is, Robert's trenchant pillory of St. Bernard as an uninformed intruder into matters beyond his competence; this suggests that pupil Robert still had some loyalty left for his master Abelard and sought to avenge his condemnation.[57]

In general, the organizational leitmotif of the *Sententie* is the same "sacramental" principle employed by Hugh of St. Victor, whom Robert regarded as a great luminary of French thought.[58] This is apparent from Robert's division of his work into two books: the first dealing with the "sacraments" of the old Law, where the author treats creation, God and the Trinity, angels and men, free will and man's fall; and the second (in its present incomplete form) dealing with the sacraments of the new Law, where he treats Christ, his nature and mission. In the second book, Robert had planned also to include the Christian sacraments, the theological virtues, and a treatise on eschatology. Robert of Melun sees a thread of systematic connection in this "sacramental" schema: "Since the canonical scriptures themselves represent the beginning and earliest institution of divine worship as well as a prefigurement of the new covenant, the order to be followed starts at the very beginning, with the sacraments of the old law."[59] The same Hugonian movement is adopted within this framework, as Robert makes explicit concerning his treatment of man: "There are five questions that are set forth firstly and principally. These are: why was 'man' created; how was he made and how was he originally constituted; how did he fall into sin and how was he restored?"[60] Thus, Robert proposes to center his theological inquiry mainly around the biblical-historical axis of the *opus conditionis* and the *opus restaurationis*.

At the same time, however, Robert represents his own version of that effort of fusion of Victorine and Abelardian theologizing, and he does this in quite an original way. The overall "sacramental" scheme he understands as corresponding to the *sacramentum* of the threefold Abelardian scheme, and within this overall scheme he makes room for the other two Abelardian principles of organization: "My proposal will be complete, if, while relating briefly the sacraments of the old and new covenants, I shall have completed the treatise on faith, hope, and charity."[61] Furthermore, an integral systematization requires such a fusion: "Herein lies a complete inventory for a *summa* of salvation for men and women: reception of the sacraments, faithful belief, and perseverance in charity." The one who follows this plan of life, says Robert, "shall surely partake of everlasting life."[62]

In an attempt to assess the methodology of Robert's *Sententie*, we are indeed fortunate to possess in at least one manuscript (Bruges 191) his preface, there entitled *De modo colligendi summas*, which provides an outstanding prospect from which to appreciate the method Robert chooses for his work. As Ghellinck has noted,[63] Robert achieves a deep and penetrating understanding of the motivation of sentential literature, his own included:

> By whatever need the books of Sentences came to
> be written, and how we ought to form our
> understanding regarding the doubtful writings of the
> holy fathers, a certain person seems to give a hint,
> saying: Now after we have escaped from the
> tortuous places up to this point, one is free to
> consider more attentively why one always, in
> considering the writings of the holy fathers, finds
> both ambivalent and meticulous sententiae, of which
> some seem to be contradictory, so that not only
> those who are intent on disputation find matter there
> for making errors but also those who wish to build
> up the Catholic faith are not able to get on with the
> job easily.[64]

In this context, Robert makes his own intention clear:
"The intention of the work that I have undertaken is to
teach those things, through which the more obscure
passages of sacred scripture would become a little more
evident to less gifted persons."[65]   In this project,
Robert seeks to avoid the mistakes of two classes of
summa-writers: those who get so bogged down in the
details that they can never catch hold of the whole and
those whose perception of the whole is independent of
very real individual problems.   How does Robert
understand his task?

> What is a *summa*? Nothing more than a short
> summary of particulars.   Therefore,   where
> particulars remain unexplained, there a *summa* is not
> to be taught; for when particulars remain unknown,
> it is impossible that a *summa* be known; if indeed a
> *summa* is the complete collection of particulars, then
> neither the one who overlooks particulars teaches a
> *summa*, nor does the one who neglects the
> knowledge of particulars come to the doctrine of a
> *summa*.[66]

Robert situates his own conception with respect to the
educational methodology current in his time and
develops a thorough critique of the contemporary
academic situation; at one point he refers to the
educational disarray as an "itch that invades a whole
herd of pigs."[67]

The principal focus of Robert's displeasure was
the use of glosses as objects of study in the schools.[68]
There are two reasons for Robert's objections. Firstly,
glosses focus on what is problematic, confused, and
difficult in a text. For this very reason, these are
unsuited for training immature minds; those who use
them are like people who seek the leaves that hide the
fruit, instead of the fruit itself.[69] This approach does
great disservice to the process of learning:

> For there is great confusion in the order of
> instruction and an intolerable inversion of learning
> when one equates the secondary with the principal,
> much less puts it ahead: those who do it will deny
> for some reason--who, putting in second place the
> text and series of books to be read, spend their
> entire effort in the study of glosses.[70]

Secondly, Robert finds fault with this employment of
glosses because they lack *auctoritas*: "They err,
therefore, who would adduce glosses as if they were
authorities for the proof or disproof of somethings,
since they are neither authorities nor in such matters
can they hold the place of authorities."[71] But,
Robert's refusal to grant *auctoritas* to the glosses does
not exhaust his understanding of how *auctoritas*
functions positively in the various books of
Scripture[72] and in the Fathers.[73] His comments on
this subject provide a valuable source for reconstructing

the role of *auctoritas* in medieval educational life.

Robert also affords us an invaluable opportunity to observe his theological methodology as he situates it with respect to secular disciplines. In an almost classical formulation, Robert states:

> The liberal arts themselves are not an ornament [of theology], but its instrument, which only begins to have something of the ornamentative when the very doctrine of divine scripture accomplishes something through it. Indeed, the liberal arts only have that one mistress, are ordered to her by a debt of subjection, are regulated by her law, when they transgress it, the arts perform either mischievously or with no fruit.[74]

Robert then produces a sketch of the ideal educational plan, his own personal "reduction of the arts to theology":

> For his [man's] instruction, all writings were made, whose parts are both sacred scripture and the humanities. The humanities, that is profane learning, both the composition of discourses and the property of things teach. The composition of discourses in the trivium, the property of things in the mathematical disciplines according to extrinsic and intrinsic [principles]: according to extrinsic, as in the quadrivium, where the instruction develops according to exterior figures; according to intrinsics, as in physics, where natures and creatures are demonstrated according to intrinsic [principles]. For we are first to be instructed by these, so that we can come to an understanding of the divine scripture.[75]

Thus, we see that Robert of Melun can be appreciative of what pagan philosophy can contribute to the theologian's performance,[76] and yet he never loses sight of the proper relation that must obtain between these human sciences and the science of Scripture: "The sayings of sacred scripture are not subject to those reasons of dialectioners."[77]

Finally, it should be noted that Robert, in a diversion before his discussion of the Trinity, translates this problem into a more formal statement concerning the relationship between faith and reason. He makes explicit that he is grappling with the Augustinian-Anselmian formula: *Credo ut intelligam*. To explain this relationship, Robert proposes a threefold sense of "faith." As regards the "faith" of the beatific vision, this is the simple understanding of the species and the real (*rei et speciei*); here faith has no role. In the believer's journey, faith precedes and leads to understanding--but never vice versa. There is, however, one sense in which understanding precedes faith: Given that faith comes from hearing, a person must be able to understand the words that are preached before he or she can assent to them in faith.[78] In view of his methodological achievement, Robert remains an important figure in his own right. In terms of his influence, however, he unfortunately presents somewhat of a backwater. It was his destiny to develop this methodology in time to have it superseded by that of Peter Lombard; thus, it is Peter Lombard and not Robert of Melun who determines the subsequent development of medieval method in theology.[79]

During the first six decades of the twelfth-century, *sententia* comes to be construed as a systematic ground; and in the work of Peter Abelard, *sententia* itself becomes a theological theme.[80] Indeed, the quest for *sententia* which was the atmosphere of twelfth-century theologizing was well suited to being exploited by Abelard's sophisticated dialectical methodology. Such a project is essentially a search for proper definitions rather than proper demonstrations. As such it corresponds to the dialectical methodology of Plato and of Aristotle's *Topics*, and its principal instrument is *divisio*. The *ratio* which is sought is the necessity with which predicated properties and accidents inhere in a subject thus defined; the approach to this *ratio* is undertaken by way of oppositions and contradictions, as is clear in Plato's *Dialogues*. The achievement of Abelard was that he was able to understand the quest for *sententia* that preceded and surrounded him as a department and function of this logic.

Indeed, it was Abelard who brought the whole movement to a crisis by understanding *sententia* in the light of dialectical methodology; the shadow of his achievement falls across the majority of the works listed above, as either a positive or negative partner in their dialogue. Even the Victorine school, which in its principal representatives lay outside the sentential movement and in opposition to it, was forced to understand itself methodologically, if only by way of contrast, and to address the question of the proper way of doing theology. We see evidence of this development, for instance, in the *Didascalion* and the *De sacramentis* of Hugh of St. Victor.[81] Of course, Hugh's fully conscious and explicit option for biblical-historical organization of Christian truth requires some investigation into and explicitation of the status of this truth as it is embodied in Scripture. To think critically along these organizational lines, moreover, puts one in contact with more primitive problems of exegesis and hermeneutic. These Hugh confronts in his *Didascalion*. Indeed, the principal characteristic of the sentential achievement that preceded the work of Peter Lombard remains precisely a combination and/or fusion of Abelardian and Victorine methodological self-understandings. Many of the works listed above attest to the fact that the project of fusion and amalgamation of the Abelardian and Victorine styles of theology was a principal concern of theologians in the first half of the twelfth-century. Only the early works ascribed to the School of Laon escape this influence--which is understandable in view of the antipathy existing between its members and Abelard because of Abelard's ridicule, especially of William of Champeaux. Still, Synan reports the following development: "The claim that theology as a scientific discipline began with Peter Abelard and Hugh of St. Victor is . . . yielding to the view that the true pioneers were Anselm at Laon and William of Champeaux at Paris, both in turn indebted to Manegold, 'the master of modern masters,' who taught at Paris and died around 1110 at Lauterbach."[82]

3. Peter Lombard

We can understand the achievement of Peter Lombard in light of the authors and methodological developments that preceded him.[83] Peter was born in the final years of the eleventh century or the first years of the twelfth, for by 1159 he is referred to as *venerabilis*. The place of his birth was Novara in Lombardy; his family's economic situation was not comfortable, so that he had to rely upon letters of introduction from personages such as St. Bernard in order to secure lodgings during his travels and during the beginning of his stay in Paris. His first studies and teaching were done at Bologna during the third and fourth decades of the 1100's, and G. Le Bras has suggested a connection with Gratian at this period.[84] In 1135-1136 Peter set out for France, staying for an undetermined period at the school of Rheims with his countryman, Lutolph of Novara. He came to Paris sometime before 1140, and here Bernard's letter of introduction was useful in putting Peter on good terms with St. Victor. It is uncertain whether he was lodged on the premises; he certainly imbibed the doctrinal atmosphere and maintained cordial relationships with that community throughout his life. On the basis of this chronology, it seems impossible that Peter could have been an *auditor* of Abelard. He was, however, an avid reader of the Abelardian *corpus* (as John of Cornwall reports) and no doubt of the current sentential literature. His rise on the Paris intellectual scene was rapid. By 1142-1143, the Lombard was sufficiently celebrated for his reputation to reach Gerhoh of Reichersberg in Bavaria. It seems likely that he taught in the school of Notre Dame, although he was not a canon there. He was influential among the *magistri* who successfully debated the Gilbertine errors and pressed for condemnation at the council of Rheims (1148), held in the presence of Pope Eugenius III.[85] This same pope provided Peter with a letter confirming him as a prebend when Peter visited Rome in 1152; the documentary evidence cannot be used to support any other visits, although it does not rule out the possibility. In a disputed election, the chapter of Paris turned to Peter and named him bishop in June/July 1158. His exercise of this office was brief. He died in July (21?) 1160.

On the basis of his extensive corpus,[86] Peter can be termed a member of the "right wing" of the Abelardian school: a representative of an Abelardianism that has gone underground and that has given itself over to the tutelage of St. Victor. The question of who, if anyone, represents a left-wing Abelardianism is hard to resolve in any definitive way. Doctrinally speaking, the chief representatives would seem to be Rolandus of Bologna and Master Omnebene. In terms of Abelardian methodology, perhaps one could look on the *Sententie divinitatis*, an amalgam of the theology of the Porretani with Abelardianism, as a representative of such a left wing.[87] In general, the situation after 1140 was hardly congenial to an open espousal of Abelardian dialectical theology.

The "conservative" counterpoint to the Lombard's venture appears nowhere more evident than in his Prologue to the *Quattuor Libri Sententiarum*. Throughout this brief prolegomenon to theologizing as Peter Lombard conceives it, there still shudders the sting of the 1140 condemnations. No doubt sensing the tenor of such times, Peter clothed this Prologue in Scriptural metaphors and references[88] and stressed the association of his own work with the "authentic" achievements of Augustine by alluding to the latter's *De Trinitate*, Bk. 3, proemium, i. He excused the *Sentences* in speaking of their motivation being not his own but the irresistible demands of his students: "Not being able rightly to resist the wishes of the studious brethren."[89] The initial sentences were intended to set the appropriate tone of hesitation, of fear and trembling. The same tone was adopted by Robert of Melun in his Preface. At this early moment of

systematization, however, it would not seem adequate
to describe such a confession of incapacity and
inability as a mere literary conceit. Yet, in addition to
these tonal subtleties, Peter was at pains to distance
himself from the contemporary theological scene,
which he caustically described as dominated by those,
"Who make it their business to collect what pleases
rather than instructs; not wishing to be taught, but to
adapt doctrine to their desires, they have indeed 'the
appearance of wisdom' . . . (Col 2:23)."[90] The focus
of this tendentiously orthodox *captatio benevolentiae* is
the pure dialectical methodology, represented by
Abelard and the Porretani, as this and other passages in
the *Sentences* make clear.[91]   A similar chord of
negativity is struck as regards pagan philosophy.[92]
All in all, this combative purpose to the *Sentences* is
well and strongly expressed in Peter's Prologue.[93]

    And yet such an exposition cannot claim to do
justice to what Peter does in fact guardedly suggest
regarding his intention. In the Prologue one catches a
phrase here and there among the polemical welter that
more truly and more profoundly illuminates what Peter
thought himself to be about in his *Sentences*. In this
more positive orientation, Peter echoed the Pauline
mystery-doctrine when he spoke of his task as being an
"opening-up" of what lay hidden in the theological
investigations of his predecessors[94] and an eager
traditio of knowledge concerning the sacraments
(presumably in the wide sense) of the Church.[95]
Further on in the Prologue, Peter declared that, for the
theologian who has grasped a proper method of
demonstrating Christian truth, such a grasp makes
possible an exposé of error without the equal danger of
rationalization of that truth.[96]   These were precisely

the two poles--a fideism incapable of answering for its own commitment[97] and a purely rational articulation of the faith--between which Peter considered his own theological endeavor to be constituted.[98]

If the reader moves beyond the Prologue, he or she is introduced into a theological current which the decidedly anti-dialectical thrust of the Prologue might not have given one reason to expect. Peter's thorough acquaintance with Abelard's work has already been noted;[99] now it becomes apparent just how fruitful this acquaintance became when Peter appropriated it to serve his own original systematization of Christian doctrine. And besides his debt to Abelard, Peter owed much to the achievements of others of his precursors: to Hugh of St. Victor, to the author of the *Summa Sententiarum* and, when he discusses Church order and turns to the sacraments, to the canonists Ivo of Chartres and his fellow professor at Bologna, Gratian. Although their anonymity is disconcerting to our modern historical interests, Peter's contemporaries are constant companions in his dialogue, here with a probing question, here with a possible resolution of a problem.[100] In this sense, the Peter who rejects the follies of contemporary theologians in the Prologue invites them to participate in his own theological project throughout the body of the *Sentences*.

But, as we have suggested already, Peter Lombard was not merely an intellectual chronicler, acquainted with what was going on around him. For in his own quest for *sententia*, he has made good use of precisely that dialectical methodology with which this goal was pursued by his contemporaries. Dialectic is not employed with a uniform vigor at each and every moment of the Lombard's investigations. Only rarely did it yield a truly original and independent *sententia* as the fruit of Peter's own penetration of the real. More often, the dialectical methodology of opposition, contradiction and division is introduced to mediate between and reconcile the competing meanings embodied in the *sententiae* of the Fathers.

It is especially the presentation of the *sententiae patrum* in a heightened measure of intelligibility that is Peter's concern in his exposé of Christian truth. This presentation goes beyond the mere motives of convenience and utility which Peter has suggested with respect to his undertaking, i.e., having a wealth of patristic materials gathered in one book, instead of many.[101] However emphatic Peter has made his adherence to *auctoritates*,[102] the dialectical methodology afforded him a tool with which to exhibit the intelligibilities of Christian faith and to penetrate its complex and often, at least superficially, contradictory meanings. In this way, a survey of the *sententiae* on a given doctrinal problem was followed by the Abelardian interjection *videtur quod non*. This critical apparatus was not introduced to indicate any purely rational repugnance in the meanings of the *sententiae*. Rather, it expresses an acknowledgement on Peter's part of actual contradictions and of the need to plumb such meanings more deeply. Ultimately, it looks toward the mystery-character of the transcendent objects of faith itself. In the course of such investigations, Peter compiled a considerable *florilegium* of his own.[103] In addition to applying the usual instruments of dialectic to this corpus, he also seems to have made use of Abelard's rules for discerning equivocals.[104] Furthermore, Peter Lombard can be considered the earliest practitioner of what comes to be called "reverential exposition" (*reverenter exponere*), in which considerable latitude is allowed in the interpretation of a particularly weighty *auctoritas*.[105]   This mode of treating *auctoritates* achieved a certain maximal sensitivity when Aquinas confronted Augustine a century later.

Besides these purely material indices of Peter's theological methodology, attention must be paid to the architectonic within which he chose to articulate Christian truth. The formalization of his theology is sketched in the first distinction of the First Book of the *Sentences*, and there (as in his Prologue) Peter chose a course that was cautionary, if not conservative. To be more specific, Peter is concerned to place his broad organizational scheme of *res--signa/frui--uti* under the explicit patronage of Augustine's own discussions in the *De doctrina christiana*.[106]   In effect, the Master of the *Sentences* has erected two axes according to whose coordinates he can plot the elements of Christian doctrine in his exposition. In the first of these, *res* is defined only negatively and by contrast with the other member, *signum*;[107] it cannot be ascertained whether the Lombard was content merely to adopt Augustine's distinction as it was or whether he lacked the equipment necessary to deepen his grasp of *res* in a more proper, positive conceptuality. A *signum* is a *res* in its own right, but is possessed of one or other functional finalities beyond what constitutes its own "reality."[108]   In terms of these functional finalities, the *signum* is directed either toward signifying another *res* or toward "justifying," that is, toward bestowing the interior assistance of grace on the believer. It was this distinction of finalities and instrumentalities which provided Peter with an organizational principle for his treatment of the Old (legalia) and New Testament (evangelica) sacraments.[109]   Treating signs solely under the aspect of instrumentality probably represents a theological, rather than a philosophical, option on Peter's part.   The extension of this distinction of finalities and instrumentalities to the *res* member of the schema was effected by superimposing the axis *frui--uti*, which also bears the stamp of Augustine's authority.[110]

With his material now biaxially coordinated, Lombard was able to perceive a fairly rich organizational texture in the "material objects" of theology. For example, the divine Trinity is that *res* to the enjoyment of which man is principally directed, while the created world offers itself as a field of instrumentality whose use by graced persons can lead to the attainment of human destiny. The theological anthropology implicit here is by no means primitive nor purely cosmological. Conscious of the destiny which is uniquely the human call, Peter had a profound appreciation of the difference being human makes. Indeed, as M. D. Chenu has commented, the *res--signa/frui--uti* serves to focus the anthropocentric dimension in Peter's theology:

> As regards the ordering of materials found in the *Sentences* of Peter Lombard and generally accepted at that time, it has the advantage of putting to work the broad Augustinian categories of *res et signa, uti et frui*, wherein are expressed a noetic and a conception of man especially helpful in explaining the soul's spiritual itinerary.[111]

The human person and the range of human excellences

lie between the objects of pure enjoyment and those for
sheer use.   The human person can be a center of
delight, but only reflexively and in view of that pre-
eminent object of delight which is the Trinity.
Likewise, the human excellences and virtues conferred
by grace constitute avenues whereby the objects of
perfect enjoyment are attained.[112]   Among the more
notable successes of this formula of systematization,
one must count the Lombard's ample and well-
integrated treatment of the sacraments and the facility
with which eschatology was subsumed under this
scheme.[113]

   At the same time, however, one cannot be too
sanguine about the effectiveness of this formula outside
of Book One, where its utility is well attested in Peter's
treatment *de Deo trino et uno*. The deficiency goes
beyond the mere absence of a treatment of certain
subject-matters which one might have expected in view
of contemporary patterns.[114]   Rather, the lack in the
Master's systematization centers on his inability to
effect any deep and thoroughgoing actualization of his
organizational scheme in the *Sentences* as a whole and
most notably in Books Two and Three.[115]   In fact,
outside of Book One, the formula *res--signa/frui--uti*
cannot be detected in the exercise of any critical or
determinative role.   From this sort of effective
organizational vacuum, three results ensued.   Firstly,
Peter was led to take some faulty steps in articulating
his material, as, for instance, in linking the treatment of
our moral life with the discussion of *de virtutibus
Christi* in Book Three.   As a second result, the
Victorine historical-biblical methodology subverts the
announced "logical" progression at certain points, e.g.,
in the discussion of man's nature in Book Two.[116]

Finally, the ensemble thus constituted gives the impression that its relation to the principles of formal structure that Peter established at the beginning of Book One is largely an extrinsic one and that those principles do not breathe through and actualize the whole.[117]   In   this   sense,   that   undeniable methodological progress the Lombard achieved as a *prospectus* of his efforts remained a promise ultimately unfulfilled as regards the work as a systematic whole. For in that whole, the flash of Peter's organizational insight was hardly exploited; the exploitation is a project left to the expository genius of those who follow Peter Lombard.

Can one credit a thinker for what remained only implicit in his thought? Whatever be the answer to that question, the first distinction of Book One does furnish evidence of two crucial insights which, although unthematized by the Master of the *Sentences*, did suggest other horizons in terms of which theology would come to understand itself and its objects methodologically. Of these promissory achievements, the first may be termed the decompression of the temporal. At the base of the Lombard's unfulfilled vision, Chenu has discovered a theory of meaning that already presaged an end to the sort of temporal "tyranny" found in the organization of Hugh of St. Victor's *De sacramentis*. This theory of meaning grew out of early nominalist logic and its meditation especially upon the *Peri Hermeneias* of Aristotle. It affirmed the possibility of an identity in propositional meanings, an identity which could not be alienated by chronologically distinct appropriations of or references in these meanings. The import of this theory of meaning is that the human person's grasp and expression of the real as intelligible need not be irredeemably subject to its sheer temporal givenness; meanings that are propositionally constituted have an actuality of their own. For theology, the *Sentences* represent in this respect (at least *in voto*) the possibility of the sort of necessitated identity of meanings which alone suffices to ground a science. Perhaps the *Sentences* themselves did not wholly escape from the exigencies of sacred history. They nonetheless hold out the possibility that theology need not be so construed.[118]

The second key "conquest," which Peter Lombard secured for theological method but was unable to make fruitful, was the adoption of an implicit discrimination of natures: that natures are possessed of different ontological densities and different necessities with respect to one another in the orders of meanings and values (*res--signa/frui--uti*). Among natures themselves a certain order obtains in their mutual implications and entailments. The Master of the *Sentences* appreciated this orchestration of being in only the most incipient fashion in affirming a cognitive attainment of the real through signs[119] and an order of priority among goods. But, what Augustine understood according to the impoverished causal explanation of Platonism, and what Peter accepted from him without thematization, would in the next century become a fertile ground for exploitation in an Aristotelian mode of causal explanation. This is the legacy which Peter Lombard left to those who succeeded him in the magisterial chair and whose pressure was only intensified by the institutionalization of the *Sentences* in the academic pursuit of theology in the thirteenth century.[120] With its positive achievements and its shortcomings, the

Sentences of Peter Lombard were delivered to theology as its principal locus for the next three centuries. One cannot minimize the decisive influence of this work for the subsequent development of theology. As Chenu has remarked,

> To take the contents of these *IV Libri* as the basic datum for a theological science, even in cases where their limits would be overstepped [e.g., via the proliferation of *quaestiones*], was . . . an undertaking grave in consequence. One reaped the benefits, but also the limitations, of a well-ordered, selected, digested, wisely assimilated patristic inheritance in which the personal inquisitiveness of the Ancients, reduced to a common denominator, was held in a precious but rather prosaic balance . . . . Any commentator on the *Sentences* was in advance committed to these perspectives.[121]

As Ghellinck has commented, even the deficiencies of this work were not without their value; such lacunae lend themselves well to commentary and provide a stimulus to truly critical, if reverential, penetration of what the Lombard left unsaid. Indeed, as regards the problem of method that has been the focus of interests in this study, Peter's own inability to render his organizational scheme actual at every turn of his exposition exercised the theologians who succeeded him in an effort to discover intelligibilities where Peter himself neglected to do so.[122]

NOTES

1.   See Edward A. Synan, "Anselm of Laon," in Joseph R. Strayer, ed., *Dictionary of the Middle Ages* (New York: Scribner, 1982), 10.315-316. For an interesting case study, see Ivan Boh, "Divine Omnipotence in the Early Sentences," in Tamar Rudavsky, ed., *Divine Omniscience and Omnipotence in Medieval Philosophy: Islamic, Jewish, and Christian Perspectives* (Dordrecht, Holland; Boston: D. Reidel, 1985), 185-211.

2.   Stephen Brown, "Theology, Schools of," in Joseph R. Strayer, ed., *Dictionary of the Middle Ages* (New York: Scribner, 1982), 10.20-22. For a critical analysis of various intellectual movements, see Stephen C. Ferruolo, *The Origins of the University: The Schools of Paris and Their Critics, 1100-1215* (Stanford: Stanford University, 1985).

3.   Marcia Colish, "Systematic Theology and Theological Renewal in the Twelfth Century," *Journal of Medieval and Renaissance Studies* 18 (1988): 155. But Jean Leclercq, O. S. B., in "Naming the Theologies of the Early Twelfth Century" (*Mediaeval Studies* 53 [1991]: 327-336), takes exception to some of Colish's suggestive conclusions. He chooses rather to emphasize the importance that provenance plays for these early theologians (335): "The distinction between 'monastic' and 'scholastic' is based on an objective fact of the sociological order of things, namely the existence of two different milieux and, consequently, two different ways of approaching the study of Christian doctrine."

4. See Colish, "Systematic Theology," 138: "As a consequence of this investigation, I have come to the conclusion that the history of theology in the first half of the twelfth century needs to be rewritten." Recently, Miss Colish has made an impressive contribution to this research by her two-volume study, *Peter Lombard* (Leiden: E. J. Brill, 1994).

5. Leclercq, "Naming the Theologies," p. 335. Still, Leclercq, in an earlier study ("The Renewal of Theology," in Robert L. Benson, Giles Constable, and Carol D. Lanham, eds., *Renaissance and Renewal in the Twelfth Century* [Cambridge, MA: Harvard University, 1982], 68-87), takes a dim view of the early sententioners as tiresome catalogers.

6. The standard works on the general intellectual and theological development of the twelfth century are: Joseph Simler, *Des sommes de théologie* (Paris: Ernest Thorin, 1871); H. Denifle, "Die Sentenzen Abaelards und die Bearbeitungen seiner Theologia vor Mitte des 12. Jahrhunderts," in *Archiv für Litteratur- und Kirchen-Geschichte des Mittlalters* 1 (1885): 402-469, 584-624; Pierre Feret, *La faculté de théologie de Paris et ses docteurs les plus célèbres,* 7 vols. (Paris: A. Picard, 1900-1910), esp. vol. 1; Martin Grabmann, *Die Geschichte der scholastischen Methode,* vol. 2: *Die scholastische Methode im 12. und beginnenden 13. Jahrhundert* (Freiburg-im-Breisgau: Herder'sche, 1909); A. Dempf, *Die Hauptform mittelalterlicher Weltanschauung: Eine geisteswissenschaftliche Studie über die Summa* (Munich: B. Oldenbourg, 1925); G. Paré, A. Brunet, P. Tremblay, *La Renaissance du XIIe siècle: Les Écoles*

et l'Enseignement (Paris: J. Vrin; Ottawa: Institut d'Études Médiévales, 1933); F. Cavallera, "D'Anselme de Laon à Pierre Lombard," in *Bulletin de littérature ecclésiastique* 41 (1940): 40-54, 103-114; J. de Ghellinck, *Le mouvement théologique du XIIe siècle: Sa preparation lointaine avant et autour de Pierre Lombard, ses rapports avec les initiatives des canonistes: Études, recherches, et documents,* 2nd ed. (Bruges: Éditions "De Tempel," 1948; rpt. Brussels: 1969); J. de Ghellinck, *L'essor de la littérature latine au XIIe siècle,* 2nd ed. (Brussels: Desclée de Brouwer, 1946, 1955²), vol. 1; A. M. Landgraf, *Einführung in die Geschichte der theologischen Literatur der Frühscholastik unter dem Gesichtspunkte der Schulenbildung* (Regensburg: Pustet, 1948); A. M. Landgraf, *Introduction à l'histoire de la littérature théologique de la scolastique,* ed. Albert-M. Landry, trans. Louis-B. Geiger (Paris: Institut d'Études Médiévales, 1973); A. Forest, F. Van Steenberghen, M. de Gandillac, *Le mouvement doctrinal du IXe au XIVe siècle,* vol. 13 of *Histoire de l'Eglise,* ed. A. Fliche and E. Jarry (Paris: Bloud & Gay, 1951); H. Cloes, "La systématization théologique pendant la première moitié du XIIe siècle," *Ephemerides theologicae lovanienses* 34 (1958): 277-329; M.-D. Chenu, *La théologie au douzième siècle,* Études de Philosophie Médiévales 45, 2nd ed. (Paris: J. Vrin, 1966); D. E. Luscombe, *The School of Peter Abelard: The Influence of Abelard's Thought in the Early Scholastic Period* (London: Cambridge University, 1969); Peter Dronke, *A History of Twelfth-Century Western Philosophy* (New York: Cambridge University, 1987). Fuller bibliographies are in Luscombe, 316-344, and Dronke, 459-486. Of course, the earlier works must be used with caution, particularly as regards chronology and attributions of anonymous works.

7.　The romanticism of nineteeth-century Gothic Revival historians, who popularized the "systematic" view, was succeeded by the rationalism of 20th-century historians of architecture, who maintained that the walls themselves could have supported the stress without the addition of buttresses (which came to be viewed as products of ornamental fancy). For a recent study which challenges this rationalism, see R. Mark, "The Structural Analysis of Gothic Cathedrals," *Scientific American* 227 (November, 1972): 90-99.

8.　So thoroughly did subsequent medieval chroniclers appreciate the common orientation and tendency at work in Gratian, Peter Comestor, and Peter Lombard that the Lombard was gradually (and gratuitously) associated with one or the other and eventually both as blood brothers.　See Ghellinck, *Mouvement théologique,* 213-214, 285; Ghellinck, "Pierre Lombard," in *Dictionnaire de théologie catholique,* ed. A. Vacant et al., 15 vols. (Paris: Letouzey & Ané, 1903-1950), 12.1942-1943.　In the fifth chapter of *Mouvement théologique* (416-547), Ghellinck traces the parallelism between the systematizing efforts of theology and canon law.

9.　For further information, see Paré, Brunet, Tremblay, *Renaissance,* throughout.

10.　*PL* 74.683-1136.　However, recent scholarship makes no mention of Paterius; see, e.g., Carole Straw, *Gregory the Great, Perfection in*

Imperfection (Berkeley, CA: University of California, 1988).

11. See Chenu, *Théologie,* 358ff. Georges Lefèvre inaugurated modern textual scholarship on Anselm of Laon (c. 1050-1117) with his edition of the *Liber Pancrisis* in 1895, but recent scholarship has established that it is no longer possible to ascribe the interlinear glosses of the *Glossa ordinaria* to Anselm and the marginal glosses to Walafrid Strabo. Yves Lefèvre, the latest editor of the *Elucidarium,* places its author, Honorius (1075/1080-c. 1156), within the "school" of Anselm of Canterbury, but this judgment is not without challenge: Colish ("Systematic Theology," 139-141) treats Honorius as a representative author of traditional monastic culture.

12. *Metalogicon,* 3.6: "Est autem . . . ratio, quicquid adducitur vel adduci potest ad statuendam opinionem vel sententiam roborandam; opinio enim plerumque labitur, et sententia semper assidet veritati."

13. See Paré, Brunet, Tremblay, *Renaissance,* 242-274. Of this evolution, M. D. Chenu, *La théologie comme science au XIIIe siècle (pro manuscripto,* 1943), comments (24): "Voici que maintenant, avec la question, et la dispute qu'elle amorce entre spécialistes, la *sententia* de déplace encore, et désigne non plus l'interprétation, même profonde, du texte, mais la solution personnelle du maître, terminant recherche et débat par sa 'détermination' . . .: disons qu'il s'agit d'une conclusion scientifique, appuyée de "raisons," et faisant à sa manière et à son plan autorité; car, dans ce

régime, le maître, pourvu de la *licencia docendi*, a mandat pour enseigner canoniquement.''

14.　Edited by Franz Bliemetzrieder, "Anselms von Laon systematische Sentenzen," *Beiträge zur Geschichte der Philosophie des Mittelalters* 18 (1919): 3-46; this editor attributed this work as well as the *Sententie Anselmi* to Anselm himself. He subsequently revised this attribution in "Théologie et théologiens de école épiscopale de Paris avant Pierre Lombard," *Recherches de théologie ancienne et médiévale* 3 (1931): 273-291, and in "L'oeuvre d'Anselm de Laon et la littérature théologique contemporaine," *Recherches de théologie ancienne et médiévale* 7 (1935): 28-51. There is now a consensus that this work is from the school of Anselm and derives from one or more of Anselm's disciples, being completed after his death in 1117; see Synan, "Anselm," pp. 315-316. For further information see H. Weisweiler, "Das Schriften der Schule Anselms von Laon und Wilhelms von Champeaux in deutschen Bibliotheken," *Beiträge zur Geschichte der Philosophie des Mittelalters* 33 (1936); H. Weisweiler, "Die ältesten scholastischen Gesamtdarstellungen der Theologie: Ein Beitrag zur Chronologie der Sentenzenwerke der Schule Anselms von Laon und Wilhelms von Champeaux," *Scholastik* 16 (1941): 230-254, 351-368; Odon Lottin, "Nouveaux fragments théologiques de l'école d'Anselme de Laon: Conclusions et tables," *Recherches de théologie ancienne et médiévale* 14 (1947): 157-185; Grabmann, *Geschichte,* 136-168; Ghellinck, *Mouvement théologique,* 133-148.

15.   The postulated *Sententie Anselmi*, also edited by Bliemetzrieder in "Anselms von Laon systematische Sentenzen," 47-153. On the possibility that the author(s) of this work may already be reacting to Abelardian positions, see Luscombe, *School of Peter Abelard*, 175-176.

16.   See Cloes, "La systématization théologique," 288-289. Cavallera, "De Anselme de Laon," notes as characteristic of this method of theologizing the fact that "les textes scripturaires qui s'y rapportent on été tournés et retournés en tous les sens pour en exprimer le contenu et ils fournissent matière à de multiples 'questions' . . ." (53).

17.   Edited by Odon Lottin in "Les 'Sententiae Atrebatenses,'" *Recherches de théologie ancienne et médiévale* 10 (1938): 205-224, 344-357. Also in Odon Lottin, *Psychologie et morale au XIIe et XIIIe siècles*, 6 vols. in 8 (Louvain: Abbaye du Mont Cesar, 1942-1960), 400-440.

18.   Odon Lottin, "Aux origines de l'école théologique d'Anselme de Laon," *Recherches de théologie ancienne et médiévale* 10 (1938): 101-122. More recently, Valerie I. J. Flint modifies some of the traditional views on Anselm and his "followers" ("The 'School of Laon': A Reconsideration," *Recherches de théologie ancienne et médiévale* 43 [1976]: 89-110).

19.   For general information, see Cloes, "Systématisation théologique," 296-298, and especially for authorship, Luscombe, *School of Peter Abelard*,

158-164; Denifle, "Sentenzen Abaelards," 420-424; Grabmann, *Geschichte*, 223.

20.   F. H. Rheinwald edited this text in Berlin, 1834; it is also in the Migne collection, *PL* 178.1659-1758.

21.   See H. Ostlender, "Die Sentenzenbücher der Schule Abaelards," *Theologische Quartalschrift* 117 (1936): 208-252.

22.   *Sententie Florianenses,* cap. 24; *PL* 178.1730B.

23.   Edited by A. M. Landgraf, *Écrits théologiques de l'école d'Abélard: Textes inédits,* in *Spicilegium Sacrum Lovaniense* 14 (1934): 1-60. See also, Luscombe, *School of Peter Abelard,* 164ff.

24.   Landgraf (*Écrits,* xxvi-xxvii) offers an analysis of the schema: "Tria sunt que ad humanam salutem sunt necessaria: fides, sacramentum, caritas."

25.   Edited by H. Ostlender in *Florilegium Patristicum,* fasc. 19 (Bonn 1929). See also Denifle, "Sentenzen Abaelards," 424-434; Grabmann, *Geschichte,* 224; E. Bertola, "Le 'Sententie Florianenses' della scuola di Abelardo," *Sophia* 18 (1950): 368-378; Cloes, "Systématization," 297-298; Luscombe, *School of Peter Abelard,* 153ff.

26.   The only modern edition is found in *PL* 176.41-174, where it is mistakenly included among the *opera* of Hugh of St. Victor. As regards the date at which this work was composed, a diversity of opinion

exists: while earlier studies place it posterior to the *Sentences* of Peter Lombard, the bulk of more recent scholarship (e.g., D. van den Eynde, "Précisions chronologiques sur quelques ouvrages du XIIe siècle," *Antonianum* 26 [1951]: 223-229) assigns it to post-1138 and prior to the *Sentences* of Peter Lombard. Also see, Colish, "Systematic Theology," 145-146.

27.   See M. Chossat, *La Somme des Sentences: Oeuvre de Hugues de Mortagne vers 1155*, in *Spicilegium sacrum Lovaniense: Études et documents* (Paris: E. Champion, 1923).

28.   The authorship of Otto was argued by B. Geyer, "Verfasser und Abfassungszeit der sogenannter *Summa Sententiarum*," *Theologische Quartalschrift* 107 (1926): 89-107; more recent scholarship has inclined to allowing at least a principal role to this Otto, who was a friend of Peter Lombard and bishop of Lucca from 1138 until 1145/1146.   Both R. Baron ("Note sur l'énigmatique 'Summa Sententiarum,'" *Recherches de théologie ancienne et médiévale* 25 [1958]: 26-42), and Odon Lottin ("À propos des sources de la *Summa Sententiarum*," *Recherches de théologie ancienne et médiévale* 25 [1958]: 42-58) have demonstrated that it is not a question of a single author or a single redaction.   For example, *tractatus* vii, "De conjugii sacramento," is in fact a work of Walter of Mortagne. J. de Ghellinck ("À propos de l'hypothèse des deux rédactions ou des deux éditions successives de la 'Somme des Sentences,'" *Recherches des sciences religieuses* 15 [1925]: 449-54) has proposed the hypothesis of two redactions, and it is quite likely that its present format was published by no author.

29. See Baron, "Note sur l'enigmatique 'Summa Sententiarum.'"

30. Luscombe, *School of Peter Abelard*, 198-213.

31. See R. Silvain, "La tradition des Sentences d'Anselme de Laon," *Archives de l'histoire doctrinale et littéraire du moyen âge* 16 (1947-1948): 1-52.

32. This feature has been commented upon by numerous authors in our century, e.g., E. Portalié, P. Claeys-Boúúaert, A. Vernet, M. Chossat, J. de Ghellinck; M. Chossat (*La Somme des Sentences,* 1), has spoken of "la fusion des deux écoles" that the *Summa Sententiarum* accomplishes, while Ghellinck (*Le mouvement théologique,* 201), views this work as "le point de convergence du courant victorin et du courant abélardien."

33. See Luscombe, *School of Peter Abelard*, 198-213.

34. *PL* 176.41: "'De fide et spe quae in nobis est, omni poscenti rationem reddere', ut ait Petrus in Epistola sua, 'parati esse debemus cum modestia et timore (1 Pt 3). Itaque, ut pariter servetur modestia in sermone, timor in assertione, 'profanas verborum novitates', ut Apostolus praecipit, 'vitemus' [1 Tim 6]; et in nullam partem praecipiti assertione declinemus. Melius est enim non eloqui . . . magna, quam definire contraria. Sed ubicumque possumus auctoritatum vestigia sequamur, ubi vero certa deest auctoritas, his

potissimum assentire studeamus, qui maxime auctoribus accedunt; et non de sensu suo praesumentes, scripturas ex pietate interpretantur.'' On the methodological import of this preface, see Grabmann's commentary, *Geschichte*, 297-298.

35.   *Summa Sententiarum, tractatus* 1, cap. 4 (*PL* 176.47B): "Duo sunt in quibus maxime fides consistit: mysterium divinitatis et sacramentum incarnationis."

36.   For another testimony to the continuing fusion of Abelardian and Victorine orientations, see the *Sententie Abbatis Bernardi*, in H. Weisweiler, "Eine neue Bearbeitung von Abaelards 'Introductio' und der *Summa Sententiarum*," *Scholastik* 9 (1934): 346-371. Methodology is hardly the strong point of this work by an unknown Abbot Bernard. The "methodology" is largely a purely material aggregation divided into three "books," God, Christ, and the teaching of the Lord. Thus, the treatment *De Deo Uno et Trino* is by and large an abbreviation of the *Theologia "Scholarium,"* while in the subsequent treatment of Christ and the teaching of the Lord the author uses the same technique to plunder the *Summa Sententiarum* for arguments against Abelard. For more information, see Luscombe, *School of Peter Abelard*, 234ff.

37.   Edited also by A. M. Landgraf in *Écrits* théologiques, 63-285.

38.   D. E. Luscombe, "The Authorship of the *Ysagoge in Theologiam*," *Archives de l'histoire doctrinale et littéraire du môyen âge* 35 (1969): 7-16.

39. On the rising twelfth-century interest in Hebrew studies, see Luscombe, *School of Peter Abelard*, 8-9.

40. For an example, see Cloes, "Systématization théologique" (285): "Sit igitur theologice doctrine elementum in natura humana, provectus in angelica, consummatio in divina."

41. Cloes, "Systematization theologique" (285): "Atque in homine quidem creationem primam, deinde lapsum, novissime restaurationem percurrere oportet."

42. See Luscombe, *School of Peter Abelard*, 236ff.

43. See Luscombe, *School of Peter Abelard*, 228-233.

44. A. M. Gietl edited the text in *Die Sentenzen Rolands, nachmals Papstes Alexander III* (Freiburg-im-Bresgau, 1891; Amsterdam, 1969); see also Grabmann, *Geschichte*, 224-227. Roland Bandinelli was born of an aristocratic family of Siena in the early years of the twelfth-century. Nothing is known of his early life and education. He held a chair of theology at Bologna in the 1140's, and was therefore present at the crucial moment which saw the birth of Gratian's *Decretum*; in his own *Stroma* on canon law he shows his substantive debt to Gratian's work. By 1149-1150, Roland had taken up residence at Pisa as a canon of the cathedral and possibly as a professor in the episcopal school. In 1150, Roland was

made a cardinal and then *camerlengo* in 1153. Finally, he ruled the Church from 1159 to 1181 as Pope Alexander III. There is a certain irony in Roland's career. An ally and follower of Abelard, he nevertheless was the one who canonized St. Bernard in 1177. One of the principal proponents of the so-called christological nihilism (expressed in the proposition "Christus secundum quod est homo non est aliquid"), he intervened three times, with varying degrees of severity, terminating in formal condemnation in 1177, in the controversy that was raging about his own doctrine.

45.   See John T. Noonan, "Who was Rolandus?" in K. Pennington and R. Somerville, eds., *Law, Church and Society: Essays in Honor of Stephen Kuttner* (Philadelphia: University of Pennsylvania, 1977), 21-48, who argues that another Roland, also a master at Bologna, is the author of the *Sentences* and that they are to be dated from 1150 or a little after; also James A. Brundage, *Law, Sex, and Christian Society in Medieval Europe* (Chicago: University of Chicago, 1987), 257 n. 3.

46.   Cited in Denifle, "Sentenzen Abaelards" (434-435): "Tria sunt in quibus humane salutis summa consistit, fides scilicet, sacramentum et caritas." On the inversion of the usual order, see the reference to the *Sententie Parisienses I* in note 1.

47.   Luscombe, *School of Peter Abelard*, 245; see also Colish, "Systematic Theology," 150.

48.   Also edited by Gietl in *Die Sentenzen Rolands* (1891). See also Denifle, "Sentenzen Abaelards," 461-469; Grabmann, *Geschichte*, 227-229; Luscombe, *School of Peter Abelard*, 253-260.

49.   See Luscombe, *School of Peter Abelard*, 17. It remains to be seen what effect Noonan's argument brings upon this judgment.

50.   Edited in *PL,* 186.639-1010. For further information, see F. Pelster, "Einige Angaben über Leben und Schriften des Robertus Pullus, Kardinals und Kanzlers der römischen Kirche," *Scholastik* 12 (1937): 239-247; A. M. Landgraf, "Studien zur Theologie des zwölften Jahrhunderts. II. Literarhistorische Bemerkungen zu den Sentenzen des Robertus Pullus," *Traditio* 1 (1943); F. Courtney, *Cardinal Robert Pullen: An English Theologian of the Twelfth-century,* Analecta Gregoriana 64 (series facultatis theologiae, § a n. 10 [1954]); Cloes, "Systématization théologique," 291 and throughout.

51.   Ghellinck, *Mouvement théologique,* 181-182.

52.   Colish, "Systematic Theology," 150.

53.   Edited by R. Martin, O. P., in *Oeuvres de Robert de Melun,* 3 vols. in 4, *Spicilegium Sacrum Lovaniense* 13, 18, 21, 25 (1932-1952). Grabmann was the first to appreciate the importance of this theologian and to furnish a thorough analysis (see "Die Sentenzen Roberts von Melun" in his *Geschichte,* 323-358).

However, Colish ("Systematic Theology," 151) shows scant appreciation for Robert's achievement.

54.   See John of Cornwall's *Eulogium ad Alexandrum Papam tertiam*, v (ed. N. M. Häring, "The 'Eulogium ad Alexandrum Papam tertium' of John of Cornwall," *Mediaeval Studies* 13 [1951]: 253ff.).

55.   *Sententie* 1.45 (cf. Martin, Oeuvres, 3.1, 45) as cited in Luscombe, *School of Peter Abelard* (283): "Duo precipui, qui tam de sacramentis fidei quam de ipsa fide ac caritate ratione inquirenda ac reddenda . . ."

56.   *Sententie,* 1.48, 47.

57.   See Luscombe, *School of Peter Abelard*, 287-290.

58.   See Elaine Golden Robison, "Robert of Melun," in Joseph R. Strayer, ed., *Dictionary of the Middle Ages* (New York: Scribner, 1988), 10.434-435.

59.   Cited in Grabmann, *Geschichte*, 333 n. 2: "Id vero non perturbate, sed ordine agendum est et a sacramentis veteris testamenti exordium sumendum, quoniam ipsum canonice scripture est principium et prima divini cultus institutio novique testamenti prefiguratio."

60.   Grabman, *Geschichte*, 334 n. 1: "Sunt autem quinque in prima et principali enumeratione proposita. Hec sunt: quare homo creatus, qualis factus et qualiter institutus, quomodo lapsus et qualiter restauratus."

61.   Grabman, *Geschichte*, 332 n. 1: "Meum itaque propositum completum erit, si sacramenta veteris et novi testamenti breviter percurrendo de fide et spe et caritate tractatum conclusero."

62.   Grabman, *Geschichte*, 333 n. 1: "In his enim summa salutis humane integre continetur: nam qui *sacramenta* susceperit *fideliterque* crediderit ac in *caritate* perservaverit profecto salutis consors erit" (emphasis added).

63.   Ghellinck, *Le mouvement théologique* 144-145.

64.   Cited in Grabmann, *Geschichte,* 354 n. 2: "Qua necessitate vero scribendi libros sententiarum inoleverit et qualiter in dubiis sanctorum patrum scriptis intellectum nostrum formare debeamus quidam videtur innuere sic dicens: Iam postquam ex confragosis locis hucusque evasimus, considerare libet attentius, cur semper hac re in sanctorum patrum tractatibus reperiuntur tam dubie tam scrupulose sententie et que sibi invicem nonnumquam contrarie videntur, ut non solum qui contendendi intentiones suas congregant materiam in eis inveniant errandi, sed et qui ex eis astruere velint fidem catholicam non facile se queant expedire."

65.   Grabmann, *Geschichte*, 339 n. 1: "Suscepti operis propositum, cuius intentio est docere ea, per que loca sacre scripture obscuriora intelligentie minus capacium aliquatenus evidentiora fiant."

66.   Grabmann, *Geschichte*, 341 n. 1: "Quid enim summa est?   Nonnisi singulorum brevis comprehensio.   Ubi ergo singula inexplicata reliquuntur, ibi eorum summa nullo modo docetur; singulis namque ignoratis summam sciri impossibile est, siquidem summa est singulorum compendiosa collectio, quia nec summam docet qui singula pretermittit nec ad summe pervenit doctrinam, qui singulorum negligit cognitionem."

67.   Grabmann, *Geschichte*, 342 n. 1: "Iam enim more porcorum pruriginis totum invasit gregem."

68.   See Grabmann's account in *Geschichte*, 343ff.

69.   Grabmann, *Geschichte*, 342 n. 1.

70.   Grabmann, *Geschichte*, 344 n. 3: "Ordinis namque doctrinalis magna confusio est et dicipline intolerabilis perturbatio secundarium principali adaequare, nedum anteponere: quod ab his fieri qua ratione negabitur, qui textu et serie legendorum librorum postpositis, totam lectionis operam in studio glossularum expendunt."

71.   Grabmann, *Geschichte*, 349 n. 1: "Peccant ergo qui glossas quasi auctoritates essent ad aliquorum comprobationem vel infirmationem afferunt, cum nec auctoritates sint nec in tali negotio auctoritatis locum obtinere possint."   See also 345 n. 1 and 346 n. 1.

72.   Grabmann, *Geschichte*, 346 n. 2 and 347 n. 2.

73.   Grabmann, *Geschichte*, 348 n. 2.

74.   Grabmann, *Geschichte*, 353 n. 1: "Non tamen ipse artes eius [theologiae] sunt ornamentum, sed instrumentum, quod tunc solum aliquid inde decoris habet, cum ipsa divine scripture doctrina per illud aliquid operatur.   Eam quippe solam artes liberales habent dominam, ei subiectionis debito famulantur, eius lege astringuntur, quam quando transgrediuntur aut perniciose aut cum nulla utilitate operantur."

75.   Grabmann, *Geschichte*, 326 n. 2: "Ad eruditionem autem ipsius omnes scripture facte sunt, quarum partes sunt tam sacre scripture, tam ethnice.   In ethnicis enim, id est gentilibus, et sermonum compositio et rerum proprietas docet.   Sermonum compositio in trivio, rerum proprietas in mathematicis disciplinis secundum extrinseca et intrinseca; secundum extrinseca, ut in quadrivio, ubi doctrina fit secundum figuras exteriores; secundum intrinseca, ut in physica, ubi nature et creature rerum secundum intrinseca demonstrantur.   His enim prius sumus instruendi, ut sic ad intelligentiam scripture divine perveniamus."

76.   Grabmann, *Geschichte*, 350 n. 2: "Nec illa philosophorum disputatio perniciosa estimanda est."

77.   Grabmann, *Geschichte*, 340 n. 1: "Locutiones sacre scripture illi rationi dialecticorum subiecte non sunt . . . ."

78.   Grabmann, *Geschichte*, 337-338 n. 2.

79.   For further information, see Ghellinck, *Le mouvement théologique*, 144, 183-185, and throughout; Luscombe, *School of Peter Abelard*, 281-298; R. Martin, "L'oeuvre théologique de Robert de Melun," *Revue d'histoire ecclésiastique* 15 (1920): 469-472; F. Pelster, "Literargeschichtliche Beiträge zu Robert von Melun," *Zeitschrift für katholische Theologie* 53 (1929): 570-574.

80.   On Abelard's methodology, see the valuable study of J. Cottiaux, "La conception de la théologie chez Abelard," *Revue d'histoire ecclésiastique* 28 (1932): 247-295, 533-551, 788-828--in particular the tables of organization Cottiaux provides. Besides the influence Abelard exercised through his *Sic et Non, Theologia "Scholarium,"* and *Theologia Christiana*, Ostlender ("Setenzenbucher," 208-252) has postulated a reprise of Abelard's theology along the lines of a *Liber Sententiarum*. Such a work would have been a basis for many of the works mentioned above and perhaps would account for certain doctrinal and organizational peculiarities (e.g., the inversions of *caritas* and *sacramentum* that occur in the threefold scheme in certain *sententie*). On the qualifications one must make regarding this hypothesis, see Luscombe, *School of Peter Abelard*, 121 and throughout.

81.   On the Hugonian organizational scheme and methodological self-understanding, see the preceding material and footnotes, where constant reference and comparison is made. Also see Grabmann, *Geschichte*, 229-323; Ghellinck, *Le mouvement théologique*, 180-197; and Luscombe, *School of Peter Abelard*, 183-197, where the relation to

Abelard's work is well brought out. See also Paré, Brunet, and Tremblay, *La Renaissance,* 219-228.

82. Synan, "Anselm of Laon," 316; also Flint, "'School of Laon.'"

83. Ghellinck provides the following biographical data of the life of Peter Lombard in "Pierre Lombard," 1941-1951. The bibliography on Peter Lombard is quite extensive and has been gathered (up to 1935) by Ghellinck in his article for the *Dictionnaire de théologie catholique,* 2017-2019. Among these, the following may be singled out: Grabmann, *Geschichte,* 359-407; Ghellinck, *Mouvement théologique,* 213-419; Luscombe, *School of Peter Abelard,* 261 280; and the short study of P. Delhaye, *Pierre Lombard: Sa vie, ses oeuvres, sa morale,* Conference Albert-le-Grand, 1960 (Montreal: Institut d'études médiévales; Paris: Librairie J. Vrin, 1961).

84. "Pierre Lombard, Prince du droit canon," *Miscellanea Lombardiana* (1957): 245, 252.

85. For a long and interesting report of the trial of Gilbert, written by the contemporary bishop Otto of Freising, see his *The Deeds of Frederick Barbarossa,* trans. C. Mierow and R. Emery (New York: Columbia University, 1953; 1966), 88-101.

86. The works of Peter the Lombard include the following.
1) *Commentarius in Psalmos davidicos, Glossae continuae.* This work was certainly produced prior to 1138-1141--that is, to his *Commentary on Paul's*

Epistles--for it represents a rather primitive achievement when compared with later works of certain date. It is basically a *catena* of patristic *sententiae* arranged so as to provide a running commentary on the Psalms; the principal *auctoritates* cited are Augustine and Cassiodorus. The work has no preface and exhibits no methodological interest (or genius). Nevertheless, it enjoyed wide influence on subsequent biblical studies. Conceived as an attempt to build upon earlier glosses, Peter's work soon replaced them and came to be known as the *Glossatura major* (to distinguish it in turn from the *Glossa ordinaria*). It was glossed by the Lombard's disciple, Peter of Poitiers. The text will be found in *PL,* 191.55-1296.

2) *Glossae in epistolis Pauli* (later known as the *Collectanea*). Recent research indicates that this work was composed after 1148 but did not reach its final form until after 1154. Once again, it was the Lombard's intention to build upon earlier glosses and Gilbert of Poitier's *Commentarius in Epistolas S. Pauli*; however, as was the case with Peter's glosses on the Psalms, this work soon supplanted the earlier efforts and came to be known as the *Glossatura magna* (also *Majores glossae epistolarum*, *Glossa continua* and *Glossa ordinaria*). For further information, see A. M. Landgraf, "Familienbildung bei Pauluskommentaren des XII. Jahrhunderts," *Biblica* 13 (1932): 169-193, along with the results of recent research as reported in *Sententiae in IV libris distinctae*, 3d ed. (Rome, 1971), 1.46*-93*. These glosses of the Lombard soon began to be the object of further glosses on themselves; for instance, see the anonymous work in *PL,* 175.431-634. The methodology of these glosses on Paul is more self-

conscious and sophisticated than that of the Psalms glosses. This is evident from the opening of the Lombard's preface: "Principia rerum requirenda sunt prius, ut earum notitia plenior haberi possit"; Peter then proceeds to situate the Pauline corpus in terms of the whole body of Scripture and to treat questions such as authorship, etc. His admitted purpose is to reconcile the apparent conflicts among the *auctoritates* that have arisen in connection with the Pauline texts. To this end, his use of *auctoritates* is more expanded than in his glosses on the Psalms. Alongside this interest, one can note the deepening of strictly theological emphases and interests in the Lombard's *quaestiones,* for with these he probes the theological import of Paul's texts. The method is dialectical, but it is used with that chaste moderation which characterizes the *Sentences* as well. Indeed, Ghellinck ("Pierre Lombard," 1957-1959) has admirably indicated the links of this work with Peter's *chef-d'oeuvre.* Of the integrity of this movement toward properly theological intelligibility, P. Mandonnet ("Bibliographie critique," *Bulletin Thomiste* 8 1931: 233) notes: "Je ne suis pas loin de penser que les quatres livres des Sentences du Lombard ne sont autre chose que les questions qu'il a soulevées ou disputées au cours de son enseignment de la Bible et qu'il a finalement ordonnées en un corps de doctrine théologique." Some reserve, however, must be expressed about the question of the Lombard's having used this gloss technique in his magisterial exposition of Scripture; the present state of our knowledge does not warrant complete certitude regarding either the glosses on the Psalms or those on Paul. The text of the glosses on Paul's epistles can be found in *PL,* 191.1297-1696, 192.9-520.

3)   Peter Lombard has also left a body of sermons, some of which he preached at St. Victor between 1140 and 1160. They are to be found (with an erroneous attribution to Hildebert of Lavardin) in *PL,* 171.339-964.

4)   On dubious and spurious works of the Lombard, see Ghellinck, "Pierre Lombard," 1961-1962.

5)   The chronology of the *Quattuor Libri Sententiarum* is rather complicated and can only be reconstructed on the basis of internal evidence. The question has for the most part been discussed in terms of the Lombard's use of Burgundio of Pisa's translation of John Damascene's *De fide orthodoxa* (post-1154). It now seems that the *Sentences* were completed during the period 1155-1158. As to the suggestion of a second edition of the *Sentences* (first made in the thirteenth century), Ghellinck ("Pierre Lombard," 1965-1967) demonstrates the very limited sense in which this view may be accepted. The modern critical text is that of the Quarrachi Franciscans, *Petri Lombardi libri IV Sententiarum*, 3rd ed., 2 vols. in 3 (Rome: 1971[1], 1981[3]); the long "Prolegomena," pp. 5*-165*, provide a wealth of critical study on the Lombard and his works.

87.   On the *Sententie divinitatis* (the title represents the Gilbertine distinction between *Deus* and *divinitas*), see B. Geyer, "Die 'Sententiae divinitatis': Ein Sentenzenbuch der Gilbertischen Schule," *Beiträge zur Geschichte der Philosophie der Mittelalters* 7 (1909); Cloes, "Systématization théologique," 301-302 and throughout; Colish, "Systematic Theology," 149. For a recent study of Gilbert of Poitiers, see Lauge Olaf Nielsen, *Theology and Philosophy in the Twelfth-*

century: A Study of Gilbert Porreta's Thinking and the Theological Expositions of the Doctrine of the Incarnation during the Period 1130-1180, trans. Ragnar Christophersen (Leiden: E. J. Brill, 1982), 25-189.

88.   For instance, the widow's mite, the good Samaritan, the shields of David, the consuming zeal for God's house, and the citations of Eph 2:2 and 2 Tim 4:4.

89.   Prologue n. 1: "non valentes studiosorum fratrum votis jure resistere . . . ."

90.   Prologue n. 3: "Quorum professio est magis placita quam docenda conquirere: nec docenda desiderare, sed desideratis doctrinam coaptare. Habent 'rationem sapientiae in superstitione' [Col 2:23]." Once again Peter Lombard's criticism of the schools of his day shows a parallel in Robert of Melun, who also was moved to indict the prevailing educational system. Interestingly enough, the Lombard's own *Sentences* become the focus for scorn directed against insitutionalized education in the next century. Then the interlocutor is Roger Bacon, who pays Peter in his own abusive coin. For this, see M. D. Chenu, *Toward Understanding St. Thomas,* trans. A. Landry and D. Hughes (Chicago: Henry Regnery, 1964), 266 and n. 3.

91.   For a succinct list of these anti-dialectic *loci,* see Ghellinck, *Le mouvement théologique,* 229 n. 3.

92.   Ghellinck, *Le mouvement theologique,* 230-231. It should be noted, however, that in other

instances Peter approves Plato for teaching that the soul is *se movens* and favors Aristotelian realism as regards the problem of the universals--e. g., Bk I, d. v, c. l; d. xxv, c. 2; d. xxviii, c. 1. At an even more basic level, Peter's theological glossary is shot through with the Aristotelian terminology of the *logica vetus*.

93.   Prologue n. 4: "Horum igitur et Deo odibilem ecclesiam evertere atque ora oppilare ne virus nequitiae in alios effundere queant . . . ."

94.   Prologue n. 2: "theologicarum inquisitionum abdita aperire." On the continuing fruitfulness of the mystery-motif as a type of theological endeavor, see M. LeGuillou, *Christ and Church--A Theology of the Mystery,* trans. C. Schaldenbrand (New York: Desclée, 1966), 138ff.

95.   Prologue n. 2: "necnon et sacramentorum ecclesiasticorum pro modico intelligentiae nostrae notitiam tradere studuimus."

96.   Prologue n. 4: "in labore multo ac sudore . . . volumen Deo praestante compegimus ex testimoniis veritatis in aeternum fundatis, in quo per dominicae fidei sinceram professionem, vipereae doctrinae fraudulentiam prodidimus: aditum demonstrandae veritatis complexi, nec periculo impiae professionis inserti in quatuor libris distinctum. In quo maiorum exempla doctrinam reperies . . . ."

97.   On the guiding role played in twelfth-century theology by the Petrine text, "De fide quae est in nobis ratio reddenda omnibus," see Ghellinck, *Le*

mouvement théologique, 280-285. This text is a principal motive for eschewing fideism and seeking some "demonstration" serviceable to faith among the twelfth-century *magistri*.

98. Prologue n. 4: "Temperato inter utrumque moderamine utentes."

99. On this, see the report by John of Cornwall in Luscombe, *School of Peter Abelard*, 279-280.

100. For a number of these texts in which the flavor of contemporary controversy is still strong, see Ghellinck, *Le mouvement théologique*, 232 and n. 1.

101. Prologue n. 5: "Non igitur debet hic labor cuiquam pigro vel multum docto videri superfluus, cum multis impigris multisque indoctis, inter quos etiam mihi, sit necessarius, brevi volumine complicans Patrum sententias, appositis eorum testimoniis, ut non sit necesse quaerenti librorum numerositatem evolvere, cui brevitas collecta quod quaeritur offert sine labore."

102. Prologue n. 4: "Compegimus ex testimoniis veritatis in aeternum fundatis . . . . In quo majorum exempla doctrinamque reperies," and "Sicubi vero parum vox nostra insonuit, non a paternis discessit limitibus." See also, Bk I, d. ix, c. 9; Bk III, d. v, c. 3 and d. ix, c. 2.

103. Augustine is not only the spiritual and doctrinal master of Peter Lombard, he is also the source of the bulk of the *sententiae* (almost one

thousand) presented by Peter; on this, see F. Cavallera, "Saint Augustin et le Livre des Sentences de Pierre Lombard," *Archives de Philosophie* 7 (1930): 438-451. For his biblical glosses, moreover, Peter depends heavily on Florus of Lyons as a major source of citations from Augustine. Among the Latin Fathers, the number of citations ranges down from Hilary of Poitiers and Saint Ambrose (both with roughly eighty *sententiae* cited). Among the Western *auctoritates* of the ninth and tenth centuries, Alcuin, Paschasius Radbert, and Haymo of Halberstadt are the most frequently cited. Understandably, Lombard's use of the *sententiae* of the Greek patristic tradition is considerably more limited: John Damscene (26 citations), John Chrysostom (20), Origen (10), Pseudo-Dionysius (2), Hermas, Athanasius, Didymus, and Cyril of Alexandria (1 each). Peter's compilation has notable lacunae that do not even faithfully represent the knowledge of the Fathers that was in fact current in the monastic centers of his time; see Ghellinck, *Le mouvement théologique*, 243. It should further be noted that, Augustine aside, the Lombard's knowledge of the *corpus patrum* was largely secondhand and derivative from earlier *florilegia*. In particular, for the application of certain *sententiae* to given theological problems, Peter is particularly dependent upon such an association already accomplished in Abelard's *Sic et Non*; see also J. Van Dyk, "The *Sentences* of Peter Lombard and Medieval Philosophy," in J. Kraay and A. Tol, eds., *Hearing and Doing: Philosophical Essays Dedicated to H. Evan Runner* (Toronto: Wedge, 1979), 149-157.

104. See Ghellinck, *Le mouvement théologique*, 233.

105. Ghellinck, *Le mouvement thèologique*.

106. See Ghellinck, *Le mouvement thèlogique* especially Bk I, chap. 2.

107. Ghellinck, *Le mouvement thèologique*, Bk I, d. i, c. 1: "Proprie autem hic res appellantur quaenon ad significandum aliquid adhibentur . . . ."

108. Ghellinck, *Le mouvement thèologique*, Bk I, d. i, c. 1: "Omne igitur signum etiam res aliqua est: quod enim nulla res est, omnino nihil est," quoting Augustine, *De doctrina christiana*, Bk 1, chap. 2, n. 2, where the *signum* is defined as "quorum usus est in signficando."

109. Ghellinck, *Le mouvement thèologique*: "Eorum [signorum] autem aliqua sunt quorum omnis usus est in significando, non in justificando; id est, quibus non utimur nisi aliquid significandi gratia, ut aliqua sacramenta legalia; alia quae non solum significant, sed conferunt quod intus adjuvet, sicut evangelica sacramenta."

110. To sanction this distinction, Peter draws not only upon the *De doctrina christiana,* Bk I, chaps. 3, 4, and 22, but also upon the *De Trinitate,* Bk X, chap. 10. In so doing, he seeks to associate himself with these influential works of Augustine's own systematic efforts.

111.   Chenu, *Toward Understanding St. Thomas,* 309-310.

112.   In locating the virtues within the *frui-uti* framework, Peter was faced with the task of reconciling opposing *sententiae,* here in Augustine and Ambrose: "Nos autem harum quae videtur auctoritatum repugnantiam de medio eximere cupientes, dicimus quod virtutes propter se pentendae et amandae sunt, et tamen propter solam beatitudinem [the proper object of *frui*]" (Bk I, d. i, c. 3). The text cited here is very valuable as a testimony of Peter's overall method: a survey of *auctoritates* whose term is the *dicimus quod,* the determination of a more profound layer of *sententiae* through the use of dialectic. For further discussion, see Cloes, "Systématization théologique," 293 n. 98.

113.   That the integration of the treatise *De ultimis* was a positive achievement on the Lombard's part can be noted precisely from its absence in the work of some of his predecessors: the School of Anselm, the *Sententiae divinae paginae,* the *Ysagoge in theologiam,* the *Sententie* of Rolando. On this, see Cloes, "Systématization théologique," 310ff.   The credit for this innovation in systematization belongs to Hugh of St. Victor, although his precedent was not rigidly followed by his successors (e. g., Robert of Melun) even within his own school (e. g., the *Summa Sententiarum*); see Ghellinck, "Pierre Lombard," 2002.

114.   For example, despite its currency in the twelfth-century anti-Jewish apologetic (e.g., the *Ysagoge*), there is no tract, *De vera religione*; nor is

there a formal treatment *De* ecclesia, in spite of the significant emphasis placed upon that subject by the twelfth-century canonists. On these critiques, see Ghellinck, "Pierre Lombard," 1979.

115.   See the lacunae cited by Ghellinck, *Le mouvement thèologique*, 1980-1981, and Cloes, "Systématization théologique," 292ff.

116.   Cloes, "Systèmatization thèologique," notes (295-296): "La conclusion s'impose: loin de nous donner l'inspiration profonde et la clef de la systématisation des Sentences, les distinctions 'res--signa, frui--uti' ne servent que de cadre extérieur ou mieux d'introduction, toute superficielle, à la synthèse; elles font figure de leçon inaugurale où le maître place son oeuvre sous le patronage d'un grand nom, 'l'egregius doctor', dont l'autorité doit garantir une distribution des matières qui ne lui est pas empruntée. Bien qu'il n'érige pas méthodiquement en principe la division 'opus conditionis-opus restaurationis', Pierre Lombard suit en réalité le fil conducteur de la synthèse historico-biblique du Victorin: création, chute, ré-demption par le Verbe Incarné et par ses sacrements, consommation eschatologique." There is a great deal of justice in the author's accusation, for Peter certainly did not understand sacred history methodologically--as Saint Thomas would subsequently be able to do. Still, Cloes' criticism is too harsh. Firstly, even among the models of systematization which Cloes regards as "purely logical" (Abelard), sacred history is built back into the logical structure by means of the distinction of the twofold objects of faith. Moreover, one wonders whether there can ever be a Christian theology that

totally disregards (as opposed to being subjected to) the historical dimension of Christian faith.

117.   The extrinsic relation which the *res--signa/frui--uti* bore to the overall systematization of Peter Lombard's *Sentences* was perceived by one of his earliest "commentators," Gandulph of Bologna, who, motivated perhaps more by traditional catechetical objectives, merely substituted the Athanasian Creed for the Lombard's organizational remarks in the first distinction and then proceeded to follow Peter's overall contours. See Ghellinck, *Le mouvement théologique*, 1981.

118.   See Chenu, *La theologie*, 68-69.

119.   Such an understanding is implicit in Peter's appropriation of Augustine's formula from the *De doctrina* christiana, viz., "Res etiam per signa discuntur" (Bk I, d. i, c. 1).

120.   This process of institutionalization seems to have been initiated by the adoption of the *Sentences* as a theological textbook by Alexander of Hales; on this, see I. Brady, "The Distinctions of Lombard's Book of Sentences and Alexander of Hales," *Franciscan Studies* 25 (1965): 91-92.

121.   See Chenu, *Toward Understanding St. Thomas*, 266-267.   In *Le mouvement théologique,* Ghellinck notes deeper influences exercised by Peter Lombard on those who followed him: "Sans doute, il a contribué pour une part notable à renforcer la note technique que prenait la théologie; sous ce rapport son

action directe ou indirecte n'a pas été sans effet. On peut le regretter. Car, avec cette tendance intellectualiste, l'élément religieux de la doctrine risquait de ne plus attirer l'attention que fort secondairement, sinon dans la trame quotidienne de la vie, du moins dans l'enseignement scolaire qui, presque seul alors, contrairement à l'époque des Pères, représentait toute la théologie. Le temps n'était plus où l'on pouvait attendre des représentants de cet enseignement ces belles envolées méditatives, non moins pieuses que théologiques, qui donnait à la dévotion, respectueuse et affectueuse, une place au moins aussi grande qu'à la considération théorique des dogmes . . . . Un profond changement marquait les tendances nouvelles, avec la prépondérance du climat scolaire et le recul de l'ancienne *lectio* biblique et patristique, des *Verba* mea, *verba Patrum*" (249).

122. Chenu, *Toward Understanding St. Thomas*, 245.

AQUINAS' MIDDLE THOUGHTS ON THEOLOGY AS "SCIENCE"

Mark D. Jordan
The Medieval Institute
University of Notre Dame

Let me take, just as given, Leonard Boyle's elegant arguments about the origin of the marginal texts in MS 95 of Lincoln College, Oxford.[1] He has shown that the texts constitute a *reportatio* of Thomas Aquinas' second or Roman commentary on the *Sentences*. This commentary, composed by Thomas in Rome during 1265-1266, treats certain topics in the first book of the *Sentences*.[2] Thomas broke off from writing it in order to invent the *Summa theologiae*. Still, the Roman *Lectura* survived: an early copy of it is reported by Ptolemy of Lucca. But since it was not included in the first catalogues of Thomas' works, it played no role in the history of Thomism. It has remained hidden for seven centuries.

We readers of Thomas, however grateful and delighted we are by this discovery, must now pose a candid question that cannot be solved by codices alone.

Does this new text show itself to have been worth the wait? I can put the question most pointedly in this form. We had before the identification of the Lincoln College text a Thomist corpus of more than eight and one-half million words, mostly unread. To hear that a few ten thousands more have now been identified might seem ambiguous news, as if it were announced that fragments of a ninety-second novel by Balzac had just come to light. By Boyle's own account, the new text is not strikingly early or late. It does not take up subjects elsewhere neglected by its author, nor does it offer some secret or scandalous teaching. It is a middle text in every respect. What, then, can we learn from it?

We can learn a great deal, I think, and not only about Thomas' thoughts on the particular topics it treats. The opening section of the Roman *Lectura* offers us important help with Thomas' authorship as a whole and especially with its culmination in the *Summa theologiae*. To suggest how this might be so, I propose two approaches to the Roman *Lectura's* remarks on the standing of theological knowledge. First, I will insert the remarks into the received chronological sequence of thematically related texts and then ask whether our sense of the sequence changes. Then, second, I will ask whether the addition of the new text alters some recent debates over the meaning of those texts. The thematically related texts are, in sequence, the opening questions of the Parisian *Scriptum* on the *Sentences,* the second question of the exposition of Boethius' *De Trinitate,* and the first question of the *Summa.* The newly identified text on theology is to be inserted immediately before the text from the *Summa.*

Two objections to my proposed procedure must be

addressed immediately. First, there are complexities
not accounted for in the received chronology. Thomas
seems to have been revising the Parisian *Scriptum*
during his second Parisian regency, and we are not yet
in a position to sort out which text is the original and
which the revised.[3] Again, the dating of the Boethius
exposition is unsteady. Leaving aside doctrinal
comparisons, which would beg our question, the sole
bit of evidence is an asserted paraphrase in the
Sentences-commentary of one of Thomas' bachelors
(See Weisheipl, *Friar Thomas*). A second objection
arises from the literary genres of the various works to
be compared. Three of the texts in our comparison are
commentaries, and their concerns must be presumed to
be dictated in some way by the underlying text.

Both objections are worth taking to heart as
cautions, but neither prohibits the kind of comparative
reading I propose. To the objection of chronological
uncertainty, I am willing to grant that the Boethius
commentary may be a few years earlier or later than
the first "published" form of the *Scriptum* on the
Sentences. It will make no difference. Later revision
of the *Scriptum* would indeed make a difference, but
there is only one passage in the question on theology
that seems to have been added later.[4] To the objection
from commentary genre, I should say that in all of
these passages we are dealing with topics imposed on
the text rather than elicited from them. So there is
little to fear from covert influences of the underlying
text.

1. Reading the *Lectura* into the Corpus

If we may justifiably proceed with a comparative

reading of the new text against its parallels, we must still know what to look for in reading. I would like to suggest comparisons at three levels: the levels of textual authorities and staple arguments, of topical order, and of pedagogical project. The interrelations of the texts are more complicated and more simultaneous than the separation of three levels would suggest, but there is no other way to lay out a reading discursively than by making such artificial divisions.

(1) The level of textual authorities and staple arguments is often one of the most revealing in Thomas. It registers not only remarkable persistences or surprising turns in the authorities used, but also the developing desire for selection and simplification. Unfortunately, the usual analysis of *auctoritates* cannot be carried out on this portion of the Roman *Lectura*. The text is not fully supplied with citations and many arguments or allusions are merely indicated, as if by gesture. Thomas would have polished the whole, particularly by filling in his footnotes, if he had prepared it for publication. One can see this, I think, by noticing points at which the Roman *Lectura* invokes a principle that is more fully cited in one of the parallel texts. So, for example, the *Lectura* offers this argument against sacred doctrine being a properly constituted body of knowledge: "Moreover, no science is of particulars, etc."[5] The reference is clearly to the argument in the Parisian *Scriptum*: "No science is of particulars, according to the Philosopher, *Posterior Analytics* 1. But in sacred Scripture particular deeds of particular men are described . . . . Therefore it is not a science" (*Scriptum super Sent*. prol. 1.3.2 arg. 1 (Mandonnet-Moos 1:11). In its finished form, the *Lectura* would presumably have given us the argument

and an authority. Even where the *Lectura* mentions an authority, it does so without the explicitness of some parallel texts: *Boetius* replaces *Boetius in primo libro De Trinitate,* and so on.[6] On the other hand, maxims pass in and out of anonymity from one text to another. Thus, the Roman *Lectura* tells us: "As the Philosopher says, the subject of a science is that of which are sought the passions and parts."[7] In the exposition of Boethius, the same maxim is used in the same way, but without the citation (*Super Boethii De Trin.* 2.2 arg. 3 [Decker 85.13-14]). It is thus impossible to carry out a comparison of authorities and arguments as if the Roman *Lectura* were a finished text or as if all authorities were explicit.

We can notice the persistence of arguments and terminologies from one Thomist text to the other. In the first two articles of the Roman *Lectura,* for example, every *argumentum* or *sed contra* has an exact precedent in the two earlier texts.[8] Many of these are not peculiar to Thomas; they can be found in the writings of his teachers and colleagues. Some of the textual continuities are peculiar to Thomas. The Roman *Lectura* mentions that a certain Simonides taught that we ought not to busy ourselves about divine things, which are too high for us. The association of this doctrine with Simonides is Thomas' own addition to an Aristotelian text (see Dondaine, "'Alia lectura,'" 313). Again, the *Lectura's* defense of the use of philosophical authorities in expounding Scripture seems almost a rearrangement of selected points from his commentary on Boethius (Dondaine, "'Alia lectura,'" 314). Indeed, the textual continuities are so strong that they might seem to argue against the importance of the *Lectura.* This brings us to the second comparison.

(2) I proposed a second comparison at the level of *topical order,* that is, of the sequence within which received topics are disposed and new topics invented. Precisely because of the strong continuities between the earlier Thomist texts and the *Lectura,* exact comparisons of their topical orders can be made. They are quite revealing. If we look backwards from the first question of the *Summa,* the Roman *Lectura* marks the point at which Thomas settled for himself the right order for raising issues about theological knowledge. He then used this order in the *Summa* to organize all of the issues that had appeared in the previous treatments.

The orders adopted in the *Scriptum* and the commentary on *De Trinitate* are variously inappropriate. The *Scriptum* begins rightly by asking whether some study beyond philosophy is necessary, but it then proceeds to ask about details of the doctrine of the Trinity before settling its fundamental character as knowledge. We ask whether it is one or many and whether it is practical or speculative before we know whether it is science.[9] The *Scriptum* further separates the question whether the needed teaching is science from the question what its subject might be (*Super Sent.* prol. 1.3.2, prol. 1.4). Again, the *Scriptum* runs together under a single query about the mode of the teaching such issues as the use of philosophical argument and the senses of Scripture (*Super Sent.,* prol. 1.5).

The commentary on Boethius does somewhat better. It takes as heading "the manifestation of divine cognition" in order to treat four issues under it: whether it is licit to investigate divine things; whether there can be science about them; whether one can use philosophical reasonings in this science; whether this science ought to speak esoterically (*Super Boethii De Trin.* 2.1-4). Still too much has been left out--the unity of the science, its character as speculative or practical, its position in the hierarchies, its being most truly wisdom, and so on.

In the Roman *Lectura,* the mature order of topics emerges, combining the features of the two previous texts while opening the way to the *Summa* (*Lectura super Sent.* prol. 1-4.4). Thomas here divides the topics into four: the doctrine as science; the object of the science; the science as speculative and practical; the mode of the science. The last is then itself divided into four *quaestiunculae,* which defend (in order) theology's narrative and poetic modes, the rational investigation of holy things, the use of philosophic authorities, and the use of theological authorities other than Scripture. In moving to the *Summa,* Thomas does little more than to break up this pattern into coordinate articles and to recall as separate certain sub-topics that had appeared separately in the earlier texts.

The gain made by the Roman *Lectura* is certainly a gain in logical rigor. This gain is passed on to the *Summa.* Still the motive of reorganization in the *Lectura* is not only rigor, but also pedagogy. Now any gain in logical rigor is a gain in pedagogy, since demonstration is the most potent means of rational instruction. I mean something more: Thomas' prudent selections and simplifications of inherited material. I can make my point clearly only by turning to the last level of comparison.

(3) I proposed, as the third and last level in reading, a comparison of pedagogical projects. A "pedagogical project" is the pattern of teaching that a whole text wants to enact for its readers.[10] We know

Thomas to have been much concerned to find the right pedagogical project for theology, and we know that this concern led him finally to the structure of the *Summa*. The chief structural accomplishment of the *Summa* is to place a clarified and grounded moral theology at the center of an introduction to the whole of Christian teaching. This accomplishment is prepared in the opening of the Roman *Lectura*.

The prologue to the Parisian *Scriptum* unfolds a verse from Ecclesiasticus to reveal Christ as the fourfold wisdom of God. To the Word of God is especially appropriated the manifestation of the divine Persons, the mediation of creation, the work of restoring creation, and the conserving of all things in their last end. These four tasks of the divine wisdom are made to explain the division into four books of Peter Lombard's *Sentences*.

The prologue to the Roman *Lectura* begins as well from a verse out of Ecclesiasticus, and ends rather more simply with a division of the Sentences into two pairs of books. In between, it represents a series of schemata, each of which insists on the double character of theology as contemplative and moral. Indeed, Thomas begins the Roman *Lectura* by announcing that the teaching of every knowledge has been governed by a double intention, the demonstration of truth and the acquisition of blessedness. Every other science is typed to one half or another of this intention. Some seek only the cognition of truth, while others seek the activities by which we come to blessedness. Theology "completely contains and teaches" (*perfecte comprehendit et docet*) both the speculative and the practical.

Abruptly the prologue seems to change direction.

Because our happiness is found only in things higher than us, Thomas argues, the speculative sciences are concerned with "sublime and elevated" (*sublimis et eleuata*) truth. There are three degrees of elevation in speculative truth. The first corresponds to the "natural accounts of particular things" (*naturales rationes rerum particularium*). The second answers to those immaterial things that are knowable by accounts drawn from natural things (*secundum se immaterialia, cognoscibilia tamen per rationes rerum naturalium*). The highest degree, the third, corresponds to those immaterial things that are above all accounts of natural things, exceeding every capacity of reason. The first degree is that of physics and mathematics; the second, of metaphysics; the third, of theology, the science of Scripture. It is theology that speaks in the verse from Ecclesiasticus: "I dwell in the heights and my throne is in the column of cloud." The verse enunciates three features of theology: the height of its matter, the certainty of its cognition, and the perpetuity of its duration.

Thomas now connects this with his starting-point. Theology not only leads to the cognition of truth, but also to the completeness of blessedness. It does so in three ways: by considering not only the things that make us blessed, but also those that lead to what makes us blessed and those that serve blessedness instrumentally. These three relations to blessedness are projected into Christ himself. His divinity is the enjoyment of blessedness. His soul is the example of the virtues that lead to blessedness. His flesh is the instrument of blessedness so far as it offers remedies against impediments to blessedness. The triple nature of theology's concern with blessedness has now been led back to the threefold Christ.

Thomas does not stop. He adds a final schema, a
final pattern of likeness by which theology is seen as
an image of Christ: Christ himself is the column of
cloud that led the children of Israel in their exodus.
He illumines and refreshes his children. More: Christ
is the column by his firmness and by the hiddenness of
his divinity. So too theology is the column leading
Israel out of Egypt. It has its throne high above all
other sciences; it stands firm on God's eternal
revelation; it consoles by pouring forth the spirit.
Therefore, Thomas concludes, this science of theology
concerns itself both with the contemplation of truth and
with showing the true way to blessedness. And so
Lombard's *Sentences* is properly divided into two. The
first part treats of God and creatures; the second, with
Christ, the virtues, the sacraments, and blessedness.

We are accustomed to associate a breathless
rehearsal of Scriptural patterns rather with Bonaventure
than with Thomas. Perhaps we need to change our
ways. Thomas has moved us, very quickly, from a
dichotomy of speculative and practical, through a
trichotomy of intelligible objects, to a trichotomy of
objects for the study of blessedness, its reduction to the
threefold Christ, who then becomes in two or three
ways the cloud of Exodus, which cloud is also a figure
for theology, which thus refuses the original dichotomy
in order to teach contemplation of truth as the activity
of blessedness. The whole succession of figures aims
to show just this--that theology is the unique science
that cannot be made either theoretical or practical. It
must be both.

Thomas does not need to repeat the same
introduction at the beginning of the *Summa* because the

very structure of the *Summa* enacts the unity of theoretical and practical. It is enough in the *Summa* to reduce the preliminary discussion of the issue to a single article, the shortest in the first Question, because the reader will see the issue resolved in reading the *Summa*, perhaps especially in grasping the order and position of the *secundae pars*. But those who need a more explicit introduction now have it, in the prologue to the Roman *Lectura*.

I would offer this relation to the *Summa* as one reason, at least, for thinking that the new text is importantly helpful to the reading of Thomas. I would also count it as one explanation for why Thomas broke off his attempt at an exposition of the *Sentences* in Rome. No matter how fine the prologue or how thorough the introduction, Peter Lombard's *Sentences* will not permit a coherent treatment of moral life. In order to complete the task that Thomas set for himself in the new prologue, he had to set aside the *Sentences* and invent a hybrid genre, at once academic and pastoral, that would be adequate to a theology both theoretical and practical. But that is another story--and one that Fr. Boyle has also had more than a small share in telling.

2. Reading the *Lectura* into Contemporary Debates

If the newly recovered text of the Roman *Lectura* helps us better to understand the development of Thomas' authorship, is it of any help in resolving disputes about Thomas' teaching on the nature of theology? This question can only be addressed piecemeal. The disputes are numerous and quick to change. But even to speak about a few of the them will help in

judging the importance of the new text.[11]   So I will
introduce the Roman *Lectura* as new evidence for three
recent scholarly discussions: (1) the disagreement
between Weisheipl and O'Brien on the context of *sacra
doctrina*; (2) Corbin's thesis about the development of
Thomas' notion of theology; and (3) the controversy
between Patfoort and Leroy over the relations between
sacra doctrina and *theologia*.

   I turn to my second case. In a brilliant and difficult
book, Michel Corbin argues that the sequence of
Thomas' texts on theology records a development in
the strictest sense.[12]   The transit from the *Scriptum* on
the *Sentences* to the *Summa* is an irreversible progress
in the resolution of dialectical tensions within conceptions of theology.   Thus Corbin can summarize his
narrative about Thomas' texts as a table of presences
and absences (Corbin, *Chemin*, 92).   Certain doctrines
or devices appear with each new Thomist text
according to an inner logic of conceptions.

   Now Corbin wrote before Boyle had identified the
report of the Roman *Lectura*. So that *reportatio* does
not figure in Corbin's table or in his considerations.
But it does provide an excellent if unplanned test of
Corbin's grand hypothesis. With the Roman *Lectura*,
we have a Thomist text about theology that falls
chronologically between the last two points on Corbin's
line.   Does it also fall on the line of doctrinal
development that he sketches?

   For Corbin, the *Scriptum* on the *Sentences* is
characterized by the structural parallel between
theology and philosophy; the commentary on Boethius'
De Trinitate by the preambles of faith; the *Contra
Gentiles* by the double mode of truth; the *Summa
theologiae* by the centrality of Scripture and tradition.

He then converts the list of characteristics into a narrative. In the *Scriptum*, the philosophy/theology parallel betrays an angelic view of the possibilities for a human *intellectus fidei*. This drives Thomas in the commentary on Boethius to see that theology is human discourse that must already contain philosophy. The *Scriptum's* external analogy of *rationes fidei* and *rationes naturales* is replaced by a division within theology between *rationes persuasoriae* and *rationes demonstrativae*. The *Contra Gentiles* takes up the doubling of the *intellectus fidei* as its basic structure, placing all the *rationes demonstrativae* before the *persuasoriae*. Since the truth of faith reflects the absolutely simple God, Thomas must reduce the doubling by tracing a movement of reason from creatures back to God. But the posterior unity of reason's ascent does not jibe with the prior unity of the truth as a gift from God. More importantly, the prior unity of theology, which uses reasons as servant, cannot be grounded by the posterior unity of reason, which tries to scale heaven by similitudes. So there is another step to be taken. The *Summa* transforms the notion of theology yet again, explaining it as the unitary interpretation of the finite course of the revealed Word of God, embodied in Scripture and tradition.

There are certainly questions to be raised about this narrative as a fair rendering of the texts it mentions. I set them aside. Is the narrative confirmed or disrupted by the identification of the Roman *Lectura*? I would argue that the narrative is disrupted in at least two ways. First, the Roman *Lectura* shows that Thomas conceived the treatment of theology in the *Summa* as a variation on topics in the *Scriptum*. The immediate background for *Summa theologiae* 1.1 is not the commentary on Boethius or the opening of the *Contra Gentiles* (which is not strictly comparable to the texts about theology), but rather the questions that Thomas had introjected into his earlier reading of the *Sentences*. Second, the Roman *Lectura* emphasizes, if more emphasis were needed, how much continuity there is in the elements from which Thomas builds his various accounts. What explains his progress is not a table of presences and absences, but a table of arrangements and rearrangements. In short, the appearance of the Roman *Lectura* has made Corbin's thesis more doubtful.

I turn to my third and final case. Albert Patfoort has written for several decades on the nature of Thomist theology and its structural implications. In 1983, versions of five of his essays were collected in a small volume as a preface or companion to the reading of Thomas.[13] The volume was reviewed by M. V. Leroy, who attacked one of its principal claims about Thomas' understanding of theology.[14] The review elicited a formal reply.[15] The heart of the controversy concerns the relations of *sacra doctrina* and *theologia* (Patfoort, "Sacra doctrina," 306, 308-315). Patfoort continues to hold that the topic of *Summa theologiae* 1.1 is *sacra doctrina*, not *theologia*. *Sacra doctrina* is the whole of Christian teaching as exemplified in the Scriptures. *Theologia* is the part of *sacra doctrina* concerned with the non-symbolic, argumentative elaboration of Christian doctrine on the basis of authorities that include, but also extend beyond the Scriptures. Hence the first quaestio of the *Summa* is not meant to secure the method of the work that follows. It is, rather, a sketch of the larger whole within which the *Summa* and its enterprise fall.

Neither Patfoort nor Leroy refer to the preliminary articles of the Roman *Lectura*. How would those articles affect their debate? Patfoort argues his case on two features of *Summa theologiae* 1.1. First, he claims, Thomas does not interchange the expressions *sacra doctrina* and *theologia,* however much he interchanges *sacra doctrina* and *haec scientia.* Second, Thomas allows to *sacra doctrina,* called *haec scientia,* the use of quasi-poetic images and symbols. Argumentative theology is denied their use. Now the Roman *Lectura* offers additional evidence on both of these points. First, although the term *theologia* is as rare in the *Lectura* as in the *Summa,* Thomas does identify it explicitly with the *sacra doctrina* of Scripture. Indeed, he begins with *theologia: ista tamen scientia, scilicet theologiae (Lectura super Sent.* prol. [fol. 2ra]). The content of the highest science of immaterials is named as the subject of the Scriptures.[16] Within the space of a few lines, *ista scientia* and *haec scientia* are frequently interchanged. Moreover, the content of *ista scientia* is divided according to the division of Lombard's *Sentences,* that is, of the authoritative reference work for *theologia.*[17] Moreover, and more strikingly, the third and fourth *quaestiunculae* of the fourth article ask whether philosophical and patristic authorities are to be used--not in theology--but in *sacra scriptura.*[18] Here, plainly, the argumentative mode of Patfoort's *theologia* is applied directly to the science of the Scriptures.

NOTES

1. Leonard E. Boyle, "'Alia lectura fratris Thome,'" *Mediaeval Studies* 45 (1983): 418-429. Fr. Boyle's essay reconsiders and supplements the evidence adduced in H.-F. Dondaine, "'Alia lectura fratris Thomas'? (*Super I Sent.*)," *Mediaeval Studies* 42 (1980): 308-336.

2. For the circumstances of its composition, see Boyle throughout, and James A. Weisheipl, *Friar Thomas d'Aquino: His Life, Thought and Works* (New York: Doubleday, 1974; reported with corrigenda and addenda, Washington: Catholic University of America, 1983), 216-217, with the addenda on 471. For a list of the topics treated by the Roman *Lectura,* see Mark F. Johnson.

3. The redactional problems afflicting the printed traditions of the Parisian *Scriptum* have long been recognized. See G. Rossi, "L'autografo di S. Tommaso del Commento al III libro delle Sentenze," *Divus Thomas* [Piacenza] 35 (1932): 532-585; Antoine Dondaine, "S. Thomas a-t-il disputé à Rome la question des 'attributs divins,'" *Bulletin Thomiste* (1933): 171-182 (with regard to the text later inserted as *Scriptum* 1.2.3); André Hayen, "S. Thomas a-t-il édité deux fois son Commentaire sur le livre des Sentences?" *Recherches de théologie ancienne et médiévale* 9 (1937): 219-236; M.-D. Chenu, *La théologie comme science aux XIIIe siècle* (Paris: J. Vrin, 1943), 82-83; P.-M. Gils, "Textes inédits de S. Thomas: Les premières rédactions du *Scriptum super tertio Sententiarum,*" *Revue des sciences philosophiques et théologiques* 45 (1961): 201-228; P.-

M. Gils, "Codicologie et critique textuelle: Pour une étude du ms. Pamplona, Catedral 51," *Scriptorium* 32 (1978): 221-230; Adolfo Robles Sierra, "Fragmento autografo de IV de las Sentencias de Santo Tomas," *Escritos del Vedat* 10 (1980): 565-579 (with regard to a fragment of *Scriptum* from 4.25.1.2 ad 2 to the end of 4.25.1.2, which contains an article not in printed tradition); R. H. and M. Rouse, in *La production du livre universitaire*.

4. This is the passage in *Scriptum super Sent.* pr[=prol.].1.2 *sol.*, "Vel dicendum quod in scientia duo est considerare . . . a qua accipit principia sua" (ed. Mandonnet-Moos [Paris: Lethielleux, 1929-1947], 1.13-14). It appears in Mandonnet-Moos, but not in the Parma edition of the same text (see *Opera omnia* [Parma: Petrus Fiaccadori). Moreover, the supplementary character of the passage is clear from its diction (*vel dicendum*) and its position *after* the reply to the first *argumentum* (*et quod objicitur, quod est de particularibus*). The insertion is noteworthy, because it represents the only passage in the *Scriptum* that uses the notion of subalternated science. I will come back to this below.

5. *Lectura super Sent.* prol. 1.2, as in Oxford, Lincoln College MS 95 f. 4ra: "Preterea, nulla scientia est de particularibus etc." For subsequent references I will simply cite the apparent textual divisions and then the foliation of this MS.

6. For the Boethius, compare *Scriptum super Sent.* prol. 1.4 arg. 1 *contra* (Mandonnet-Moos 1:15) and *Lectura super Sent.* prol. 3 arg. 4 (f. 4va).

7. *Lectura super Sent.* prol. 2 arg. 2 (f. 4va): "Preterea, sicut dicit Philosophus, subiectum scientie est cuius queruntur passiones et partes."

8. Thus, *Lectura super Sent.* prol. 1 arg. 1 = *Scriptum super Sent.* prol. 1.3.2 arg. 2 and *Super Boethii De Trin.* 2.2 arg. 5; *Lectura* prol. 1 arg. 2 = *Sent.* prol. 1.3.2 arg. 1; *Lectura* prol. 1 arg. 3 = *Sent.* prol. 1.1 arg. 1; *Lectura* prol. 1 arg. 4 = *Sent.* prol. 1.2 arg. 1; *Lectura* prol. 1 sc = *De Trin.* 2.2 sc 1; *Lectura* prol. 2 arg. 1 = *Sent.* prol. 1.2 arg. 1; *Lectura* prol. 2 arg. 2 = *De Trin.* 2.2 arg. 3; *Lectura* prol. 2 arg. 3 = *De Trin.* 2.3 *corp.*; *Lectura* prol. 2 arg. 4 = *Sent.* prol. 1.4 arg. 1 *contra* and *De Trin.* 2.2 arg. 3; *Lectura* 2 sc = *De Trin.* 2.2 *corp.* and throughout.

9. Recall the order of *Super Sent.* prol. 1.2, prol. 1.3.1, and prol. 1.3.2.

10. To understand Thomas' pedagogical projects, it is not enough to rehearse or to attempt to classify his very familiar remarks on the Augustinian puzzles about the causality of human teaching. See, for example, Christoph Schönborn, "Die Autorität des Lehrers nach Thomas von Aquin," in *Christian Authority: Essays in Honour of Henry Chadwick,* ed. G. R. Evans (Oxford: Clarendon Press, 1988), 101-126. At a minimum, an account of Thomas on teaching must include what he has to say about acquiring habits, as in Wolfgang Schmidl, *Homo discens: Studien zur pädagogischen Anthropologie bei Thomas von Aquin,* Österreichische Akademie der Wissenschaften, Philosophisch-Historische Klasse, Sitzungsberichte 487 (Vienna: Verlag der Österreichische Akademie, 1987), 91-134.

But Thomas' pedagogical projects can only be seen as they are carried out. A reader who is interested in understanding Thomas as teacher will not neglect the achieved order of his pedagogical works in favor of his brief remarks on pedagogy. Just so the reader interested in Thomas' notions of theology will not ignore the actual procedure of the *Summa* in order to concentrate only on the few pages of its opening *quaestio*.

11. I select the disputes partly for their interest, partly for their precision. Much of what is written about Thomas on theology is too general to be affected by the discovery of new textual evidence. See, for example, Johannes Stöhr, "Theologie als 'Sacra doctrina' bei Thomas von Aquin und in neueren Auffassungen," in *Veritati catholicae: Festschrift für Leo Scheffczyk zum 65. Geburtstag,* ed. Anton Ziegenaus, Franz Courth, and Philipp Schäfer (Aschaffenburg: Pattloch, 1985), 672-696 (the essay does provide an introduction to early modern Thomistic commentary); and Otto Hermann Pesch, *Thomas von Aquin: Grenze und Grösse mittelalterlicher Theologie, Eine Einführung* (Mainz: Matthias-Grünewald, 1988), 108-144.

12. Michel Corbin, *Le chemin de la théologie chez Thomas d'Aquin,* Bibliothèque des Archives de Philosophie NS 16 (Paris: Beauchesne, 1974). I tried to provide a fuller response to Corbin in "The Modes of Thomistic Discourse," *The Thomist* 45 (1981): 80-98. In what follows, I assume the essential correctness of my earlier reading.

13. Albert Patfoort, *Saint Thomas d'Aquin: Les clés d'une théologie* (Paris: Éds. FAC, 1983). The two essays now in question appeared originally as "Théorie de la théologie ou réflexion sur le corpus des Écritures?," *Angelicum* 54 (1977): 459-488, and "La concezione della teologia secondo S. Tommaso," *Sapienza* 35 (1982): 259-270.

14. M. V. Leroy, review of Patfoort, *Revue Thomiste* 84 (1984): 298-302. See also the reviews of the original versions of Patfoort's essays by Clemens Vansteenkiste in *Rassegna di letteratura tomista* 13 (1980), # 695, and 18 (1985), #525.

15. Albert Patfoort, "*Sacra doctrina,* théologie, et unité de la *Iᵃ pars,*" *Angelicum* 62 (1985): 306-319. Compare Clemens Vansteenkiste's review of this essay, *Rassegna di letteratura tomista* 21 (1988): 231-232, #533.

16. *Lectura super Sent.* prol. (fol. 2ra): "Tertius gradus [*scil.* scientiarum] est quia aliqua sunt in se immaterialia et super autem omnes rationes naturalium rerum. . . . Et de hiis est sacra scriptura, quia illa tradit nobis que superant capacitatem rationis."

17. *Lectura super Sent.* prol. (fol. 2ra): "Sic igitur in ista scientia uersatur circa duo, scilicet circa contemplationem in altitudine veritatis et ostensionem uere beatitudinis. Et inde est quod Magister in duas partes diuidit librum istum sententiarum." Compare *Lectura* prol. 4.1 arg. 4, where the argument holds that if *hec scientia* is sufficiently given in Scripture, then books such as the Lombard's are superfluous. The

argument would not have force unless the one science embraced both the Scriptures and academic theology.

18. *Lectura super Sent.* prol. 4.3-4 (fol. 6ra-rb): "Hic queritur utrum in sacra scriptura liceat uti auctoritatibus philosophorum"; "Hic queritur utrum in sacra scriptura liceat uti auctoritatibus sanctorum."

MAIMONIDES, AQUINAS, AND THEOLOGISM

William Dunphy
St. Michael's College,
University of Toronto

Medieval philosophy was largely concerned with the efforts of thinkers from the Jewish, Christian, and Islamic communities to come to terms with the polytheistic, non-creational, and deterministic elements of the classical Platonic, Aristotelian, and Neoplatonic traditions. What was required for these communities, to say the least, were major modifications, if not transformations, of those elements.

While the *demiurgos* of Plato's *Timaeus* appeared to some as adaptable to the Creator of Genesis, the world of Aristotelian natures seemed to be incompatible with a world that was created. The exigencies of an eternally ordered and necessarily produced world seemed to demand a "God" that was utterly bereft of any freedom in producing, ordering, and, indeed, even knowing such a world.

Thus, it was a major problem for any Jewish,

Christian, or Islamic thinker who wished to keep the marvelous "baby" of the orderly, regulated, and rational Greek world, while throwing out the "bathwater" of implacable necessitarianism. They had to transform Aristotle's "unmoved mover" into something it was not, namely, the freely creating personal God of Genesis and the *Qur'an,* for whom no falling sparrow escapes the divine providential care.

Indeed, for some of their co-religionists, this was more than just a major problem: it was a self-contradictory impossibility. These began by affirming their religious conception of God as the omnipotent and radically free, voluntary Creator of everything that existed and then set about to construct a philosophical view of the created world that would not compromise any of these divine attributes.

Etienne Gilson devoted a chapter of his book, *The Unity of Philosophical Experience,* to this approach and labelled it "theologism." Based on his 1936 lectures at Harvard University, Gilson understood the "experiences" in his title to be a series of attempts in history to use points of view or methodologies of non-philosophical disciplines to deal with properly philosophical problems, leading inevitably, in his view, to the near destruction of philosophy. He described one of those attempts, theologism, as follows:

> When theologians attempt to remodel philosophy to suit their own beliefs [and] . . . where the revealed truth is, by hypothesis, absolute truth, the only way to save philosophy is to show that its teaching is substantially the same as that of revealed religion. (*Unity,* 36-37)[1]

He observed further that, regardless of the various

times, places, and civilizations in which such "theologians" arose, they were all "thoroughly intoxicated with a definite religious feeling . . . of the Glory of God," and thus, Gilson noted:

> The better to extol the glory of God, pious-minded theologians proceed joyfully to annihilate God's own creation. God is great and high and almighty; what better proof could be given of these truths than that nature and man are essentially insignificant, low and utterly powerless creatures.[2]

But why would any theologian feel compelled to hold such an extreme view? One answer might be that they saw in philosophy or in certain philosophical positions a serious threat to the very foundation of their religion.

One such threat from Greek philosophy, for example, was that of the so-called "eternal world," that is, one whose duration was without beginning or end. Now, one religious truth common to Judaism, Christianity, and Islam is the affirmation of the temporal creation of the world. This would seem directly to contradict the philosophers' view of an eternal world with its necessary production or emanation from a First Cause, for which view they claimed to have irrefutable demonstrations. This situation would account for the proliferation and collections of arguments throughout the Middle Ages which attempted to demonstrate either that the world is eternal or, conversely, that it had a beginning.

The latter set of arguments were developed by religious thinkers who came to be known as the men of *kalam* or *mutakallimun,* that is, those who sought to give a rational account of, or to study, *theos,* the divine, or God, where the term *kalam* is equivalent to the Greek term *logos*. Indeed, these thinkers literally could be called theologians, provided one restricts that meaning to a basically apologetic usage. These theologians turned to philosophy's rational argumentation in an effort to discover positions that could be used to shield their religious doctrines from philosophical attack.

Regarding the so-called eternal world controversy, these *mutakallimun* of the three faiths regarded the philosophers' purported demonstrations of the world's eternity as a blatant denial of the existence of a personal, creating God. As we shall see, they developed philosophical world views that entailed the existence of an absolutely free, omnipotent, personal God, creator of everything else that exists. In their view, then, the *kalamic* arguments for the world's temporal beginning and the philosophical arguments for its eternity were mutually exclusive.

Two major theologians, however--one Jewish, Moses Maimonides (1135-1204), the other Christian, Thomas Aquinas (1225-1274)--refused to see those opposed positions as truly disjunctive. Because of their basic metaphysical and epistemological principles, they argued that the *kalamic* proofs were merely probable at best, and, in most cases, sophistical or fallacious. At the same time, they mounted refutations of the philosophers' proofs for the world's eternity. In doing so, both thinkers clearly separated the question of the world's duration, whether *ab aeterno* or *de novo,* from the question of its origin, namely, whether it was a creature or not. It must be admitted, parenthetically, that their own contemporaries and centuries of later historians have had difficulty in recognizing this distinction and the fundamental importance it has to an understanding of the thought of both Maimonides and Aquinas.[3]

The *mutakallimun* of the three faiths also perceived, in varying degrees to be sure, that a stable world of nature, as elaborated in Aristotle's *Physics,* was the very foundation of the philosophers' demonstrations that the world is being perpetually moved and requires, therefore, a Prime Mover or necessary First Cause. Such a stable world of nature consisted of various substantial entities, each modified in various accidental ways (quantitatively, qualitatively, relationally, etc.). These entities possessed a stable, intelligible nature or essence from which flowed certain essential traits and activities that ground scientific accounts of the world.

If, therefore, to a pious-minded theologian of the sort we are describing, the accepted philosophical view of the world necessarily led one to the view of an eternal world necessarily moved by God, as its unmoved mover or First Cause, then their task was clear: devise a different world view that would be compatible with the notion of the omnipotent, free, creating God of revelation. In such a view, all causal power would be vested in a Creator who could just as easily will that fire cool as that it heat, or that an elephant be the size of a flea.

In this paper, then, I would like to explore two related instances of what Gilson called theologisms, one largely Islamic, the other Christian, and present the strong, contemporary reactions to them by the twelfth-century Jewish thinker, Moses Maimonides, and the thirteenth-century Christian, Thomas Aquinas.

Maimonides

Moses Maimonides, who died in 1204, was known to the medieval west exclusively through latin translations of his *Guide for the Perplexed.* This work was intended to show religious Jewish intellectuals, already perfect in moral virtue and well trained in science, that, in the presence of scriptural passages seemingly contradicting scientific conclusions, they did not have to choose between their religion and their science.[4]

Part of this task involved Maimonides presenting and then refuting the views of those who espoused what Gilson called theologism and to whom Maimonides, and indeed history, referred as *mutakallimun* or men of *kalam.* In Latin translations of works dealing with these *mutakallimun,* they were variously referred to as *loquentes in lege Maurorum* (or *Saracenorum*), meaning the practitioners of a rational account of the religion of Islam.

According to Maimonides' summary history of *kalam* in chapter 71 of part one of his *Guide,* it first arose in Greek and Syrian Christian communities as the learned among them came to realize that some of the positions of the philosophers, who were both widely known and respected, could destroy the very foundations of their faith. Thus they began to develop rational premises that would be useful both in establishing the truth of those foundations and shielding them from philosophical attack. Maimonides mentions the sixth-century Christian, John Philoponus, in this regard. This theologistic approach to philosophy was continued when Islam superseded Christianity in these areas and, to a lesser extent, was adopted by some Jewish thinkers within Islamic jurisdictions.[5]

As Maimonides saw it, then, what all these men of *kalam* had in common was the search for philosophical positions that could support religious doctrines and then conform their views of reality to those positions. They "considered how being ought to be in order that it should furnish a proof for the correctness of [their] opinion" rather than to "conform in their premises to . . . that which exists." They could proceed in this way, Maimonides tells us, because they believed that "no consideration is due to how that which exists is, for it is merely a custom; and from the point of view of the intellect, it could well be different" (*Commentary*, 178-179). Just why these "men of *kalam*" had to deny the evidence of their senses and to deny the existence of any stable world of nature becomes clear in Maimonides' presentation of their fundamental philosophical premises and purported demonstrations of the world's beginning in time.

He lists twelve premises common to all *loquentes* while recognizing the diversity of their opinions and the multiplicity of their arguments. The premises include the views that the world is made up of individual particles, called atoms, that exist in a vacuum and in indivisible instants of time. And while they use the language of "substance" and "accidents," it is certainly not the same as Aristotle's (*Guide*, as in chapter seventy-three). For example, they claim that an accident, which subsists in a substance, does not last during two units of time. What appears to be a continued existence of a species of accident is, in reality, the continued, successive creation by God of that kind of accident as long as He wills it to be, and to be in that way. As Maimonides put it:

> They assert that when a man moves a pen, it is not
> the man who moves it; for the motion occurring in
> the pen is an accident created by God in the pen.
> Similarly, the motion of the hand, which we think of
> as moving the pen, is an accident created by God in
> the moving hand.   (*Guide*, 202-203)

And, of course, an observer who habitually associated
the moving hand as being the cause of the moving pen
has that habituation created in his knowledge by God
as well.

In sum, Maimonides says that they wish to assert
that there is no corporeal entity endowed with the
power of action. The ultimate and, indeed, the only
agent is therefore God. This entails the further view
that when I think that it is I who wills to move the
pen, it is actually God who created the volition in me,
along with the motion of the hand and of the pen.
Conversely, God has to create, continuously and
successively, accidents of rest in the pen (or rather,
successions of created pens) for as long as there is no
moving pen.

A major foundation of the *kalamic* positions is,
for Maimonides, the tenth premise that "anything that
may be imagined is an admissible notion for the
intellect." For example, it is possible to have an
elephant created in the size of a flea, and vice versa.
Indeed, that fire burns and water cools could equally
well be reversed by the will of the all-powerful God.
The only limitations to God's omnipotence would be
those entailing contradictions. Experiential evidence is,
therefore, totally beside the point. In short, what is the
case now with every reality we experience could very
well be its opposite at another time. There are no
natures of things, no laws of nature, and no truly

causative actions in that which exists (*Guide*, 206-212).

The twelfth and final premise in Maimonides' systematic ordering of the *mutakallimun* positions, is that the senses do not lead one to the truth of the matter. This provides them, he claims, with a blanket defense against any critic who might appeal to sensory evidence in order to refute their assertions (*Guide*, 213-214). He notes that this whole approach constitutes a reversal of the correct procedure. He would agree rather with Themistius who put it that "that which exists does not conform to the various opinions, but rather the correct opinions conform to that which exists" (*Guide*, 179).

When it came to adducing rational proofs for the existence, oneness, and incorporeality of God, all of the men of *kalam,* according to Maimonides, insisted on starting with proofs that the world had a beginning in time. Since he was convinced that neither a temporal creation nor an eternal world could be cogently demonstrated ("it is a point before which the intellect stops"), Maimonides confessed to feeling a very strong aversion in his soul to their approach:

> For every argument deemed to be a demonstration of the temporal creation of the world is accompanied by doubts and is not a cogent demonstration except among those who do not know the difference between demonstration, dialectics, and sophistic argument. (*Guide*, 180).

Maimonides himself chose not to base his demonstrations of the existence, oneness, and incorporeality of God on such weak and necessarily flawed arguments for a temporal beginning of the world. Rather, prescinding from the question of whether the world's duration be *ab aeterno* or *de novo,* he preferred to side with those philosophers who, starting with an already existing, sensibly perceived, world of nature, constructed therefrom proofs that God exists, is one and incorporeal. He would deny, however, that they have any valid demonstrations that such a created world is *ab aeterno,* any more than the *loquentes* have any valid demonstration that it is *de novo.*

Now, while Maimonides would agree with the men of *kalam* and against the philosophers that the world, indeed, is created *de novo,* he did so as a matter of religious faith. In this, however, he would have more sympathy for the philosophers than for the men of *kalam.* His reason for doing so is at the very heart of the title of this paper. Unlike the philosophers, whose attempted demonstrations are derived from the very nature of perceived existence, the *mutakallimun* contradict the manifest nature of existents and even deny that there is a world of natures. Bad philosophy does not make for good theology.

Aquinas

When, during the mid-1250s, Thomas Aquinas was preparing himself to teach in the faculty of theology at the University of Paris, he was already acquainted with *The Guide for the Perplexed* and regularly cited Rabbi Moses in his early work, a *Commentary on the Sentences of Peter Lombard.* He adopted positions similar to those of Maimonides on the undemonstrability of a temporal creation of the world and on the utter stupidity of those *mutakallimun* who would deny any causal efficacy or power to creatures. Early on in the *Second Book on the Sentences* (1.1.4), Aquinas had occasion to summarize their position:

> God immediately effects all things so that nothing other [than God] is the cause of anything. This is so much the case that they claim that fire does not burn but God [is the cause]; nor is the hand moved except as God causes its motion, and so with other examples. This position, however, is stupid since it removes order from the universe and takes away from things their proper activity and does away with the judgment of [our] senses.[6]

In the same place, in answering the question "Whether the world is eternal," Aquinas listed nine *kalamic* arguments for the negative. He pointed out their weakness and claimed that the eternal world advocates had already effectively refuted them. In turn, he presented fourteen arguments of the philosophers before refuting them as non-demonstrative. Aquinas concluded that neither the temporal beginning of the world nor its eternity is susceptible of strict demonstration. He there also expressed his concern at those of his contemporaries who would use such dubious arguments to bolster the religious claim that creation is *de novo*. Rather than a confirmation of faith, it could subject it to ridicule (cf. *Guide* [1.1.5], 33).

In a somewhat later work, his *Summa Contra Gentiles,* Aquinas repeated this approach to the question. After noting the lack of cogency and validity of the *kalamic* arguments for creation *de novo*, he again expressed his deep concern at anyone who would use such questionable arguments to promote religious faith. It could very well, he said (2.38), have the opposite effect if an inquirer into the Catholic faith thought the whole of our faith rested on such inept reasoning, rather than on the unshakable basis of divine teaching.[7]

Later still, in the *Summa theologiae* (1.46.2), Aquinas reiterated this concern.[8] In addition to providing his own arguments to show that creation *de novo* is an article of faith and completely indemonstrable, he took a swipe at those who "presumptuously undertook to demonstrate what is of faith" and instead introduced non-necessary arguments. His reason is clear. Non-believers who are sophisticated in recognizing the difference between demonstrative, probable, and sophistical reasoning could take the occasion to ridicule Christian believers, thinking that the entire faith rested on such dubious foundations.

It is worth noting that Aquinas was not thinking just of the *mutakallimun* of Maimonides' text. A famous contemporary of his student days at the University of Paris, Bonaventure, in his *Commentary on the Sentences* (1.1.1.2), praised the *kalamic* proofs for the temporal creation of the world as self-evident to both reason and philosophy (*per se notae*).[9] In fact, Bonaventure continued, "To maintain that the world is eternal or eternally produced, while maintaining [at the same time] that everything is produced *ex nihilo,* is completely against truth and reason." This is so much the case, he added, that he did not believe that any philosopher, of even the most minuscule intelligence, had held such a view. The reason is clear for Bonaventure: "It entails a manifest contradiction" (*Commentary*, 15).

It is worth noting that Aquinas, in a still later work, his *De aeternitate mundi contra Murmurantes,* pointedly remarked that, if to maintain that something made by God always existed involved a logical contradiction, it is absolutely amazing that the great Augustine had not seen that. Otherwise, remarked Aquinas, he could have spared his considerable efforts to disprove an eternal world in books 11 and 12 of his *City of God.* He noted further that it was also amazing that the most noble philosophers (those who, according to Augustine, surpassed all others in prestige and authority) did not recognize this so-called manifest contradiction.[10] Not content with these ironical thrusts, Aquinas then lapsed into what for him was a most uncharacteristic sarcasm: "Those who so subtly espy such a contradiction stand out among mankind in such a way that wisdom could be said to originate with them" (*De aeternitate mundi*, 59).

There are also many places where Aquinas criticized *kalamic* positions that would deny all causal power to creatures, the better to safeguard the freedom and omnipotence of the Creator. I intend to focus on a series of chapters from book 3 of the *SCG*, where his theme is divine providence (*SCG*, 3, 64-65, 97).

By showing that God as the conserver of all things in existence (ch. 65) follows on establishing that God is the ruler of all through his providence (ch. 64), Aquinas claimed to have thereby refuted the position of the Islamic men of *kalam* (*loquentes in lege Maurorum*). They claimed to have established God as the conserver of all things in existence by holding that all forms were accidents and that no accident lasts through two instants of time. For Aquinas, these positions are patently absurd (*Quae omnia patet esse absurda--SCG*, 65, 299).

After concluding in chapter 68 that God is said to be everywhere and in all things precisely through his power, that is, in the manner in which an agent cause is present to its effect, Aquinas noted, in chapter 69, that some have erred in their understanding of this. These Islamic men of *kalam* thought it entailed denying to all mere creatures any active role in the production of effects in nature, so that fire does not cause heat, but rather God causes heat in the presence of fire, and similarly regarding all other effects in nature. These *loquentes* hold that no accident can pass over from one subject to another, and so regarded as impossible that heat go from one hot body into another body (supposedly) heated by it (*SCG*, 69, 303).

Their conclusion that all accidents of everything are created by God leads inevitably, Aquinas argued, to a number of inappropriate conclusions. For example, to claim that God is the sole agent in nature would not explain the uniformity in natural actions that appears to our sensible experience. Cooling, he noted, does not result from the presence of a hot thing, while warming does. Likewise, human semen does not result in the generation of the anything but human beings. So, Thomas concluded, the causality of these effects ought not to be credited to the sole power of God, thereby obliterating creature causality. Further, it is against the very nature of wisdom that a wise agent would act in vain, which would be the case if God produced a world of creatures apparently producing their own effects while these were, in fact, solely produced by God. Further, Aquinas argued, since the perfection of an effect points to the perfection of its cause, to detract from the perfection of creatures is actually to detract from the perfection of the divine power.

Another inappropriate entailment of this *kalamic* position would be that it destroys the possibility of any natural science. This is so, Aquinas argued, because the nature of a cause is not known through an effect unless its power is known through that effect, and if created things have no actions productive of effects, it would follow that no natures could be known by us starting from effects, which is especially the way followed by natural science (ibid., 303-304; I have summarized four of the nine "inappropriate conclusions" that Aquinas treats in this chapter).

Later on, in chapter 97, in which Aquinas dealt with arguments to prove that God's providence followed a rational plan, he had occasion to refute two erroneous views. One of which held that all things follow from the pure will of God without any rational plan, while the other held that there is an order of causes which comes forth under divine providence, but by way of absolute necessity (*SCG*, 97, 345-346).

It is instructive for us to note how Aquinas dealt with the first erroneous view, which he identified as that of the *mutakallimun*.[11] As with their position on creation *de novo,* he agreed partly or wholly with their conclusion but completely disagreed with their efforts to establish it by pseudo-philosophical reasoning. Once again we see his point: bad philosophy does not make good theology.

Thus, in seeking to find a properly rational explanation of a natural effect, for example, "Why wood is heated in the presence of fire," Aquinas might appear to agree with the *loquentes* in answering, "because God willed it." There would be, however, a world of difference in their respective meanings.

"According to them," Aquinas had said, "it makes no difference whether fire heats or cools unless God wills it so." Aquinas even adds citations of texts from Scripture and Augustine that seem to support that view. But that is not the case, he noted, for these texts do not remove reason from the dispensation of providence. The appropriate answer to the question must include rather than exclude the entire order of secondary, creature causes.

Aquinas outlined that answer as follows: "'Because heating is the natural action of fire,' and this is so 'because heat is its proper accident.' But this is the result of its proper form, and so on, until we come to the divine will" (*SCG*, 97, 345-46). It is interesting to note here that Bonaventure did not follow the extreme *mutakallimun* annihilation of the order of secondary causality within creation. However his understanding of the role of secondary causes, couched as it is in the context of what Augustine had called seminal reasons (*rationes seminales*),[12] reveals some similarities with the *kalamic* attempts to safeguard the absolute omnipotence of the creator. Bonaventure touched on the question of the causality of creaturely agents in the second book of his *Commentary on the Sentences* (190-194). The question treated there (7.2.2.1) was "Whether the induction of every form be from the creator or could some particular or created agent induce some form," where the verb *inducere* (later *educere*) refers to the coming-into-being of all forms of reality. In the course of answering the question, he lists a variety of philosophical positions on it. One position, held by "some of the more recent philosophers" was that the creator is the source of all forms. If one were to interpret this to mean that God is the *principal* producer and efficient cause of every form, it would be for Bonaventure the true position. If, however, one were to hold that God is the *total* efficient cause of every production of form, with particular agents limited to merely disposing matter for the reception of form, it is untenable and, indeed, irrational (*Commentary*, 192: *quare ista positio non est rationabilis*).

There was one position of the philosophers that Bonaventure thought to be closer to the truth and which ought to be held "Not only because reason persuades us," but also "because it is confirmed by the authority of Augustine." It holds that the very essences (*veritates*) of all the forms that are to be produced naturally are to be found in the potency of matter. And when such a form is actually produced, no new quiddity or essence (*veritates essentiae*) but rather a new disposition is given to it so that what was in potency comes to be in actuality, the way a rosebud comes to be a rose. This is not to say, Bonaventure explains, that these are diverse quiddities but rather diverse dispositions of the same quiddity. So that, he adds, "If a created agent has the power to make what is [already] in one way to be in another way, this is no great thing [*hoc non est magnum*]" (*Commentary*, 192-193). This phrase, *hoc non est magnum,* is a most revealing one. While this illustrious contemporary of Aquinas avoids the more extreme *kalamic* denial of any causality to creatures, Bonaventure's position here reveals a fundamental sharing of the concerns of all "theologisms" to safeguard the glory of the omnipotent, creating God. So that, while he judges the *kalamic* denial of secondary causality to be unreasonable, he still manages to downplay the causal efficacy of creatures in nature--for, after all, "It is no great thing."[13]

Conclusion

The topic of this paper has not been yet another quaint or exotic scholastic disputation, but rather a central point, namely, whether there is any room for genuine, rational or philosophical speculation within a religious faith based on a divine revelation. The *mutakallimun* of the three related monotheistic religions appear to me to have shared a failure of nerve in this regard in assuming that philosophy and science are in an adversarial position toward religious faith, though they were correct in seeing the philosophers' notion of an eternal world as a critical issue. If the received philosophical view of the world led one to an impersonal God that necessarily and therefore eternally caused the world, a true believer in the Genesis or *Qur'an* accounts must utterly disagree. One choice might be to adopt a complete and utter fideism. The *mutakallimun* of the three faiths, however, sought other rational explanations of reality to support their religious view of an omnipotent personal God who freely creates the world *ex nihilo* and *de novo*.

Yet Maimonides and Aquinas were convinced that the source of human reason and of revelation was one and the same and that therefore no conflict between an article of faith, properly understood, and any properly demonstrated conclusion of science or philosophy could exist. As we have seen, both thinkers felt a strong aversion to the pseudo-philosophical theologism of the men of *kalam*. In the matter of the eternal-world controversy, both carefully distinguished between the question of whether or not the world is created *ex nihilo* and the question of its duration, *de novo* or *ab aeterno*. As to the first question, both of them thought that philosophy was able to demonstrate the fact of creation. Regarding the world's duration, both agreed that the matter ultimately rested on the liberty and volition of God and was, therefore, necessarily indemonstrable.

Aquinas and Maimonides adduced refutations of the philosophers' purported demonstrations that the world is eternal. (Aquinas' use of the *Guide* as source for both the substance and the ordering of these refutations is especially clear in *SCG* 2.32-37 [see Maimonides' *Guide,* 2.14.17-18].) And, although they both agreed with the *mutakallimuns'* position that the world had a beginning, they both ridiculed their attempted demonstrations of it, remarking that, at best, some were merely probable and, at worst, most were fallacious.

They also were both appalled at the powerless creatures of the omnipotent, sheerly voluntary Creator of the *mutakallimun.* The pious annihilation of the world of nature and the destruction of the very foundations of all scientific accounts of the created world evoked caustic comment from both Aquinas and Maimonides. We have already noted their use of terms such as "absurd," "foolish," "ridiculous," "irrational," etc.

In conclusion, their ultimate rejection of what Gilson later dubbed "theologism" can be summed up, it seems, in the judgment noted above: "Bad philosophy never makes for good theology."

NOTES

1.   Etienne Gilson, *The Unity of Philosophical Experience* (New York: Scribner's, 1948), ch. 2.

2.   Gilson, *Unity*, 37-38.

3.   See my article, "Maimonides and Aquinas on Creation: A Critique of Their Historians," in *Graceful Reasons: Essays in Ancient and Medieval Philosophy Presented to Joseph Owens, C.SS.R.* (Toronto: Pontifical Institute of Mediaeval Studies, 1983), 361-379.

4.   The *Guide for the Perplexed* was composed by Maimonides in Arabic. It was translated into Hebrew by Samuel ibn Tibbon in 1204. A second Hebrew translation by the poet Judah al'Harizi followed. A latin translation of al'Harizi's hebrew version was circulating at the University of Paris during the late 1220s. Bishop Agostino Giustiniani published an edition of the *Guide* at Paris in 1520, based on several manuscripts of that latin translation.

5.   *Guide*, 177.   This and all subsequent citations of the *Guide* are from the excellent English translation by S. Pines (Chicago: The University of Chicago Press, 1963).

6.   Thomas Aquinas, *Second Book on the Sentences* (Paris: R. P. Mandonnet, 1929), 24.

7.   Thomas Aquinas, *Summa Contra Gentiles* (Rome: Leonine Commission's Manual Edition, 1934), 128.

8.   All references are to the Ottawa edition: Thomas Aquinas, *Summa theologiae* (Ottawa, Ont.: Ottawa Dominican College, 1941), 297a.

9.   Bonaventure, *Commentary on the Sentences, editio minor* (Quaracchi, 1938), 13.

10.   Thomas Aquinas, *De aeternitate mundi,* in *Opuscula Philosophica,* ed. J. Perrier (Paris, 1949), 58-59.

11.   *De aeternitate mundi,* Aquinas explicitly cites Rabbi Moses as his source here for the erroneous view of the *loquentes in lege Saracenorum.*

12.   See Armand Maurer, *Medieval Philosophy* (Toronto: Random House, 1982), 15: "According to St. Augustine, God created everything at once, although not in the same perfect state. In the beginning some things existed in perfect form, while others were created in embryo or in 'seed' *(rationes seminales)*. . . . God implanted the seminal principle of each species in matter, so that in the course of time . . . each might come . . . to full flower."

13.   Gilson, however, in his chapter on "Theologism and Philosophy" *(Unity,* 53-54), goes somewhat farther in his criticism of Bonaventure's views on efficient causality: "An effect, says Bonaventure, is to its cause as the rose is to the rosebud. It is permissible to appreciate the poetic quality of his comparison and the religious purity of his intention, without overlooking its philosophical implications. If, in the beginning, God created,

together with all that was, all that was to be, the end of
the world story was in its beginning, and nothing can
really happen to it; in such a system God is the only
efficient cause, and this world of ours is a completely
barren world, just as in the doctrine of [the *mutakallimun*]."

ONTOLOGY

The Theological Character of Aquinas' Five Ways

Mark Johnson
St. Joseph's College

It would be easy to show that the overwhelming part of the seemingly innumerable studies devoted to St. Thomas Aquinas's five ways for proving the existence of God, found in his *Summa theologiae*, part 1, question 2, article 3, consider them from a philosophical perspective.[1] This fact is understandable, since it was Pope Leo XIII who hoped that his 1879 encyclical, *Aeterni patris*, would reinstaurate a Christian philosophy--and particularly a Thomistic philosophy--better able to meet the philosophical challenges arising from the Enlightenment, especially as those challenges concern God.[2] No wonder, then, given such ecclesiastical approbation, and the innate attractiveness that Thomas' hardheaded rationalism offers, that believing philosophers should turn in numbers to Thomas' *quinque viae* as a point of departure for a philosophically-based consideration of God. After all, it was a constant refrain of Thomas', on the authority of St. Paul in Romans (1:20), and because

of the precedence of earlier philosophers, that the
human mind can come to a demonstrative knowledge
of the existence of God, and of some of his essential
attributes, without dependence upon revelation.[3]

Yet this fact is somewhat sad--'sad' because,
within the Christian context, such heavy emphasis
upon, and controversy surrounding, the five ways
considered by unaided reason, runs the risk of
separating the God found there from the God of faith,
the God we worship. And this gives substance to the
very complaint we find in believers like Pascal and
Bergson. Athens may indeed have something to do
with Jerusalem, but the god of Athens is not the God
of Jerusalem, because philosophy does not know the
God of Abraham.[4]

My intent here is to show that there is a definite
theological character to Thomas' five ways for proving
the existence of God, a character, it might surprise, that
goes beyond the mere theological context of the work
in which they are found to the very internal logic of
the arguments themselves. I shall begin, then, by
discussing the nature and purpose of the *Summa
theologiae*, turning thereafter to a consideration of the
five ways.[5]

The Nature and Purpose
of the *Summa theologiae*

The *Summa theologiae*, "the crown of Thomas'
genius," as James Weisheipl put it,[6] was a work born
out of frustration. There existed no complete treatment
of Christian teaching that to Thomas' mind was free
from some pedagogical defect. At the outset of his

career he wrote a *scriptum* on Peter Lombard's *Sentences*, as was the custom for students in theology in his day, so the disorder found there can be attributable both to the structure of the *Sentences* and to the nature of a *scriptum*.[7] At the end of his first regency in Paris he undertook the writing of the *Summa contra gentiles*, whose structure and purpose lay solely with him,[8] but for all that he had to break with the order he originally intended, thus perhaps calling into question the wisdom of the two-part division of the work on the basis of what can be known without faith, and what requires faith in order to be known.[9] The incomplete *Compendium theologiae*, though usually dated late, could well be dated in the mid-1260's, and its tripartite structure of faith, hope, and charity, seems also a forced, perhaps artificial, scheme for teaching the entire expanse of sacred theology.[10]

In 1265, Thomas was instructed to open a *studium personale* at Santa Sabina in Rome, where he taught students selected to study especially with him, and, so far as we know, where he was to be in complete charge of the curriculum.[11] We have no sure idea as to the content of Thomas' classroom activity, save the fact that, for a short time, he lectured on Book 1 of the *Sentences*.[12] Precisely why Thomas did not continue teaching from the *Sentences* at this *studium personale* in Rome is anyone's guess, but one can easily imagine him throwing his hands up in despair over using Lombard's work as an appropriate schoolroom text for his purposes. The Trinity before the divine nature and attributes? *Uti* and *frui* without any discussion whatsoever of the good? Add to this his own concern that the heavy moral emphasis of Dominican teaching be placed within the context of the whole of theology, dogmatic as well as sacramental, and it became clear to Thomas that he would have to take matters into his own hands.[13]   The *Summa theologiae* is the fruit of that decision, a decision to produce a systematic account of the whole of theology, an account that in turn would avoid the pitfalls of existing works, cluttered as they were with useless articles, needless repetition, and disorder.[14] He would fill the void with a work that would finally keep the needs of the novice in mind, providing the students of sacred doctrine with a work that presents the truths of the Catholic faith in an order befitting both the subject matter and the exigencies of sound teaching.[15]

Thomas' first order of business in the *Summa theologiae* is to set the limits of the presentation, which he does by explaining the subject matter of sacred doctrine in question 1 of the *Prima pars*.[16] This question has been the subject of much study and indeed controversy. What is the subject of the first question? Is it scholastic theology, or faith? Could it be the very process of Christian instruction? Many distinguished Thomists have wrestled with the question--the names of Cajetan, Báñez, John of St. Thomas, Chenu, Van Ackeren, and Weisheipl, come to mind.[17]   All students of Thomas' theology inevitably take a particular stand on all of this, and I have adopted the general view of Weisheipl, according to whom the subject of the first question is the content of Christian instruction under its widest possible consideration. Adding to this, largely because of the comments of Muñiz, Ramírez, and Wallace,[18] I would emphasize that sacred doctrine is to be viewed not merely as a science--doing so can lead to awkward claims about what Thomas is really doing--but as a wisdom, not unlike the wisdom of metaphysics. Sacred doctrine's tasks go beyond the drawing of conclusions virtually contained in the articles of faith, an activity that characterizes "science." They extend to a consideration of the articles of faith themselves, their intelligible order relative to one another, and the intellectual notions requisite to these just-mentioned tasks. Sacred doctrine does draw conclusions, true, but it does so because, as a wisdom, it possesses preeminently the functions of science and understanding, and these latter form the basis of scientific investigation in the lower disciplines.[19]

The wisdom of sacred doctrine differs from the wisdom of first philosophy, or metaphysics, because its consideration of God is direct, whereas first philosophy considers God only as the principle of substance, the subject of its distinctive inquiry. But it is under the aspect of God, *sub ratione dei*, that all things have their intelligibility in the discipline of sacred doctrine.[20] Hence the massive *Secunda pars* of the *Summa theologiae* is not, strictly speaking, about the human person, but rather about "the image of God," in action.[21] For Thomas, then, the subject-matter of the *Summa theologiae* is God, but this includes both what reason learns and what faith hears.[22] For Thomas, of course, the principal source of the content of faith is sacred scripture,[23] so it is reasonable to expect that a major part of his pedagogical strategy depends very heavily upon biblical language, as well as upon received notions and texts, themselves heavily indebted to, and imbued with, such language.[24] And the importance of this I shall now suggest, turning to the five ways.

The Five Ways

That there are arguments to prove the existence of God in the *Summa theologiae* at all is the result of the Aristotelian epistemology that Thomas employs in his understanding of human knowing, for the presence of question 2 would not be necessary if the existence of the subject of sacred doctrine, God, were intuitively known to exist. The inquiry into the immediacy of our knowledge of God's existence is the topic of article 1, where Thomas fields several arguments urging the immediacy of God's existence in our knowledge. Yet in the face of these arguments, one of which is an appropriation of the argument of Anselm,[25] he refuses to budge. For him the existence of God must be demonstrated, because our immediate knowledge is of sensible, material things, not spiritual things.[26]

Once we do grant, as Thomas would have us do, that the existence of God cannot be immediately known, we must next address the concern of article 2: "Whether, that God is, is demonstrable." It is important to note the technical character of the word "demonstrable" here, for in Thomas' vocabulary *demonstratio* and its related adjectives refer to the act of the human mind by which it produces *scientia*, which is knowledge about something "that cannot be other than it is."[27] It would be a gross exaggeration to say that article 2 is a synopsis of the *a posteriori* demonstrative logic detailed in Aristotle's *Posterior Analytics*, but students of Thomas' thought who know that work, and his own later exposition of it, are bound to feel at home in the description of how he thinks we can demonstrate the existence of God.[28]

As Thomas sees it, we demonstrate the existence of God by using the second of the two types of demonstration he outlines in the response to article 2. While the first type proceeds from cause to effect, this second type of demonstration proceeds through an effect to its cause, which Thomas thinks is required here, since effects are usually first and best known to us, though in the order of existence the cause precedes the effect.[29] But to be successful in his venture, Thomas must overcome the second objected difficulty presented to him at the outset of the article. Granted that we have to do with scientific demonstration here, we recall that the medium of demonstration is the "notion" of a thing, its *quod quid est*. But, the difficulty reminds us, we cannot know the *quod quid est* of God, so it would seem that whole demonstrative effort is impossible with respect to him.[30]

In responding to this difficulty, whose substance he largely grants, Thomas turns to use some of the techniques of the *Posterior Analytics*. When one demonstrates the cause of something from its effect, one does *not* use the "notion" of a thing, its *quod quid est*, in demonstrating its existence. One rather uses the effect in the place of the definition of the cause, which in turn serves as the reason for the inference of the cause from the effect. Finding out the real definition of a thing, its *quod quid est*, is an investigation to be undertaken *after* we show the thing to exist in the first place. The question "what is it?" follows upon the question "is it?," and it is the latter question that is the present concern. Is there a God, at all? In the absence of the *quod quid est* or real definition, we use the effect as a sort of "stand-in definition" of the cause, or, more precisely, we use the effect as a notion for what the name of the cause means, its "nominal definition." Thomas' reply merits a full citation:

> It should be said that when a cause is demonstrated through an effect, it is necessary to use the effect in the place of the definition of the cause in order to prove the existence of the cause, and this is especially the case with God. Because, for showing that something exists, it is necessary to take as the middle term "what the name means," but not "what it is," because the question asking "what is it?" follows the question asking "is it?" Now the names of God are imposed from effects, as shall be shown later. Hence, in demonstrating God's existence from an effect, we can take what the name "God" means as the middle term.[31]

This complex explanation can be illustrated, interestingly, by what Thomas actually does in article 1 as regards Anselm's "ontological argument," whose demonstrative character he denies. In dealing with Anselm's argument, he does not complain at all about what he would call a nominal definition of God, "that than which nothing greater can be conceived" (*id quo maius nihil cogitari potest*). After all, Thomas' own doctrine of the divine names asserts that our analogical predication of positive attributes amounts to much the same thing, since for him the predication of some positive attribute of God really means: "God has all of

this, and more than we can comprehend."[32]   Thomas
complains that the conviction that the name "God"
means "that than which nothing greater can be
conceived" means that something exists "out there," *in
rerum natura*, that corresponds to, or in the case of a
person, answers to, the name "that than which nothing
greater can be conceived." For Thomas, when he uses
the term "God" it means "that than which nothing
greater can be conceived". Thomas' point is that just
because that is what the term "God" means does not
necessarily entail that it refers to something real. But
if we discover something in the world that is, in fact,
greater than which nothing can be conceived, then we
can say not only that "God" *means* something, but also
that God *is* something.[33]

The five ways in article 3 all preserve the method
he sketches in article 2, and avoid the problems he
thinks are found in the approach taken by Anselm.
Each of the five ways begins from an effect known to
us--the first way's starting point, Thomas points out, is
known by sensation--and the effect supplies a nominal
definition of the term "God": first mover, first efficient
cause, first necessary being, first cause of being and
goodness, intelligent director of things. Once we have
shown that there must be a first mover, a first efficient
cause, and so on, we then have warrant for asserting
that the term "God" has both meaning and reference,
which is why Thomas claims only at the end of each
of the five ways "and this we call God."[34] And thus
the demonstrations for the existence of God all depend
heavily upon the meaning given to the term "God" at
the outset of the demonstration--what the term "God"
signifies.[35]

At this point, though, we should ask the question: "signifies to whom?" Thomas' earlier suggestion, in article 2, ad 2, that there might be some who would have no clue regarding to what Anselm's "that than which nothing greater can be conceived" refers is an indication that when discussing the significance, the meaning, of a particular term, we must know who the audience is that is using that term in its discussion. Who is the audience Thomas is addressing in the *Summa theologiae*? Who must have in place a nominal definition of the term "God" in order that Thomas may proceed in the five ways? Indeed, who must have already in place an understanding of the term "God" that is operative in every article of question 1 of the *Prima pars*, where Thomas describes the nature and scope of the undertaking of sacred doctrine? The answer is straightforward. The audience is the Dominican students for whom Thomas undertook the writing of the *Summa theologiae*, the *incipientes* whom he likens to Paul's "little ones in Christ," the ones the Apostle fed with milk, not meat, in 1 Corinthians (3:1).[36]

These Dominican students were the ones Thomas taught at Santa Sabina in Rome in the mid-1260's, and it is quite likely that Thomas intended his *Summa theologiae* to be a sort of general theological *summa* for the teaching not only of these particular students, but for all Dominican students, a legacy he would leave to his religious community. It is true that Thomas continued to write the work even after the circumstances at the University of Paris snatched him from the midst of regular Dominican education in 1269, but at the outset of writing the *Summa* in 1266 he had no idea that in three years he would return to hold for a second time a chair in theology, something quite extraordinary.[37]

What did the term "God" mean to the Dominican students who were the originally intended audience of the *Summa theologiae*? That the meaning of the term "God" was deeply formed by Christian teaching and practice is, I think, a foregone conclusion. These Dominicans were to be involved, after all, in preaching and the hearing of confessions, the *cura animarum* that was the special apostolate of the Order of the Preachers--their decision to join the Order was presumably the result of a desire to serve God through the Dominican charism. The Order's heavy emphasis upon study led to the need for such preaching aids as the *concordantiae sancti Iacobi*, a biblical concordance undertaken by the Dominican community at St. Jacques in Paris, most likely under the direction of Hugh of St. Cher, around 1239.[38] Young Dominicans during their novitiate in the Order were to memorize the entire Psalter, the Gradual, and the Divine Office. They were to hear read to them writings of Hugh of St. Victor, and Bernard of Clairvaux's *De diligendo deo*, in addition to the primary, mandated lectures on the Bible.[39] As members of a religious community they were of course involved in the liturgy, an enterprise shot through with biblical language about "God": *Deus in adiutorium meum intende . . . Confiteor Deo omnipotenti . . . Credo in unum Deum . . . Agnus Dei . . . Misericors Deus . . . Te Deum, laudamus . . . .*[40] And should a young Dominican be sent to a *studium generale* for further studies, his principal subject of study there would be the Bible,

since the Bible was the textbook of medieval
theology.[41] In fact, Thomas' own biblical
commentaries, not his *Summae* or Aristotelian
expositions, were the direct result of his classroom
teaching as a master in theology at Paris, and as a
lector in Orvieto and Naples.

Biblical Language and the Five Ways

The point I would like to make is that the context in
which Thomas wrote the *Summa theologiae*, and the
audience for whom he wrote it--this goes as well for
the work's wider audience after Thomas chose to
publish it through the stationers at the University of
Paris--indicate that those who came to the work had an
understanding of the term "God" that was biblically
based, informed by subsequent Christian reflection
upon the contents of the Christian faith. The
Dominican student who came to the work, or the
university student--even the Christian who comes to the
work today!--understands the word "God" used in
questions 1 and 2 to refer to a host of possible names,
or predicates, found in the Christian deposit of faith. It
is true that the nominal definitions found in the five
ways might have a different origin for a nonbeliever,
and in fact Thomas does attribute the argumentative
"shape" of some of the ways to various non-Christian
philosophers in other works.[42] But the Christian who
comes to the *Summa theologiae*, having an intimate
knowledge of the text of sacred scripture, realizes that
the notions of "prime mover," "first efficient cause,"
and the rest, are not at all foreign to the Christian
heritage. The Bible regularly uses language that says,

in its own way, much the same thing. In a word, the believer sees an immediate affinity between, say, the "first necessary being" and the God he has read or heard about from the time he was on his mother's knee: "I am God, and I do not change" (Mal. 3:6); "In the beginning God created the heavens and the earth" (Gen. 1:1); "I am God, the Almighty" (Gen. 17:1); "O Lord, God of hosts, who is like you? Mighty you are . . ." (Ps. 89:9); "All wisdom is from the Lord God" (Sir. 1:1); "But you, Father, govern all things with providence" (Wis. 14:3); "Nothing is impossible for God" (Lk 1:37); "I am the alpha and the omega, the beginning and the end, says the Lord God" (Rev. 1:8). Passages such as these, passages from the liturgy or offices, indeed, entire sections of the sacred scriptures, like the creation narrative in Genesis, would immediately come to mind as the reader of the *Summa theologiae* approached the five ways, familiar with the nominal definition they contain because of his upbringing in a world of biblical language.[43] It would in fact be astounding if they did not come to mind.

Conclusion

The argument *sed contra* in *Summa theologiae*, I, question 2, article 3, provides what the Christian reader takes to be an absolutely unassailable answer to the question asking whether God exists: "From the person of God it is said: 'I am who am.'" Though much metaphysical mileage has been gotten out of the response of *Ego sum qui sum*, there is theological mileage to get as well. The *sed contra* is not merely a citation of some received authority whose writings have commanded, and continue to command, respect from the theological community. It is rather the direct testimony of the authority of all authorities, God himself, speaking to us as students in his school,[44] telling us directly about himself.

Important for us here is seeing that the medium of God's testimony here is the text of sacred scripture, Exodus 3:14. While the very presence of a scriptural passage commands immediate respect from the believer, the believer also knows that no scriptural passage can be understood alone--it is inevitably part of a larger story. And the Dominican student or university student in Thomas' day who encountered the passage from Exodus 3:14 immediately recalled that the story there is God's commanding Moses to announce to the people of Israel their coming exodus from Egypt: "'But,' said Moses to God, 'when I go to the Israelites and say to them 'The God of your fathers has sent me to you,' if they ask me 'what is his name?' what am I to tell them?' God replied, 'I am who am'" (Ex. 3:13-14). More than this, the student also knew well that in the story God goes on to identify himself further, in the passage used as the epigraph for this article: "God spoke further to Moses, 'Thus shall you say to the Israelites: the Lord, the God of your fathers, the God of Abraham, the God of Isaac, the God of Jacob, has sent me to you'" (Exodus 3:15). This is, I think, extremely important for our understanding of the theological character of the five ways. The God we encounter in the argument *sed contra* in article 3 is not by any means "the god of the philosophers." The context of the biblical passage, and the setting of

Summa theologiae, indicate quite clearly that the God we encounter here, even before we take up the intellectual offerings of the five ways, is the God of Abraham, Isaac, and Jacob, the God of salvation history, and, ultimately, the Triune God who becomes incarnate in the person of Jesus Christ.

Thomas' five ways are, from beginning to end, theological in intent, form, and matter. They are to lead the *incipientes* in sacred doctrine to some understanding of the Christian God, and to do this they employ the strict demonstrative policies of the *Posterior Analytics*, according to which, in *a posteriori* demonstration, we use a nominal definition for the reality we intend to prove exists. Yet in this case the nominal definition is taken from biblical language and biblically inspired language, a common heritage of Christians. It is true that in the five ways Thomas appropriates philosophical sources, and it is also true that these theological arguments stand or fall with the solidity of the argumentative strength of these philosophical sources. But in the end, the arguments for proving the existence of God, as they are found here in the *Summa theologiae*, are theological.[45] In other contexts, the arguments might be considered philosophical, and in their remote origin the five ways might also be considered philosophical. Given Thomas' theological purpose, however, and given the fact that for a believer approaching the five ways the nominal definition of "God" will always be that of the God of faith, the five ways, if anything, amount to an instance of taking the water of philosophy and changing it into the wine of theology.[46]

NOTES

1.   This is based upon an examination of the following: V.J. Bourke, *Thomistic Bibliography, 1920-1940* (St Louis: The Modern Schoolman, 1945); T. Miethe, *Thomistic Bibliography, 1940-1978* (Westport, Conn.: Greenwood Press, 1980); *Bulletin thomiste* (Soisy-sur-Seine, France: Société thomiste, 1924-1965); *Rassegna di letteratura tomistica* (Napoli: Edizioni Dominicane Italiane, 1965); P. Mandonnet, *Bibliographie thomiste*, 2nd éd, rev. et complétée par M. D. Chenu (Paris: J. Vrin, 1960); R. Ingardia, *Thomas Aquinas: International Bibliography 1977-1990* (Bowling Green, Ohio: Philosophy Documentation Center [Bowling Green University], 1993) -- the last is devoted to strictly philosophical studies.

2.   For more on this papal encyclical and its relation to Thomistic philosophy, see the articles in *One Hundred Years of Thomism. Aeterni Patris and Afterwards: A Symposium*, ed. V. B. Brezik (Houston: Center for Thomistic Studies, 1981).

3.   See *In I Sent.*, d. 3, q. 1, a. 1, in *Sancti Thomae Aquinatis Opera Omnia*, ed. P. Mandonnet (Paris: Lethielleux, 1929), vol. 1, pp. 90-92; *In Boethii de trinitate*, q. 1, a. 2, in *Sancti Thomae de Aquino Opera Omnia*, ed. Leonine (Romae: Ad Sanctae Sabinae, 1992), pp. 83-85; *Summa contra gentiles*, lib. 4, cap. 1, in *Sancti Thomae Aquinatis Liber de Veritate Catholicae Fidei contra Errores Infidelium*, eds. C. Pera and P. Marc (Turin: Marietti, 1961), vol. 3, pp. 242-44, nos. 3335-49; *In I ad Romanos*, lect. 6, in *Sancti Thomae Aquinatis Super Epistolas Sancti Pauli*

Lectura, ed. P. Cai (Turin: Marietti, 1953), vol. 1, pp. 19-23; *Summa theologiae*, I, q. 12, a. 12, in *Sancti Thomae de Aquinas Summa Theologiae*, ed. Ottawa (Ottawa: Medieval Institute, 1953), vol. 1, p. 73. For some passages in which Thomas allows for a certain, spontaneous reasoning to Gods existence, which falls short of true demonstration, see *Summa contra gentiles*, lib. 3, cap. 38, no. 2161; and *Summa theologiae*, II-II, q. 85, a. 1.

4.   It is this seeming disengagement of the god of philosophy from the God of Abraham in Thomas' thinking that leads Michael Buckley to suggest that Thomas' manner of dealing with God in the *Summa theologiae* may have been an origin of modern atheism! See his *At the Origin of Modern Atheism* (New Haven: Yale University Press, 1987), p. 55. For a response to Buckley, see Nicholas Lash, "When Did the Theologians Lose Interest in Theology?," in *Theology and Dialogue: Essays in Conversation with George Lindbeck*, ed. Bruce Marshall (Notre Dame: University of Notre Dame Press, 1990), pp. 131-47. Judging from his response to Buckley, Lash would support, I think, the tenor of my argument here.

5.   My purpose is not to denigrate the many philosophical works on the five ways, works from which I have profited. The bibliography on the five ways is massive, with new considerations appearing regularly. Those interested in the five ways should consult   the   annual,   authoritative   Thomistic

bibliography, *Rassegna di letteratura tomistica*, under its heading of *Theologia: de deo uno*. Works treating of the five ways that I have consulted for this paper include the following: Leo J. Elders, *The Philosophical Theology of St. Thomas Aquinas* (Leiden: E.J. Brill, 1990), esp. pp. 130-3; Fernand Van Steenberghen, *Dieu caché: comment savons nous que dieu existe?* (Louvain: Publications universitaires de Louvain, 1961); Jules A. Baisnée, "St. Thomas Aquinas' Proofs of the Existence of God Presented in Their Chronological Order," in *Philosophical Studies in Honor of the Very Reverend Ignatius Smith, O.P.* (Westminster, Maryland: The Newman Press, 1952), pp. 29-64; Wayne J. Hankey, *God in Himself: Aquinas' Doctrine of God as Expounded in the Summa Theologiae* (Oxford: Oxford University Press, 1987), esp. pp. 36-56; Francisco P. Muñiz, "La 'quarta vía' de Santo Tomás para demonstrar la existencia de Dios," *Revista de Filosofía* 3 (1944) 385-433; 4 (1945) 49-99; Joseph Owens, *St. Thomas Aquinas on the Existence of God: The Collected Papers of Joseph Owens*, ed. John R. Catan (Albany: SUNY Press, 1980); David B. Twetten, "Why Motion Requires a Cause: A Foundation for a Prime Mover in Aristotle and Aquinas," in *Philosophy and the God of Abraham: Essays in Memory of James A. Weisheipl, O.P.*, ed. R. James Long (Toronto: Pontifical Institute of Mediaeval Studies, 1991), pp. 235-54; Anthony Kenny, *The Five Ways: St. Thomas Aquinas' Proofs of God's Existence* (Notre Dame: University of Notre Dame Press, 1980); Thomas C. O'Brien, *Metaphysics and the Existence of God* (Washington, D.C: The Thomist Press, 1960); Niceto Blazquez, "El valor de las cinco vías de Santo

Tomás," *Studium* 26 (1986) 77-103. My own understanding of the five demonstrations is heavily indebted to the following articles of my former teacher, Lawrence Dewan: "The Number and Order of St. Thomas' Five Ways," *Downside Review* 92 (1974) 1-18; "The Distinctiveness of St. Thomas' 'Third Way'," *Dialogue* 19 (1980) 201-218; "'Something Rather than Nothing' and St. Thomas' Third Way," *Science et Esprit* 39 (1987) 71-80; "The Interpretation of St. Thomas' 'Third Way'," in *Littera, Sensus, Sententia: Studi in onore del Prof. Clemente J. Vansteenkiste, O.P.* (Milano: Massimo, 1991), pp. 189-200; "St. Thomas' 'Fourth Way' and Creation," and "St. Thomas' Fifth Way: Directedness," both as yet unpublished.

6. James A. Weisheipl, *Friar Thomas d'Aquino: His Life, Thought, and Work,* 2nd ed. (Washington, D.C.: Catholic University of America Press, 1974), p. 361, now rivaled by J.-P. Torrell's *Initiation à saint Thomas d'Aquin: Sa personne et son oeuvre* (Fribourg: Éditions Universitaires Fribourg en Suisse, 1993). Interestingly, there has been little work done on the precise title of this work, and it is possible that Thomas could have intended another name for it, since there is no place in the work where he actually refers to it by name. It is clear that he considers the work to be theological, and uses the word *theologia* or *theologus* to refer to the study and the practitioner respectively (see *Summa theologiae* I, q. 1, a. 1; q. 78, *in capite*; I-II, q. 7, a. 2; II-II, q. 1, a. 5, ad 2), and the work's genre is definitely that of a *summa*, as were

those of Phillip the Chancellor and William of Auxerre, and, later, Albert the Great. For more on this see P. A. Walz, "De genuino titulo *Summa theologiae*," *Angelicum* 18 (1941) 142-51. The work is listed under the name *summa fratris Thome de Aquino super theologiam* in the 1286 listing of the Parisian stationer, William of Sens (See H. Denifle, ed., *Chartularium Universitatis Parisiensis*, [Paris: Delalain, 1889], vol. 1, p. 646). Richard and Mary Rouse, "The Book Trade at the University of Paris, ca. 1250-ca. 1350," in *La Production du livre universitaire au moyen age: Exempla et pecia*, ed. L.-J. Bataillon et al. (Paris: Éditions du Centre National de la Recherche Scientifique, 1988), 41-114, esp. pp. 56-62, make a strong case that the oft-cited taxation list is, in fact, for the stationer, William of Sens, who specialized in Dominican, and Thomistic, texts.

7.   Marcia Colish's giant *Peter Lombard*, 2 vols. (Leiden: E. J. Brill, 1994), is concerned to give to Lombard his due place in the history of medieval thought, and to defend him from accusations ranging from his being a mere compiler to his being a bland thinker. See vol. 1, pp. 33-90, esp. 77-90, for an account, then defense, of the ordering of his *Libri sententiarum*. My claim here reflects what I take to be Thomas' ultimate judgement of the suitability of Lombard's construction for his personal aims.

8.   For more on the *Summa contra gentiles*, see Weisheipl, *Friar Thomas*, pp. 130-34 359-60; Torrell,

Initiation à saint Thomas d'Aquin, pp. 148-70; and especially Mark D. Jordan, "The Protreptic Structure of the *Summa contra gentiles,*" *The Thomist* 50 (1986) 173-209.

9.   Thomas originally intended that the first three books of the *Summa contra gentiles* be ordered on the basis that arguments found in them concern "what faith professes and reason investigates," while the substance of book 4 concerns "the manifestation of [divine] truth that exceeds reason" (*Summa contra gentiles,* book 1, cap. 9, nos. 55-58). Yet the goal of completeness in his presentation of the moral life in book 3 requires Thomas to discuss the beatific vision (caps. 51-63), miracles (caps. 101-7), mortal sin and damnation (caps. 143-45), and divine grace and predestination (caps. 147-43). In the course of writing the work, I suspect, Thomas realized that the division of "what reason can know" and "what reason cannot know" does not serve the sweep of God's knowledge well. The *Summa theologiae* makes no such use of these notions as ordering principles.

10.   For the usual dating of this work, see Weisheipl, *Friar Thomas,* pp. 317-38, 387-38, 484; and Torrell, *Initiation à saint Thomas d'Aquin,* pp. 239-43. The Leonine edition of this work is found in *Sancti Thomas de Aquino Opera Omnia,* ed. Leonine (Rome: Ad Sanctae Sabinae, 1979), vol. 42, pp. 77-205. The editor, Hyacinthe Dondaine, provides an account of the variety of dating on p. 8, par. 5, and accepts with

caution the suggestion of Van Steenberghen that the section *de fide* was written in the mid-1260's, while the section *de spe* was begun later, perhaps in Naples in 1272-1273. If this is the case, the structure of the work would almost assuredly have been in place before Thomas began the first writing, in the mid-1260's.

11.   For more on this see Weisheipl, *Friar Thomas*, pp. 216-17; Torrell, *Initiation à saint Thomas d'Aquin*, pp. 66-69; and most especially L. E. Boyle, *The Setting of the Summa theologiae of St Thomas*, (Toronto: Pontifical Institute of Mediaeval Studies, 1982).

12.   A student report, or *reportatio*, of these Roman lectures survives, and is now called, somewhat misleadingly perhaps, the "Roman commentary"--"misleadingly" because we are not at all sure whether Thomas ever intended his classroom lectures to form a written work, or that he ever reviewed and corrected the student's report, thus making it an *ordinatio*. For an account of this *reportatio* or "Roman commentary" on Book 1 of the *Sentences*, along with a list of the new texts to be found in it, see my "*Alia lectura fratris thome*: A List of the New Texts of St Thomas Aquinas found in Lincoln College, Oxford, MS. Lat. 95," *Recherches de théologie ancienne et médiévale* (1990) 34-61. Thomas does not provide a series of arguments in the Roman Commentary for the existence of God, but he does give three articles that correspond to *Summa theologiae*, I, q. 2, a. 1, q. 2, a. 2, and q. 32, a.

1, respectively, one of which asks *utrum ex creaturis possit veniri in cognitionem dei.* See Johnson, "Alia lectura," p. 46, nos. 22-24. He also provides a lengthy treatment *de deo uno*, corresponding particularly to distinction 8 of Book 1 of the *Sentences* (See ibid., pp. 50-51, nos. 39-47).

13.   Boyle rightly cautions *(The Setting of the Summa theologiae* [pp. 15-20, esp. 18-19]), that we should not assume that Thomas' eventual decision to break away from the *Libri sententiarum* meant that it was the sole target of his complaint in the prologue to the *Summa theologiae*--it is quite likely that the difficulty of using existing Dominican works, like Peraldus's *Summa de virtutibus et vitiis* or Raymond of Peñafort's *Summa de casibus*, helped furnish the occasion as well.

14.   Thomas explains his rationale as follows: "Consideravimus namque huius doctrinae novitios in his quae a diversis conscripta sunt plurimum impediri; partim quidem propter multiplicationem inutilium quaestionum, articulorum et argumentorum; partim quidem etiam quia ea quae sunt necessaria talibus ad sciendum non traduntur secundum ordinem disciplinae, sed secundum quod requirebat librorum expositio, vel secundum quod se praebebat occasio disputandi; partim quidem quia eorundem frequens repetitio et fastidium et confusionem generabat in animis auditorum" *(Summa theologiae*, I, *prologus).*

15.   In his *Summa theologiae*, I, *prologus*, Thomas writes: "Haec [impedimenta] igitur et alia huiusmodi evitare studentes, tentabimus, cum confidentia divini auxilii, ea quae ad sacram doctrinam pertinent breviter ac dilucide prosequi, secundum quod materia patietur."

16.   Again, Thomas writes in his *Summa theologiae*, I, *prologus*: "Et ut intentio nostra sub aliquibus certis limitibus comprehendatur, necessarium est primo investigare de ipsa sacra doctrina, qualis sit, et ad quae se extendat."

17.   For the various authors see: Thomas de Vio (Cajetan), *Commentarium in primam partem summae theologiae Sancti Thomae Aquinatis*, q. 1, in *Sancti Thomae Aquinatis Opera Omnia*, vol. 4, ed. Leonine (Rome: Propaganda Fidei, 1888), pp. 6-26; Domingo Báñez, *Scholastica commentaria in primam partem Summae Theologiae S. Thomae Aquinatis*, ed. Luis Urbano (Madrid: Editorial F.E.D.A., 1934), pp. 7-99; John of St. Thomas, *Cursus theologicus*, ed. Solemnes (Paris: Desclée, 1931), vol. 1, pp. 143-219, 305-410; J. Fr. Bonnefoy, *La Nature de la Théologie selon Saint Thomas d'Aquin* (Paris: Vrin, 1939); M. D. Chenu, "La Théologie comme Science au XIIIe Siècle," *Archives d'Histoire Doctrinale et Littéraire du Moyen-âge* 2 (1927) 31-71; G. Van Ackeren, *Sacra Doctrina: The Subject of the First Question of the Summa Theologica of St. Thomas Aquinas* (Rome: Catholic Book Agency, 1952); J. A. Weisheipl, "The Meaning

of *Sacra Doctrina* in *Summa theologiae* I, q. 1," *The Thomist* 38 (1974) 49-80; T. C. O'Brien, "*Sacra Doctrina* Revisited: The Context of Medieval Education," *The Thomist* 41 (1977) 475-509.

18.   See Francisco Muñiz, "De diversis muneribus S. Theologiae secundum doctrinam D. Thomae," *Angelicum* 24 (1947) 93-123; J. M. Ramírez, *De hominis beatitudine*, in *Jacobus M. Ramírez, O.P.: Opera Omnia*, ed. Victoríno Rodríguez, tomus 3, vol. 1 (Madrid: Consejo Superior de Investigaciones Científicas, 1972), p. 7, n. 1; William A. Wallace, *The Role of Demonstration in Moral Theology: A Study of Methodology in St. Thomas Aquinas* (Washington, D.C.: The Thomist Press, 1962), pp. 57-70.

19.   I take the liberty of referring to my *The Sapiential Character of Sacra Doctrina in the Thought of St. Thomas Aquinas: The Appropriation of Aristotle's Intellectual Virtue of Wisdom*, unpublished doctoral dissertation (Toronto: University of Toronto, 1990). A shorter presentation is my "The Sapiential Character of the First Article of the *Summa theologiae*," in *Philosophy and the God of Abraham: Essays in Memory of James A. Weisheipl, O.P.* (Toronto: Pontifical Institute of Mediaeval Studies, 1991), pp. 85-98. Other comments can be found in my Why Five Ways?," in *Religion and the Virtue of Religion: Proceedings of the American Catholic Philosophical Association* (Washington, D.C: American Catholic Philosophical Association, 1992), pp. 107-121.

20.   Summa theologiae, I, a. 1, a. 7, *in corp.*:
"Omnia autem pertractantur in sacra doctrina sub
ratione Dei, vel quia sunt ipse Deus, vel quia habent
ordinem ad Deum, ut ad principium et finem. Unde
sequitur quod Deus vere est subiectum huius scientiae."

21.   See *Summa theologiae*, I-II, *prol.* This is
also why, at the outset of the *Prima secundae*, Thomas
is able to say precisely where the completeness of the
image of God is to be found--in the direct vision of
God himself--while a similar investigation in the
Nicomachean Ethics is delayed until book 10. See
Summa theologiae, I-II, qq. 1-5, esp. q. 3, a. 8.

22.   See *Summa theologiae*, I, q. 1, a. 7, ad 2:
"Dicendum quod licet de Deo non possimus scire quid
est, utimur tamen eius effectu, in hac doctrina, vel
naturae vel gratiae, loco definitionis, ad ea quae de Deo
in hac doctrina considerantur. . . (my emphasis)."

23.   See *Summa theologiae*, I, q. 1, a. 8 ad 2:
*Auctoritatibus autem canonicae Scripturae utitur [sacra
doctrina] proprie, ex necessitate argumentando.* See as
well *Super evangelium Iohannis,* 22, lect. 6, ed. R. Cai
(Turin: Marietti, 1952), p. 488, no. 2656: ". . . Sola
canonica scriptura est regula fidei." It is well known
that Thomas regularly uses *sacra doctrina* and *sacra
scriptura* interchangeably. See the following texts: *In
I Sent.*, prol., q. 3, a. 2, arg 1 and *sed contra*; *In*

Boethii de trinitate, q. 2, a. 3, *in corp.*, ad 5 and ad 8; ibid., q. 5, a. 4, *in corp.*, and ad 3; *Summa theologiae*, I, q. 1., a. 2, arg. 2, and ad 2; a. 4, arg. 2; *Summa theologiae*, I, q. 1, a. 7, arg. 2 and ad 2; I, q. 1, a. 9, ad 1.

24.   For discussions on the role of authority--which is really the rubric under which this falls--see the account given by M.-D. Chenu, *Introduction a l'Etude de Saint Thomas d'Aquin* (Paris: J. Vrin, 1950), pp. 106-131. Leo Elders also has some helpful comments in his "Structure et fonction de l'argument *Sed Contra* dans la *Somme Théologique* de Saint Thomas," *Divus Thomas* 80 (1977) 245-60, where he shows, based upon the count of the Leonine edition of the *Summa theologiae*, that the overwhelming majority of textual authorities in the work are from sacred scripture, with second place given to the received authorities of the fathers. Others include the gloss, canon law--usually mediated through Dominican authors such as Raymond of Peñafort and William of Peraldus--and even liturgical sources (e.g., *Summa theologiae*, I, q. 31, a. 4, obj. 4; I, q. 52, a. 1, *sed contra*; I-II, q. 113, q. 9, *sed contra*; II-II, q. 82, a. 3, ad 2; ibid., a. 4, *sed contra*; ibid., q. 83, a. 17, *in corp.*; ibid., q. 124, a. 2, *in corp.*; ibid., q. 154, a. 5, *in corp.*; ibid., q. 176, a. 2, obj. 1; III, q. 1, a. 3, ad 3). My own count of question 1 results in twenty-seven distinct references to sacred scripture, with eighteen references to received authorities (e.g., Augustine, Dionysius, etc.). In question 2, our concern henceforth, I count six references to scripture, and eight to received Christian

authorities. Philosophical authorities are far fewer in number. This shows on a material level, I think, Thomas's appropriation of the received language of the tradition.

It is also interesting, and important, to note with Mark Jordan (*The Alleged Aristotelianism of Thomas Aquinas* [Toronto: P.I.M.S., 1992], pp. 7-8, 32-41) that Thomas never uses the term "philosopher" to denote someone he knows to be a Christian thinker. This suggests to me--though it would take a separate paper to establish this with any rigor--that he would hold that ones Christian faith enters one's thinking internally, such that the resulting theorizing is always influenced in some positive way, and not merely a negative way, by faith. This is, of course, the problematic of the "Christian philosophy" controversy. I am inclined to say that "Christian philosophy" is really theology, since, in a Christian, the habit of faith illumines, both positively and negatively, premises employed in argumentation--*talis est demonstratio qualis est medium.*

25.   See *Summa theologiae*, I, q. 2, a. 1, arg. 2, and ad 2, where Thomas addresses the argument of Anselm without referring to him by name. In the newly-found Roman commentary he mentions Anselm's name explicitly, twice directly and once by pronominal reference. See Johnson, "*Alia lectura*," p. 46, no. 2. The objected difficulty, and Thomas's reply, as found in the MS (Oxford, Lincoln College MS Lat. 95), run thus: [fol. 12va] "Preterea. Quod non potest cogitari non esse est per se notum. Sed nullus potest

cogitare deum non esse, ut Anselmus dicit. Ergo deum esse est per se notum. Probatio medie. Deus est illud quo maius cogitari non potest. Aut ergo deum esse est [est] tantum in corde tuo aut in corde et in re. Si in corde tantum tunc non est maius quo cogitari non potest, quia maius est quod est in re et in corde. Similiter nec in re tantum, quia maius est quod est in re simul et in corde. Ergo deum esse est in corde et in re. Et sic nullo modo potest cogitari deum non esse. Ergo id quod prius . . . . [fol. 12va in calce] Ad secundum dicendum quod quicquid dicit Anselmus, potest tamen cogitari deum non esse, sicut habetur in psalmo, dixit insipiens in corde suo; et multi sunt qui nichil sciunt de deo. Et ratio sua ad hoc non valet, quia licet non possit cogitari deum non esse, quia nichil potest cogitari maius deo, propter hoc non sequitur nisi quod deus sit in mente ut cogitatum. Vel dicendum quod quantum in se est, est ita per se notum quod non potest cogitari non esse". For other texts where Thomas employs the argument of Anselm, see *In I Sent.*, d. 3, q. 1, a. 2, ad 4; *De veritate*, q. 10. a. 12, ad 2; *Summa contra gentiles*, lib. 1, caps. 10-12; ibid., lib 3, cap 38. The *Proslogion* of Anselm is found in *Sancti Anselmi Cantuariensis Archiepiscopi Opera Omnia*, ed. F. S. Schmitt (Seckau: Styria, 1938), vol. 1, pp. 93-122, with Gaunilon's reply on pp. 125-29, and Anselm's response to Gaunilon on pp. 130-39.

26.   For more on this, see Thomas' account of human knowledge in *Summa theologiae*, I, qq. 84-89. Thomas' commitment to this view of human knowing separates   him   from   St.   Bonaventure,   whose

understanding of human knowing is much like what
Thomas would attribute to angelic knowledge. See
Lawrence Dewan, "St. Thomas, St. Bonaventure, and
the Need to Prove the Existence of God," in
*Philosophy and Culture: Proceedings of the XVIIth
World Congress of Philosophy*, in 5 vols, ed. V.
Cauchy (Montreal: Éditions Montrarency, 1983-1988),
vol. 3, pp. 341-34.

27. See Aristotle, *Liber posteriorium
analyticorum*, lib. 1, cap. 2, 71b9-12, in *Sancti Thomae
de Aquino Opera Omnia*, vol. 1/2, 2nd ed., ed. Leonine
(Romae: Ad Sanctae Sabinae, 1989), p. 17: "Scire
autem opinamur unumquodque simpliciter, set non
sophistico modo, quod est secundum accidens. Cum
causam quoque arbitramur cognoscere propter quam res
est, et quoniam illius causa est, et non est contingere
hoc aliter se habere."

28. For more on demonstration, see James A.
Weisheipl, *Aristotelian Methodology: A Commentary
on the Posterior Analytics of Aristotle* (River Forest,
Ill.: Dominican House of Studies, 1958); Melvin P.
Glutz, *The Manner of Demonstrating in Natural
Philosophy* (River Forest, Ill.: Studium Generale of
Saint Thomas Aquinas, 1956); Wallace, *The Role of
Demonstration in Moral Theology*, pp. 15-70; T. C.
O'Brien, *Metaphysics and the Existence of God: A
Reflection on the Question of God's Existence in
Contemporary Thomistic Metaphysics* (Washington,
D.C.: The Thomist Press, 1960).

29.   See *Summa theologiae*, I, q. 2, a. 2, *in corp.*: "Respondeo. Dicendum quod duplex est demonstratio. Una quae est per causam, et dicitur propter quid, et haec est per priora simpliciter. Alia est per effectum et dicitur demonstratio quia, et haec est per ea quae sunt priora quoad nos; cum enim effectus aliquis nobis est manifestior quam sua causa, per effectum precedimus ad cognitionem causae".

30.   See *Summa theologiae*, I, q. 2, a. 2, arg. 1: "Praeterea. Medium demonstrationis est quod quid est. Sed de Deo non possuimus scire quid est, sed solum quid non est, ut dicit Damascenus. Ergo non possumus demonstrare Deum esse."

31.   See *Summa theologiae*, I, q. 2., a. 2, *ad 2*: "Ad secundum. Dicendum quod cum demonstratur causa per effectum, necesse est uti effectu loco definitionis causae ad probandum causam esse, et hoc maxime contingit in Deo. Quia ad probandum aliquid esse, necesse est accipere pro medio quid significet nomen, non autem quod quid est, quia quaestio quid est, sequitur ad quaestionem an est. Nomina autem Dei imponuntur ab effectibus, ut postea ostendetur: unde, demonstrando Deum esse per effectum, accipere possumus pro medio quid significet hoc nomen Deus." See also, though it postdates the present discussion in the *Summa theologiae*, Thomas's *Expositio libri posteriorum*, l. 1, cap. 2, ad 71a11, in *Sancti Thomae de Aquino Opera Omnia*, vol. 1/2, 2nd ed., ed. Leonine

(Romae: Ad Sanctae Sabinae, 1989), p. 11: ". . . Et non dicit [Philosophus]: 'quid est' simpliciter, sed 'quid est quod dicitur,' quia antequam sciatur de aliquo an sit, non potest proprie sciri de eo quid est (non entium enim non sunt diffinitiones), unde questio 'an est' precedit questionem 'quid est'; set non potest ostendi de aliquo an sit nisi prius intelligatur quid significatur per nomen; propter quod etiam Philosophus in IV Metaphysice, in disputatione contra negantes principia, docet incipere a significatione nominum."

32.   See *Summa theologiae*, I, q. 13, a. 2, *in corp.*: ". . . Cum igitur dicitur: Deus est bonus, non est sensus: Deus est causa bonitatis, vel: Deus non est malus; sed est sensus: id quod bonitatem dicimus in creaturis, **praeexistit in Deo, et hoc quidem secundum modum altiorem** (my emphasis)." Actually, Thomas does note the possibility that someone who hears the name "God" might not know it means "that than which nothing greater can be conceived." See *Summa theologiae*, I, q. 2, a. 1, ad 2: "Dicendum quod forte ille qui audit hoc nomen Deus, non intelligit significari aliquid quo maius cogitari non possit . . . ."

33.   See *Summa theologiae*, I, q. 13, a. 2, *in corp.*: ". . . Dato etiam quod quilibet intelligat hoc nomine Deus significari hoc quod dicitur, scilicet illud quo maius cogitari non potest; non tamen propter hoc sequitur quod intelligat id quod significatur per nomen, esse in rerum natura, sed in apprehensione intellectus tantum. Nec potest argui quod sit in re, nisi daretur

quod sit in re aliquid quo maius cogitari non potest, quod non est datum a ponentibus Deum non esse."

34.   See *Summa theologiae*, I, q. 13, a. 3, *in corp*. Father Dewan ("The Number and Order of the Five Ways", wonders, on p. 18, note 50), whether the fact that the first three ways arrive at what *all* call God (*quod omnes dicunt Deum*) and the last to way arrive at what *we* call God (*quod dicimus Deum*) is significant. I do not think so. Each and every one of the ways begins by including the reader in the investigation, such that Thomas' description of the effect known to us in the first and most manifest way is *certum est . . . et sensu constat, aliqua moveri in hoc mundo*, while the second and third claim that *invenimus in istis sensibilibus* or *invenimus in rebus*, which leads to what *omnes Deum nominant*, or *omnes dicunt Deum*. The fourth way, while it does not claim that "we" find diverse gradations in things, nonetheless holds that *invenitur in rebus aliquid magis et minus bonum*, which leads to something that "we" call God: . . . *et hoc dicimus Deum*. But in the fifth way *videmus quod aliqua quae cognitione carent*, and this, too, leads to the reality of which we say, *et hoc dicimus Deum*. It does not seem to me that Thomas is commenting here on the extent to which others, outside his Christian audience, are able to approach God through reasoning.

35.   It is interesting to note that even the first objected difficulty in *Summa theologiae* I, a. q, a. 3, employs a *quid nominis* of God, which in this case is

that of 'infinite good', in order to suggest that there is
not a God: "Videtur quod Deus non sit. Quia si unum
contrariorum fuerit infinitum, totaliter destruetur aliud.
Sed **hoc intelligitur in hoc nomine Deus**, scilicet quod
sit quoddam bonum infinitum. Si ergo Deus esset,
nullum malum inveniretur. Invenitur autem malum in
mundo. Ergo Deus non est (my emphasis)."

36.   See *Summa theologiae*, I, *prologus*: "Quia
catholicae veritatis doctor non solum provectos debet
instruere, sed ad eum pertinet etiam incipientes erudire,
secundum illud Apostoli I ad Cor. III, 'Tamquam
parvulis   in   Christo,   lac vobis potum dedi, non
escam' . . . ."

37.   See Boyle, *The Setting of the Summa
theologiae*, pp. 15-20.

38.   See R. H. and M. A. Rouse, "A Verbal
Concordance to the Scripture," *Archivum Fratrum
Praedicatorum* 44 (1974) 5-30.

39.   See Marian   Michelle   Mulchahey,
*Dominican Education and the Dominican Ministry in
the Thirteenth and Fourteenth Centuries*, in 2 vols.,
unpublished doctoral dissertation (Toronto: Centre for
Medieval Studies, 1988), part 2, chap. 3, "The Order's
Institutional Response to Its Ministry: Dominican
Schools," vol. 1, pp. 119-272. See also William A.
Hinnebusch, *The History of the Dominican Order*:

Origins and Growth to 1500, in 2 vols. (Staten Island: Alba House, 1966), especially the chapter entitled "Dominican Bible Studies," vol. 2, pp. 99-115. Much of the specification is attributable to Humbert of Roman's revision of Dominican education, during Thomas' early period as a Dominican. See E. T. Brett, *Humbert of Romans: His Life and Views of Thirteenth-Century Society* (Toronto: P.I.M.S., 1984), pp. 41-56.

40.   For more on Dominican liturgical life, see the magisterial study of Ansgar Dirks, O.P., "De liturgiae dominicanae evolutione," *Archivum Fratrum Praedicatorum* 50 (1980) 5-21; 52 (1982) 5-76; 53 (1983) 53-145; 54 (1984) 39-82; 55 (1985) 5-47. See also Gonzalez Fuente, *La vida liturgica en la Orden de Predicatores. Estudio en su legislacion: 1216-1980* (Rome: Ad Sanctae Sabinae, 1981) and W. R. Bonniwell, *A History of Dominican Liturgy* (New York: J. F. Wagner, 1944), esp. pp. 9-193. Maura O'Carroll has reestablished the propers for the Dominican Rite in Thomas' day in "The Lectionary for the Proper of the Year in the Dominican and Franciscan Rites of the Thirteenth Century," *Archivum Fratrum Praedicatorum* 59 (1979) 79-103, and it would be very interesting to search the Biblical texts mandated there for instances of *Deus*. A similar effort with Simon Tugwell's "Dominican Profession in the Thirteenth Century," *Archivum Fratrum Praedicatorum* 53 (1983) 5-52, is profitable; references to God (pp. 45-48) concern subjection, thanksgiving, desire to please God, all coming from Biblical passages ranging from Kings to the Psalms to Luke.

41.   See Henri Denifle, "*Quel livre servait de base a l'enseignement des Maîtres en Théologie dans l'Université de Paris*," *Revue Thomiste* 2 (1894) 129-61.

42.   See Jules A. Baisnée, "St. Thomas Aquinas' Proofs," mentioned above in note 5.

43.   The *Concordantiae Bibliorum Sacrorum iuxta Vulgatam* (Stuttgart: Fromann-Holzboog, 1977), vol. 2, cols. 1214-79, has roughly 5400 occurrences of the word *Deus*. Given the interchange between *Deus* and *Dominus*, one could also consult the later term as well, as above in *Concordantiae Bibliorum*, cols. 1497-607. An examination of reference to *Deus* in the *Concordantia sancti Iacobi* would be instructive--for Thomas' time one would have to find the first or second of the three concordances (see Rouse and Rouse, "A Verbal Concordance," pp. 6-8)--but the variety of different readings in manuscripts makes anything approaching a "critical edition" of the *Concordantia* almost impossible.

44.   See *Summa theologiae*, II-II, q. 2, a. 3, *in corp.*: ". . . Per modum addiscentis a Deo doctore . . . . Unde ad hoc quod homo perveniat ad perfectam visionem beatitudinis praeexigitur quod [fidelis] credat Deo tanquam discipulus magistro docenti."

45.   Muñiz ("De diversis muneribus," p. 113) makes the suggestive claim that philosophical elements used in sacred theology are like the elements a living body takes in as nutrition; they continue to have their original properties, but are formally part of the whole that has assumed them: "In ordine naturali corpora viventia nitriuntur accipiendo ab extrinseco elementa ipsis extranea, quae, semel incorporata et assimilata, vivificantur et informantur eadem anima eademque vita suppositi viventis."

46.   See *In Boethii de trinitate,* q. 2, a. 3, ad 5: ". . . Unde illi, qui utuntur philosophicis documentis in sacra doctrina redigendo in obsequium fidei, non miscent aquam vino, sed aquam convertunt in vinum."

AVERROES ON GOD'S KNOWLEDGE OF BEING *QUA* BEING[1]

Thérèse-Anne Druart
The Catholic University of America

Aristotle's claim in *Metaphysics* 12.9 is still puzzling: "it must be itself that [divine] thought thinks [since it is the most excellent of things], and its thinking is a thinking on thinking [*noēsis noēseos*]."[2] Averroes' reflections on this particular claim and on the whole issue of God's Knowledge are even more puzzling. Scholars disagree not only about what Averroes' view is but also about how well he handles this difficult theme.

Kogan, working mainly on the *Tahafut al-Tahafut* (*Destructio destructionis* or *Incoherence of the Incoherence*), concurs with S. Van den Bergh's view that the theory expressed there at first glance "makes the term 'knowledge' as applied to God not only incomprehensible but meaningless."[3] Kogan then tries to rescue Averroes by proposing a more subtle interpretation of God's causal knowing, but he concludes that "when the theory of causal knowing is recognizably epistemic, it is not causal, and when it is causal, it is not epistemic."[4]   Jolivet, who works on the *Long Commentary on the Metaphysics*, claims that Averroes departs from Aristotle in his handling of God's thinking.[5] Rosemann, on the other hand, argues that Averroes is a faithful Aristotelian in his commentary on God's thinking about thinking.[6] Finally, Flynn shows how deep is the influence of Averroes on Thomas Aquinas' reflections on God's Knowledge, noting the points on which Aquinas quotes Averroes either as an authority to be followed or as an adversary to be fought.[7]

These scholars have brought to light many interesting points but have not really focused on the core of Averroes' position on the divine thought and, in particular, on how God may have any Knowledge of the sublunary world. In the four main relevant texts, i.e., the *Tahafut al-Tahafut* (*The Incoherence of the Incoherence*), the *Fasl al-Maqal* (known as *The Decisive Treatise* or *On the Harmony of Religion and Philosophy*), the *Damima* (known as the *Appendix*, a brief treatise on God's Knowledge), and the *Long Commentary on the Metaphysics*, Averroes consistently claims that God's Knowledge is neither particular nor universal.[8] He also asserts that the word "knowledge" is said of God's Knowledge and of ours only equivocally.[9] The equivocity is grounded in the fact that God's Knowledge is the cause of beings, whereas beings are the cause of our knowledge.[10] All these negative views are well known, but in one passage Averroes offers something positive besides the famous claim that God's Knowledge is causal.   The *Commentary* on *Metaphysics* 12.51 brings a new and very interesting note which will be the focus of my reflections: "The First, may He be praised, is the one who knows the nature of being inasmuch as it is being without qualification [*bi-'itlaq* or *simpliciter*] which is Himself [or: his essence]."[11] This sounds very much as if God's Knowledge is metaphysics, and this Knowledge is supposed to solve all the puzzles raised by our difficulty in understanding God's truly eternal Knowledge of everything outside himself and especially of what is here below.

Reflecting on this claim and some of its implications, I would like to retrace the arguments in order to elucidate the meaning of this statement as well as to determine whether Averroes' final claim in this commentary on 12.51 does indeed solve all the puzzles. Rosemann claims that it does, but he also hints that Averroes' position may be somewhat inconsistent ("*Noesis Noeseos*," 557 n. 41).

First, I shall address the issue of what is meant by the claim that God's Knowledge and ours are equivocal, since this general assertion is the underpinning for the view that God's Knowledge is neither universal nor particular. Second, I shall examine what it means to claim that God's Knowledge is neither particular nor universal. Third, I shall discuss some points related to the denial of God's Knowledge of particulars. Fourth, I shall reflect on the denial of God's Knowledge of universals. Finally, I shall examine the claim that God knows being inasmuch as it is being and in this way cannot be said to be ignorant of all things. How is it that such a Knowledge is neither universal nor particular? Is Thomas Aquinas, who was fascinated by this passage, right in his view that such Knowledge is no proper knowledge at all?

The Equivocity between
Human and Divine Knowledge

In *On the Harmony* (10-11, English 54), the *Appendix* (44, English 74-75), *Incoherence* (e. g., 462, English 280), and the *Commentary* on *Metaphysics* 12 (1708, English 197), Averroes forcefully asserts that God's Knowledge is very different from ours. In some of these passages the technical expression "equivocal"[12] is used. Flynn ("St. Thomas and Averroes," 30 n. 16) claims that there is every reason to believe that Averroes is using the term "equivocal" in the sense of "analogous" or "ambiguous," as it was called by the Arabic philosophers. This would mean that it is not a complete equivocation but simply a *pros hen* one. Rosemann follows suit (*"Noesis Noeseos,"* 556 n. 38).

Yet it seems to me that what is meant is complete equivocity and not a *pros hen* equivocation. Averroes is, of course, very aware of *pros hen* equivocation, as his commentary on 4.2 (where Aristotle introduces this type of equivocation) shows most clearly. Furthermore, *pros hen* equivocation is explained in the *Incoherence* (387-388, English 233-234). The *Commentary* on 12.28 (1554, English 133) speaks of terms used neither homonymously nor equivocally, but nevertheless as related. Yet in chapter 51 and in every other text I am aware of in which he is speaking of God's Knowledge and ours, Averroes uses the term "equivocation" or "equivocal" without further qualification, which suggests that only a *pros hen* equivocation is meant.

Flynn's main text to justify his interpretation of *pros hen* equivocation is located in *Incoherence*, discussion 7 (387-388). This passage tells us that there

are things which have a single name not by univocal or
equivocal commonality of name but by community of
names related to one thing ambiguously. A characteristic of these things is that they lead upwards to a
first in that genus, which is the first cause for all those
things to which this name refers; for example, heat is
said of fire and of all other hot things.

Flynn asserts that this applies to God's
Knowledge and ours because one of the illustrations
that follows this statement is "the name intellect, which
according to people is said of the separate intellects
according to priority and posteriority since in them a
first intellect is cause of the others" (388). Yet this
text speaks of intellect, not knowledge; it is about
separate intellects, which do not include the human
intellect; and it claims that a first intellect is the cause
of other intellects, whereas Averroes does not claim
that God's Knowledge is the cause of our knowledge.

In fact, in all four of the texts that I am
considering, Averroes does not ground the equivocity
in a relation of cause and effect between God's
Knowledge and ours, nor in a difference of degrees (as,
for instance, in fire and hot things). Rather, the source
of the equivocity is that the two knowledges are
different kinds. God's Knowledge causes beings,
whereas ours is caused by beings. One could object
that the contrast holds of the proximate cause and its
effect: since God's Knowledge causes the beings which
cause our knowledge, reference to the remote cause
solves the problem--exactly as fire causes heat in the
water boiling on the stove, which in its turn will warm
the teapot into which it is poured. Yet the cases are
not similar, since in the case of fire and hot things it is
always a question of transmitting heat directly or

through a certain number of intermediaries, whereas in the case of God's Knowledge and ours, the intermediary beings act on the human mind as beings and not as knowing. The intermediary beings may even be totally deprived of knowledge, such as a tree or a cat.

Averroes always insists on the gap between human and divine knowledge. The *Incoherence*, for instance, explains this in striking terms (468):

> According to the philosophers, it is impossible that His Knowledge be analogous to our knowledge since our knowledge is caused by the beings whereas His Knowledge is their cause. It is not true that eternal Knowledge is in the image ['ala surat] of originated knowledge. Anyone who holds the latter position does indeed make of God an eternal human being and of the human being a generable and corruptible God. In sum, as has already been shown, what pertains to the First's Knowledge is opposite [muqabil] to what pertains to human knowledge. I mean that it is His Knowledge which produces the beings and that it is not the beings which produce His Knowledge.

The two types of knowledge are not said merely to be different but are said to be opposite. This opposition is expressed still more strongly in *On the Harmony:*

> . . . Our knowledge of them [particulars] is an effect of the object known, originating when it comes into existence and changing when it changes; whereas Glorious God's Knowledge of existence is the opposite of this: it is the cause of the object known, which is existent being. Thus, to suppose the two kinds of knowledge are similar to each other is to identify the essences and the properties of opposite

things, and that is the extreme of ignorance. And if the name of "knowledge" is predicated of both originated and eternal knowledge, it is predicated by *sheer equivocity* [italics added: *bi-'ishtirak al-'ism al-mahd*], as many names are predicated of opposite things, e. g., *jalal* of great and small, *sarim* of light and darkness. Thus there exists no definition embracing both kinds of knowledge at once, as the theologians of our time imagine.

Again, the *Appendix*, treating of the usual confusion between these two types of knowledge, says (43, English 74): "The mistake in this matter has arisen simply from making an analogy between the eternal Knowledge and originated knowledge, i.e., between the suprasensible and the sensible; and the falsity of this analogy is well known." This refers to *Metaphysics* 10.51, where Averroes, in his commentary (1387), claims that the corruptible and the incorruptible are said equivocally, since they are contraries (*mutadadan*) which have nothing in common except the name. He then gives as example the term "body" as used for corruptible and incorruptible beings. The same principle applies to God's eternal and therefore incorruptible Knowledge and ours. Therefore, the complete equivocity between God's Knowledge and ours is grounded not only in the fact that God's Knowledge is causal while ours is caused but also in the equivocity following from the radical difference between the corruptible and the incorruptible (*Metaphysics* 10.51).

The radical equivocity of knowledge is even transferred to ignorance. "He [God] is qualified neither by the knowledge which is in us, nor by the ignorance which is its opposite, [for] one ascribes none of these two to something such that it is not in its nature that any one of them would exist in it" (ibid., 1708). Aquinas' paraphrase of this passage in the first book of his *Commentary on the Sentences*, dist. xxxv, qu. 1, art. 3, shows clearly that he understood this equivocity to be complete: "And from this according to him [Averroes] it does not follow that God is ignorant, since His Knowledge is not of the genus of our knowledge; and therefore the opposite ignorance does not apply to Him, just as one does not say of a stone that it has sight or is blind."[13]   This equivocity of ignorance will allow Averroes to avoid saying that, since God's Knowledge is not particular, God must be ignorant of all things.   The radical equivocity between divine and human knowledge and ignorance explains why God's Knowledge is neither universal nor particular, since these two terms characterize only human knowledge.

God's Knowledge
Is Neither Particular nor Universal

The *Incoherence* (462, English 280), *On the Harmony* (19, English 55), and the *Commentary on the Metaphysics* 12.51 (1708, English 197) all assert that God's Knowledge cannot be described as particular or universal.   As for the *Appendix,* it claims that eternal Knowledge is "a knowledge of beings which is unqualified" (44, English 75), and Hourani interprets this as Knowledge neither universal nor particular (*Metaphysics*, 118 n. 209).

The assertion that God's Knowledge is neither particular nor universal is sometimes presented with variations.   For instance, the end of the eleventh discussion in the *Tahafut* formulates it in the following manner: "In the same way, in what concerns the universals and the particulars, it is true that He, may He be praised, knows them and does not know them" (446). This formulation, which simultaneously both affirms and denies God's Knowledge of universals and particulars, is an application of a far-reaching previous claim, viz., that God's Knowledge cannot be divided into the opposites "true" and "false" and that therefore, in the case of God, two propositions are simultaneously true: (1) God knows what he knows, and (2) God does not know what he knows.[14] This further claim reinforces the view that God's Knowledge and ours are utterly different.

Another variation on the theme to which Kogan has drawn attention (*Averroes and the Metaphysics of Causation*, 230) is found in the sixth discussion of the *Tahafut*. There Averroes tells us that, "Since for us knowledge of particulars is actual knowledge, we know that His Knowledge resembles more particular knowledge than universal knowledge, even though it is neither universal nor particular" (Arabic 345). The reason given for this surprising further precision reflects a point made again and again, namely, that God's Knowledge is pure actuality; and it reinforces Averroes' attack on Avicenna, who had claimed that, though God does not know particulars, he does know universals (*Tahafut,* 347, English 208). Curiously enough, this further precision is based on some kind of comparison with human knowing and shows that Averroes' view of the complete equivocity between divine and human knowledge is either not fully tenable or gives rise to some inconsistencies, at least in the arguments used to make some points. In some cases

Averroes may have been sloppy, and in others he may have wanted to hide how radical some of his positions were.

Beyond the variations on the theme, there lurk further questions. Is Averroes simply denying that God knows particulars in a particular way and universals in a universal way (that is, is he simply denying human modes of knowing all the beings)? Or is his claim still more radical: is he asserting that God does not know at all either particulars or universals? For instance, the last text we quoted focuses on particular and universal knowledge, qualifying the mode of knowing but not explicitly referring to the objects of knowing themselves. In the same way, the claim that it is both true and false that God knows what he knows might be used to affirm that God both knows and does not know universals and particulars, since he would know them but not in a particular or universal mode.

The *Appendix,* which focuses on knowledge of particulars, seems to make a distinction between the objects known and the mode of their being known: "The philosophers have been accused of saying . . . that the Glorious One does not know particulars. Their position is not what has been imputed to them; rather they hold that He does not know particulars with originated knowledge" (44, English 75). This text seems to affirm that God knows particulars but not in the particular mode of originated knowledge, since originated knowledge is caused by the beings, whereas eternal Knowledge causes them.

On the other hand, other passages do not hesitate to deny to God Knowledge of both universals and particulars, and not simply the different human modes of knowing them. The *Commentary* 12.51 is particularly enlightening, since it denies the particular and universal modes of knowing as well as knowledge of particulars and universals: "His Knowledge, may He be praised, cannot be qualified as universal or particular, for the one whose knowledge is universal knows only potentially the particulars which are in act" (1708). And a bit further down, the text adds: "It is even clearer that His Knowledge is not particular, since the particulars are infinite, and no knowledge encompasses them" (*Commentary*, 12.51).

Needless to say, I do think that in fact Averroes denies God's Knowledge of universals and particulars, and not simply the particular or universal modes of knowing them. The texts which seem to open the door for knowing particulars in another mode of knowing, such as the passages we quoted above from the *Appendix* (see p. 137 in the edition as above) and the *Tahafut* (see p. 136 in the edition as above), may be considered as popular and as not revealing Averroes' considered view. In other words, they may be trying to hide radical claims rather offensive to religious feelings.

In the *Commentary on Metaphysics* 12.51, while refuting Themistius' view that God thinks many intelligibles at once, Averroes makes it clear that God does not think anything outside himself, and this again explains why he claims that God knows neither particulars nor universals:

> This is what escaped Themistius when he allowed that [God's] intellect thinks many intelligibles at once. This is contrary to our statement that He thinks Himself [or: His essence] and does not think anything outside Himself, and that the intellect and what it thinks are one in every respect. For he

[Themistius] says that He thinks all things inasmuch
as He thinks that He is their principle. All of this
is the statement of someone who does not
understand Aristotle's demonstrations here. (1706-
1707)

Themistius' suggestion that God knows other things at
least inasmuch as he is their principle is rejected by
Averroes in the *Tahafut,* as we shall see in a moment.

After this examination of the general assertion
that God's Knowledge is of nothing outside himself
and is neither particular nor universal, I would like to
look more carefully at the difficulties raised by each
part of this double claim. Since Averroes asserts that
God's Knowledge is closer to particular knowledge, I
begin with the denial of knowledge of particulars.

The Denial of God's Knowledge of Particulars

The most straightforward denial of God's
Knowledge of particulars is found in a technical work,
the *Commentary* on *Metaphysics,* 12.51 (1708): "It is
even clearer that His Knowledge is not particular since
the particulars are infinite and no knowledge
encompasses them." This statement is altogether
peculiar and unique. It begins by asserting that the fact
that God's Knowledge is not particular is clearer than
the fact that it is not universal, but Averroes also says
that God's Knowledge is closer to particular
knowledge. However, a greater degree of clarity for an
argument denying God's Knowledge of particulars does
not preclude that God's mode of knowing whatever he
does know is closer to the particular mode, since this
mode is actual.

Even more surprising is the reason given for denying God's Knowledge of particulars, viz., that particulars are infinite and so cannot be known. This rests on the utter impossibility for the infinite to be known. To my knowledge, this is the only passage in which Averroes uses this argument. Besides, a passage in the sixth discussion of the *Tahafut* provides a way to refute it:

> In us apprehension of what is actually infinite is prevented, because in us the objects of knowledge are distinct from one another. Yet, if there is a knowledge in which objects of knowledge are unified, then with respect to such knowledge, the finite and the infinite are equivalent. (345)

The whole problem, of course, is whether such a unifying knowledge exists; and, if it does, whether this type of knowing would respect the individuality of the particulars and allow us to still speak in a meaningful way of knowledge of particulars. I think that Averroes attempts this through knowledge of being inasmuch as it is being, but this will be discussed shortly. At the moment, let us consider the arguments used to deny to God a knowledge of particulars.

The main arguments against God's Knowledge of particulars are: (1) such knowledge is sensory; (2) it would introduce multiplicity in the divine knowing; and (3) it would interfere with the immutability of the divine eternal knowing, since particulars are changeable.[15] Two of these three reasons would not apply to a consideration of universals, since they are not apprehended by sensation and are not changeable, though they are multiple. Averroes is fully aware of this, but still holds that God cannot know universals either (461-462, English 280).

The Denial of God's Knowledge of Universals

Averroes often chides Avicenna for maintaining that God knows universals. His principal argument to oppose such view is that knowledge of universals is only potential knowledge of particulars; therefore, it is inconsistent with the claim that God's Knowledge is purely actual:

> His Knowledge, may He be praised, cannot be qualified as universal or particular, for the one whose knowledge is universal knows only potentially the particulars which are in act. So his object of knowledge is necessarily potential knowledge, since the universal is simply knowledge of the particulars. Since the universal is potential knowledge and there is no potentiality in His Knowledge, may He be praised, then His Knowledge is not universal. (*Commentary*, 1708)

The issue of potentiality is also at the root of the problem raised by the multiplicity of universals, as is shown in the sixth discussion of the *Tahafut* (345): "Therefore, one says that the First Knowledge must be actual knowledge and that in it there is no universality at all nor multiplicity arising from potentiality, such as the plurality of species arising from the genus."

Let us observe that multiplicity seems to be a derivative of potentiality and that the insistence on the actuality of God's Knowledge has been at the root of the claim that, though God's Knowledge is not particular, yet it resembles more knowledge of particulars than knowledge of universals. Let us also keep in mind that here Averroes denies to God any knowledge of species. We will return to this point later.

On the other hand, two passages have been brought up which seem to go against the assertion that God does not know the universals, and both are found in the *Commentary on the Metaphysics* 12. The first implies that God knows forms, and the other speaks of God's providence for the species.

First, does God know forms? Are they really present in the divine intellect? Chapter 18, commenting on the end of chapter 3, criticizes Avicenna's "Giver of forms" and theological views about the creation of forms out of nothing. Averroes concludes what he considers to be a digression with the following statement: "It is said that all proportions and forms exist potentially in prime matter and actually in the first mover in a manner similar to the actual existence of the artifact in the soul of the craftsman" (Arabic 1505).

The formula "it is said" may indicate that Averroes is simply reporting some view without agreeing with it. Furthermore, the previous dispute with the theologians centered on their affirmation that God creates forms out of nothing. The view that Averroes reports here rebuts this very claim but is rather suspicious, since it focuses on an analogy between the first mover and a craftsman. The whole third discussion in the *Incoherence* is a bitter attack against the validity of this very analogy, and already al-Ghazali had perfectly understood that the philosophers were rendering this analogy utterly meaningless. As for Averroes himself, he states: "He who tries to compare heavenly with earthly existence, and believes that the Agent of the divine world acts in the way in which an agent in this sublunary world works, is utterly thoughtless, profoundly mistaken, and in complete error" (Arabic 193, Van den Bergh 116).

The second statement which seems incompatible with the claim that God does not know universals is the assertion that his providence deals with species but does not concern itself with individuals *qua* individuals:

> This is the source of God's providence for all beings, i.e., that He protects their species since individual protection is not possible. As for those who think that God's providence concerns itself with each individual, what they say is true in some respect but false in another. It is true insofar as no *condition* is found in some individual which is not also found in a class of this species. As for providence for the individual in the way it shares with none other, this is something the divine excellence does not require. (*Commentary*, 1607, cf. *Tahafut* 504, English 308).

Yet in a previous text (p. 142 above) we saw that Averroes specifically denies that God knows species. So we have to assume that God exercises providence without knowing it. And he does so since what is really causal is not his Knowledge of beings but their knowledge of him as final and formal cause. God causes in being an object of knowledge for the separate intellects: "Therefore, there is nothing to prevent that which is in itself intellect and intelligible from being cause for the various beings insofar as its various aspects are thought" (*Commentary*, 1649).

Of course, Averroes understands that these

various aspects are various to us but in God are one
and the same: "Therefore, one must understand from
our claim that He is living and that He possesses life
[that he] is one and the same with regard to the subject
but two with regard to the point of view"
(*Commentary,* 1620). So, the different ways in which
the beings themselves look at the first cause, God, and
their other causes, if any, determine their forms and
species.

God Is Not Ignorant of Things of This World Since He Knows Being Inasmuch as It Is Being

As we have seen, on the one hand Averroes
insists that God's knowing is utterly different from ours
and that God therefore knows neither particulars nor
universals. On the other hand, he does not want to
claim that God is truly ignorant of the things of this
world. His solution is to claim that in knowing
himself, God knows the existence which is cause of the
beings and that, in knowing being *qua* being, he in
some way knows the beings.

Refuting the view that God is ignorant of what is
here below, the *Long Commentary* 51 claims to offer
the truth. This passage deserves careful reading.

> The truth is that, inasmuch as He knows only
> Himself, He knows the beings through existence,
> which is the cause of their existences. An example
> of this is someone who knows only the heat of fire.
> For it is not said of him that he does not to know
> the nature of the heat existing in hot things. Rather
> such a person is the one who knows the nature of
> heat inasmuch as it is heat. In the same way the
> First, may He be praised, is the one who knows the

nature of being inasmuch as it is being without
qualification (*bi'itlaq, simpliciter*), which is Himself
[or his essence].   For this reason, the name
"knowledge" is said equivocally of His
Knowledge, may He be praised, and of ours . . . .
(1707-1708; the Latin [which is fairly different]:
Junctas, vol. 8, f. 337 r.)

The wording is very important.   God is *not*
ignorant of what is here below but is not said to know
it. What he does know is the nature of being inasmuch
as it is being without qualification. He therefore is
said to know the beings through the existence which is
their cause. God does not, then, know the beings but
their cause, which is his own existence, i.e., himself.
Yet he does not know that his existence is the cause of
anything, because God does not even know he is a
cause. God cannot know what he is related to nor his
own relation to anything else. The *Tahafut al-Tahafut*
says so in the thirteenth discussion:

> The first intellect is pure act and a cause, and there
> is no resemblance between His Knowledge and
> human knowledge. So, insofar as He does not
> know something other than Himself *qua* other, He
> is not passive Knowledge. And insofar as He
> knows something other inasmuch as it is His own
> essence, He is active Knowledge. (462)

Since God does not know anything else as
differing from himself, he cannot know something as
caused, and therefore he cannot know that he is a
cause. This application is spelled out in the reply to
the second objection in the third discussion:

> The First does not think anything else about His
> own essence than His very own essence and not
> anything relating to it, i.e., being a principle . . . .
> His being a principle is a relational aspect and it is
> not correct that it is exactly the same as His
> essence.   If He were to think of His being a
> principle, He would think that of which He is a
> principle according to the manner of the existence
> proper to the latter.   And if this were the case the
> most noble would be perfected by the inferior since
> the object of thought is the perfection of the thinker.
> (*Tahafut al-Tahafut*, 202-203)

This text shows not only that God does not know he is
a principle or a cause but also that he cannot know
this; for such knowledge would imply (1) that God has
knowledge of inferior things and (2) that God's
Knowledge is perfected by the object he is thinking--
and that would make of his Knowledge a caused
knowledge and not a causal one.

All this leads to the conclusion that God does not
know the beings but rather his own existence which
happens to cause the beings, though he does not know
there are other beings and therefore does not know
himself as a cause. Now, how would such knowledge
of the existence which is the cause of the beings ensure
that somehow God is not ignorant of the beings he
does not know of? The *Long Commentary* explains
this:

> An example of this is someone who knows only the
> heat of fire. For it is not said of him that he does
> not know the nature of the heat existing in hot
> things. Rather such a person is the one who knows
> the nature of heat inasmuch as it is heat. In the
> same way, the First, may He be praised, is the one

who knows the nature of being inasmuch as it is
being without qualification, which is Himself.
(1707-1708)

Now, God is said to know not only the existence which
is the cause of the beings (though he is unaware of
this) but also the nature of being inasmuch as it is
being without qualification. Similarly, someone who
knows only the heat present in fire cannot be said not
to know the nature of the heat present in hot things.
But it seems that in this case the one who knows only
the heat in fire certainly knows neither hot things nor
that there are degrees of heat. The analogy of course
comes from *Metaphysics* 2.1; this passage for Averroes
and the Arabic tradition is the very beginning of the
Metaphysics, since in their text book 2 comes before
what they had of book 1. In his commentary on this
passage, Averroes, referring to this analogy, simply
says (*Metaphysics*, 14): "Since fire is the cause of heat
in things, it is the first among all hot things in what
concerns the name and meaning of heat."[16] Notice
that the passage in book 2 indicates that fire is the
cause of heat, but the passage in book 12 does not
allude to this but rather shifts to knowing the nature of
heat inasmuch as it is heat. Yet knowing the nature of
heat inasmuch as it is heat does not in itself lead to
knowing that there are various degrees of heat or that
there are other things than fire which exist and which
are hot.

Using this analogy of the knowledge of heat
inasmuch as it is heat, Averroes goes back to the
Knowledge that God enjoys and states that he is the
one who knows the nature of being inasmuch as it is
being without qualification, which is himself. Leaving

aside the question whether God's essence can really be equated with the nature of being inasmuch at it is being without qualification, one can readily wonder whether God's knowing the nature of being inasmuch as it is being without qualification (making him, be it noted, the perfect metaphysician) ensures any real knowledge of things. Furthermore, knowledge of being inasmuch as it is being is given now as the very reason for the equivocity between God's Knowledge and ours. Why is this so? Is it because true knowledge of being inasmuch as it is being is not knowledge of things, and we human beings can no more completely put aside knowledge of things when we try to reach knowledge of being inasmuch as it is being than we can put aside knowledge of other things when we try to focus on self-consciousness (*Commentary*, 1700-1701, English 194)? Does it mean that human beings cannot really reach knowledge of being inasmuch as it is being? Or does it mean that ordinary human knowledge, because it is completely blind to being inasmuch as it is being, cannot in any way be compared to God's knowledge; but metaphysical knowledge can and therefore can truly be called divine knowledge--not only because it has God for one of its objects but also because it imitates God's very own way of knowing? If this is the case, then the metaphysician is more than human.

Yet, leaving aside these fascinating questions, I would like to discuss whether God's Knowledge of being inasmuch as it is being without qualification solves Averroes' problems. Knowledge of being inasmuch as it is being is certainly not knowledge of particulars and is not knowledge of universals (plural); yet it seems to be knowledge of *a* universal, being, but in a very peculiar mode which thereby transcends the usual meaning of universal. Knowledge of being inasmuch as it is being is not knowledge of universal "being" in the way such knowledge would become truly actual only by means of knowledge of particular beings. It focuses on the very universality of the universal. Averroes may have thought that such a mode is neither particular nor universal in the ordinary sense and that it therefore transcends these divisions as it transcends the ten predicaments.

But can God really know being inasmuch as it is being if he only knows of himself, a particular being, albeit the most perfect and the cause of all other beings, particularly since he does not know himself as a cause?

Even if one grants such knowledge to God, can it really yield some proper knowledge of the beings? Rosemann seems to imply that it does to some extent (559-561), whereas Thomas Aquinas denies it in the *Commentary on the First Book of the Sentences,* dist. 35 qu. 1 art. 3. For him it is no proper knowledge at all, and he understands Averroes as claiming in the very passage we commented upon the complete equivocity between God's Knowledge and ours:

> However, one must know that the Commentator in *Metaphysics* 2 [*sic, scil.* 12], text 51, says that God does not have knowledge of things other than Himself, except inasmuch as they are beings. For, since His being is the cause of existence for all things, inasmuch as He knows His own being, He is not ignorant of the nature of the *essence* [italics added] found in all things. In the same way the one who would know the heat of fire would not be ignorant of the nature of the heat existing in all hot things. Yet he would not know the nature of this

and that hot thing inasmuch as it is this or that. So God, by His knowing His own essence, though He knows the existence of all things inasmuch as they are beings, does not know things inasmuch as they are this or that. And from this, according to him, it does not follow that God is ignorant, since His Knowledge is not of the genus of our knowledge; and therefore the opposite, ignorance, does not apply to Him, just as one does not say of a stone that it has sight or is blind. But this view is shown to be doubly false--first, because He is not the cause of things only inasmuch as their being in general is concerned, but also inasmuch as everything that is in the thing is concerned.[17]

Another, later text of Aquinas' *ST,* 1.14.6, "whether God knows things other than Himself by proper knowledge," deals with the same topic but transforms Averroes' analogy with the person who knows only the heat of fire:

Some have erred on this point, saying that God knows things other than Himself only in general, that is, only as beings. For as fire, if it knew itself as the principle of heat, would know the nature of heat, and all things else in so far as they are hot, so God, through knowing Himself as the source of being, knows the nature of being, and all other things in so far as they are beings.[18]

After criticizing this view, Aquinas concludes: "We must therefore say that God knows things other than Himself with a proper knowledge, not only in so far as being is common to them, but in so far as one is distinguished from the other."[19]

Though here Aquinas makes the parallel with fire more complete by the *per impossibile* hypothesis that fire could know itself as the principle of heat, and though he therefore assumes that God can know himself as the source or principle of the beings which Averroes denies, he still claims that a knowledge of common being is no proper knowledge. Such knowledge Aquinas considers a universal knowledge; yet Averroes, who speaks of the nature of being inasmuch as it is being (which Aquinas does not here directly address) seems to think such knowledge is not really universal but transcends the division between universal and particular and, therefore, does not involve any potentiality. Knowledge of being inasmuch as it is being is somehow also actual knowledge of the cause of all the beings and of the actual being of the caused beings, at least if God were aware of them.

This seems a clever but rather unsatisfactory answer to the problems raised by God's Knowledge of anything outside himself. Even if God is a metaphysician, and therefore metaphysics is the divine way of knowing, it still does not ensure true knowledge of things here below.

NOTES

1.   Published also in *Anaquel de estudios árabes* (Madrid) 5 (1994) 39-57.

2.   1074b33-35, in *The Complete Works of Aristotle: The Revised Oxford Translation*, ed. Jonathan Barnes, trans. W. D. Ross (Princeton: Princeton University Press, 1984 [Bollingen series 71-72]), vol. 2, p. 1698.

3.   Barry S. Kogan, *Averroes and the Metaphysics of Causation* (Albany: State University of New York, 1985), p. 230.

4.   Kogan, *Averroes*, p. 246. See also his "Some Reflections on the Problem of Future Contingency in Alfarabi, Avicenna, and Averroes," in *Divine Omniscience and Omnipotence in Medieval Philosophy*, ed. Tamar Rudavsky (Dordrecht: D. Reidel, 1985), p. 100.

5.   J. Jolivet, "Divergences entre les metaphysiques d'Ibn Rusd et d'Aristote," *Arabica* 29 (1982): 235.

6.   Philipp W. Rosemann, "*Noesis Noeseos* und 'Ta'aqqul at-ta'aqqul.' Das Aristotelische Problem der Selbstbezuglichkeit des unbewegten Bewegers in der Kommentierung Ibn Rusds," *Zeitschrift für philosophische Forschung* 40 (1986): 543-561.

7.   J. G. Flynn, "St. Thomas and Averroes on the Knowledge of God," *Abr-Nahrain* 18 (1978-1979): 19-32.

8.   Since I will be citing both the Arabic and English versions of these four works throughout the paper, I give them here in tabular form, so that future citations can be referred here for full bibliographic information. Each work will hereafter be mentioned according to the simplified titles given below.

Tahafut:
>   Arabic: Averroes, *Tahafot at-Tahafot,* ed. Maurice Bouyges, Bibliotheca Arabica Scholasticorum, serie arabe 3 (Beirut: Dar el-Machreq, 1930 [rpt. 1987]).

Incoherence:
>   English: Averroes, *Averroes' Tahafut al-Tahafut (The Incoherence of the Incoherence),* trans. Simon Van den Bergh, 2 vols., E.J.W. Gibb Memorial, n.s. 19 (London: Luzac, 1969).

Kitab Fasl al-Maqal:
>   Arabic: Ibn Rushd (Averroes), *Kitab Fasl al-Maqal with Its Appendix (Damima) and an Extract from Kitab al-Kashf 'an Manahij al-Adilla,* ed. George F. Hourani (Leiden: E. J. Brill, 1959), pp. 3-40.

On the Harmony:
>   English: Averroes, *On the Harmony of Religion and Philosophy,* trans. George F. Hourani, E.J.W. Gibb Memorial, n.s. 21 (London: Luzac, 1976), pp. 44-71.

Damima:
>   Arabic: Ibn Rushd (Averroes), *Kitab Fasl al-Maqal with Its Appendix (Damima) and an*

Extract from Kitab al-Kashf 'an Manahij al-Adilla, ed. George F. Hourani (Leiden: E. J. Brill, 1959), pp. 41-45.

Appendix:

English: Averroes, *On the Harmony of Religion and Philosophy,* trans. George F. Hourani, E.J.W. Gibb Memorial, n.s. 21 (London: Luzac, 1976), pp. 72-75.

Tafsir:

Arabic: Averroes, *Tafsir ma ba'd at-Tabi'at ou "Grand Commentaire" de la 'Metaphysique' d'Aristote,* ed. Maurice Bouyges, S.J., 3 vols. (Bibliotheca Arabica Scholasticorum, serie arabe 7 (Beirut: Dar el-Machreq, 1938-1952 [rpt. 1973]). (The commentary on book 12 is in vol. 3, but pagination is continuous throughout the 3 volumes.)

Commentary:

English: Averroes, *Ibn Rushd's Metaphysics: A Translation with Introduction of Ibn Rushd's Commentary on Aristotle's Metaphysics, Book Lamda,* trans. Charles Genequand, Islamic Philosophy and Theology: Texts and Studies 1 (Leiden: E. J. Brill, 1984).

9.   *Tafsir* 1708, English 197; *Damima* 130-131, English 74-75; *Tahafut* 462, English 280. It is because of this equivocity that when speaking of God's Knowledge I am capitalizing "knowledge."

10.   *Tafsir* 170, English 197; *Damima* 130, English 74; *Tahafut* 468, English 285.

11.   *Commentary* 1708, ll.1-2.   Since the context helps in understanding what is at stake, and since the text of the medieval latin translation is rather shaky, I am here providing a translation of part of the end of ch. 51 (pp. 1706-1708): "This is what escaped Themistius when he allowed that the intellect [of the unmoved mover or God] thinks many intelligibles at once. This is contrary to our statement that He thinks Himself and does not think anything outside Himself and that the intellect and what it thinks are one in every respect. For he [Themistius] says that He thinks all things inasmuch as He thinks that He is their principle. All of this is the statement of someone who does not understand Aristotle's demonstrations here. But this entails an objectionable consequence, i.e., that the deity be ignorant of what is here below. Therefore, some people said that He knows what is here below by means of universal knowledge and not by means of particular knowledge. The truth is that inasmuch as He knows only Himself, He knows the beings through the existence which is the cause of their existences. An example of this is someone who knows only the heat of fire. For it is not said of him that he does not know the nature of the heat existing in hot things. Rather such a person is the one who knows the nature of heat inasmuch as it is heat. In the same way the First, may He be praised, is the one who knows the nature of being inasmuch as it is being without qualification which is Himself.   For this reason, the name knowledge is said equivocally of His Knowledge, may He be praised, and ours because His Knowledge is the

cause of being whereas being is the cause of our knowledge. Hence, His Knowledge, may He be praised, cannot be qualified as universal or particular . . . ."

12.   *Commentary* 1708 (*bi-ishtirak al-'ism*). Medieval Latin: *equivoce* (*Aristotelis Opera cum Averrois Commentariis*, vol. 13 [Venice: Junctas, 1562 (rpt., Frankfurt: Minerva, 1962)]), f. 337r. The medieval latin translation of the end of 12.51 as printed in this edition is rather garbled.

13.   *Scriptum super libros sententiarum*, ed. Mandonnet (Paris: Lethielleux, 1929), vol. 1, p. 817: "Nec ex hoc sequitur, ut ipse dicit, quod sit ignorans: quia scientia sua non est de genere scientiae nostrae: inde nec ignorantia opposita sibi potest convenire; sicut nec de lapide dicitur quod sit videns vel caecus."

14.   *Scriptum*, ed. Mandonnet, 445, but following the correction Van den Bergh adopts in his translation, p. 269, and cf. p. 371.

15.   These three arguments can be found in the thirteenth discussion of the *Tahafut*, 460-463, English 279-281. Arguments two and three can also be found in *Commentary* on *Metaphysics* 12.51, especially 1693-1708, English 191-198.

16.   For the latin text, see: Averroes (Ibn Rusd), *In Aristotelis librum II metaphysicorum commentarius*, ed. Gion Darms, Thomistische Studien 11 (Freiburg: Paulus Verlag, 1966), 58 l. 26-59, l.28: "Verbi gratia quoniam ignis est causa in rebus calidis,

ideo etiam magis est dignus habere hoc nomen calidum
et eius intentionem quam omnia alia calida.''

17.   *Scriptum*, ed. Mandonnet, pp. 816-817:
''Respondeo dicendum, quod Deus certissime proprias
naturas rerum cognoscit.   Sciendum tamen, quod
Commentator in II [*sic, scil.* 12] *Metaph.*, text. 51,
dicit, quod Deus non habet cognitionem de rebus aliis
a se, nisi inquantum sunt entia: quia enim esse suum
est causa essendi omnibus rebus, inquantum cognoscit
esse suum, non ignorat naturam essentiae inventam in
rebus omnibus; sicut qui cognosceret calorem ignis,
non ignoraret naturam caloris existentis in omnibus
calidis: non tamen sciret naturam hujus calidi et illius,
inquantum est hoc et illud.   Ita Deus per hoc quod
cognoscit essentiam suam, quamvis cognoscat esse
omnium rerum in quantum sunt entia, non tamen
cognoscit res inquantum est haec et illa.   Nec ex hoc
sequitur, ut ipse dicit, quod sit ignorans: quia scientia
sua non est de genere scientiae nostrae: inde nec
ignorantia opposita sibi potest convenire; sicut nec de
lapide dicitur quod sit videns vel caecus.   Sed haec
positio dupliciter apparet falsa: primo, quia ipse non est
causa rerum quantum ad esse ipsorum solum commune,
sed quantum ad omne illud quod in re est.'' Thomas'
rephrasing at times is closer to the Arabic than the
Junctas text, but the analogy with the stone seems to be
his own creation.

18.   Anton Pegis, *Introduction to St. Thomas
Aquinas* (New York: Modern Library, 1948), p. 137.
Latin (Marietti's edition, 1928): ''. . . Circa hoc
quidam erraverunt, dicentes quod Deus alia a se non
cognoscit nisi in communi, scilicet inquantum sunt

entia. Sicut enim ignis, si cognosceret seipsum, ut est principium caloris, cognosceret naturam caloris, et omnia alia, inquantum sunt calida; ita Deus, inquantum cognoscit se ut principium essendi, cognoscit naturam entis, et omnia alia, inquantum sunt entia.''

19. Pegis, *Introduction to St. Thomas Aquinas*, 137. Latin: "Oportet igitur dicere quod alia a se cognoscat propria cognitione; non solum secundum quod communicant in ratione entis, sed secundum quod unum ab alio distinguitur."

ANTHROPOLOGY

AQUINAS ON THE IMMEDIACY OF THE UNION OF SOUL AND BODY[1]

Kevin White
The Catholic University of America

Although the number of texts in which Saint Thomas Aquinas argues that the rational or human soul is "immediately" united to a body seems to leave no doubt about the importance of this point in his account of human nature, students of his thought might be tempted to slight it for two reasons. In the first place, he usually makes the case for it polemically, in response to certain adversaries who hold that there "are" intermediaries between soul and body, so that his conclusion, as the privative term "immediately" also suggests, appears to be merely negative. Secondly, he most often presents this conclusion as either a part or a direct consequence of the Aristotelian teaching that the soul is a substantial form, so that it might seem to be the drawing out of an aspect or implication of Aristotle's view rather than a statement of a distinct point of doctrine with an interest and significance of its own. As a corrective to this temptation, the following discussion offers an examination of Aquinas' texts on the question of the immediacy of the union of soul and body, while attempting to clarify the similarities and differences among his various statements with a view to tracing a development in his thinking on the question. This last point calls for comment.

Since at least as long ago as 1926, the year in which Joseph de Guibert's *Les doublets de saint Thomas d'Aquin*[2] appeared, the notion that Aquinas' vast corpus of writings presents either a simply homogeneous or an incoherent teaching on any of the questions which it repeatedly addresses has given way to the more nuanced and historically informed view that his various treatments of a question or, in the jargon of his editors, his *"loca parallela"* are to be neither opposed as contradictory, as his thirteenth-century adversaries suggested, nor shown to conform to the standard of the *Sentences* commentary, as the early *concordantiae* attempted to do. Aquinas' various treatments should rather be understood in terms of his developing or evolving reflection on the particular question. Case-studies by Guibert and by subsequent authors who adopted this view have tended to confirm that changes in Aquinas' thinking on particular points are indeed "developments of doctrine" in the sense given this expression by Cardinal Newman, displaying as they do the latter's "seven notes" of "genuine development": preservation of type, continuity of principles, power of assimilation, logical sequence, anticipation of the future, conservative action on the past, and chronic vigor.[3] Now, the discernment of an instance of development in Aquinas' thought would seem to require not only a literary and historical sensitivity and a grasp of theological and philosophical principles, but also, and more fundamentally, some reliance on firm historical conclusions concerning the chronology of his works. Conversely, however, the study of a particular development can, if managed with sufficient skill, contribute to an understanding of this chronology, as Anton C. Pegis demonstrated in 1974 with his "The Separated Soul and Its Nature in St. Thomas."[4] In light of Pegis's example, the following study suggests that certain differences among Aquinas' treatments of the question concerning the immediacy of the soul's union with a body point to a development in his thinking on this question which may have ramifications for our understanding of the chronology of his writings. This suggestion will be offered somewhat diffidently, however, since the differences in question are significantly less drastic than those, for example, which Pegis pointed out in Aquinas' various treatments of a different topic.[5]

Aquinas addresses the question with which we are concerned in six works: two early ones, *Scriptum super libros Sententiarum* (*In Sent.*) and *Summa contra Gentiles* (*SCG*), whose dates of origin--1252-1256 and 1259-1264 respectively--are well-established;[6] and four later ones, *Quaestio disputata de anima* (*QDA*), *Summa theologiae* (*ST*) 1, *Quaestio disputata de spiritualibus creaturis* (*QDSC*), and *Sentencia libri de anima* (*SLA*), the historical order of which is less certain.[7] The three last-mentioned works were certainly composed during Aquinas' three-year stay, beginning in September 1265, at Santa Sabina in Rome. Furthermore, *QDSC's* third article, the one of special interest here, was composed after March of 1266; the *prima pars* was begun during the academic year 1266-1267; and *SLA* was composed during 1267-1268.[8] As to *QDA,* although historians have long been divided over whether to date it during Aquinas' time at Santa Sabina or during his second Parisian sojourn from late 1268 to September 1272, an important recent scholarly opinion not only dismisses the latter possibility, but places *QDA* relatively early in Aquinas' Roman period.

In an article published in 1974, René-A. Gauthier suggested that *QDA* originated at Rome as an exercise preparatory to composition of questions 75-89 of the *prima pars.*[9] Gauthier mentioned two manuscripts which explicitly state that *QDA* was disputed at Paris, but noted that they are mediocre witnesses to a Parisian family of manuscripts whose archetype certainly did not contain any such statement. He added that, although Aquinas indeed knew of and used the Moerbeke translation of the *De anima* when composing *QDA,* he more frequently quotes from the older translation in this work. While this can be explained by his habit of quoting texts from memory, Gauthier reasoned, the relative neglect of the new translation would be too great--and the contrast with the *De unitate intellectus* too violent--in a work composed at a time and place, that is, during 1269-1270 in Paris, in which a rigorous use of the Aristotelian text was unavoidable. On the other hand, this neglect is understandable if *QDA* was composed at Rome before Aquinas had become imbued with the new translation of the *De anima* by composing his commentary on it. In a final parenthetical comment, stating that *QDSC* is more attentive than *QDA* to an exact use of the new translation, Gauthier seemed to imply that *QDA* was composed before *QDSC* as well as before *ST* 1.75-89.[10] By way of confirming Gauthier's dating of *QDA* as prior to Aquinas' move to Paris, the Leonine editor of *QDA,* Bernardo Carlos Bazán, has noted his discovery of an independent Italian family of manuscript witnesses to *QDA* which antedates the Parisian exemplar of the work.[11]

There seems to be good reason to accept the conclusion of these scholars that *QDA* was composed at Rome and not Paris. On the other hand, in what follows here, we shall be taking issue with the suggestion that *QDA* was composed prior to both *ST* 1.75-89 and *QDSC* by arguing, on the basis of Aquinas' *ipsissima verba,* that *QDA* 9 was in fact the last of his discussions of the question of intermediaries to be composed. It will be left to the reader both to judge the strength of our argument, which is certainly not apodictic, and to decide how it might be reconciled with Gauthier's observation concerning the infrequent use of the *nova translatio* of the *De anima* in *QDA.*

The argument will be that *QDA* 9 is, in significant ways, unique among Aquinas' six treatments of the question of soul-body intermediaries; that this uniqueness is, more precisely, a superiority, one which seems to be a consequence of a decision by Aquinas to improve on the approaches to the question in the other five texts; and that *QDA* 9 thus has the appearance of being his last word on the question.

1. *In 2 Sent.* **1.2.4** *ad* **3**

The theme of intermediaries between soul and body first arises in Aquinas' writings in his reply to an objection which occurs early in his commentary on the second book of the *Sentences*. In response to the question "whether the rational soul should be united to a body," this objection argues that, because soul and body "stand as far apart as possible from one another," they cannot be conjoined in the manner of the greatest union, which is that of form and matter:

> Moreover, things which stand as far apart as possible from one another can be joined in only the weakest union. But soul and body do stand as far apart from one another, as the text says. Therefore, since the joining of form to matter is according to the strongest union, it seems that the soul is not able to be united to a body in the way that form is to matter.[12]

Here the metaphorical expression *maxime distant* calls attention to itself both because it is crucial to the objector's argument against the Aristotelian definition of the soul as the form of a body, and because it does not (as the confirmation of the minor premise here asserts it does) occur in the passage of the *Sentences* under discussion. Its meaning is clarified by a treatment of the *distantia* between soul and body in a work composed at Paris a generation before Aquinas arrived there to comment on the *Sentences* in 1252, namely Philip the Chancellor's *Summa de bono*:[13]

> Next the question is raised, What kind of dispositions are needed in order for perfections of this kind to be joined to perfectibles other than themselves? For this question, one must understand the "distance" of the first and rational soul from a body. Not that this distance is complex. For the rational soul has three ways in which it is opposed to its body: for it is

simple, bodiless, and incorruptible, but the body is composite, bodily, and corruptible. Accordingly, on account of its excessive distance from the body, the rational soul could not be joined to the body unless there were added certain dispositions or adaptations serving as intermediaries for joining these two to one another.[14]

This account of the "distance" between a rational soul and a body presents the Platonic theme of the opposition of properties between the two (compare *Phaedo* 78b-80b). Philip identifies three such oppositions, namely, simple-composite, incorporeal-corporeal, and incorruptible-corruptible, oppositions which, he argues, need to be overcome by certain "dispositions or adaptations" serving as "intermediaries" (*media*) in the uniting of soul and body. The hypothesis of intermediaries between soul and body is also maintained, with some variation, by a number of later thirteenth-century theologians, notably the author of the *Summa Duacensis*[15] and two Franciscans who also use the term *distantia* in this regard, John of Rochelle and Saint Bonaventure.[16] Bonaventure, in fact, presents the theory while treating precisely the passage of the *Sentences* under discussion in Aquinas' *In Sent*.

Lombard's passage occurs in book 2, in the sixth chapter of the first *distinctio,* where, after considering the reason for the creation in general of rational beings (angels and men), he takes up the question of why the human soul was united to a body.[17] Echoing the vivid biblical contrast between the "earthy" and the "spiritual" elements in man (see Gen 2:7 and 1 Cor 15:45-49), he argues that God made man "from a twofold substance" (*ex duplici substantia*), joining a spiritual soul made of nothing to a body made of earth, in order to provide a sign of, and an assurance of the possibility of, two no less radically different things, namely, Himself and the human spirit.[18] At one point in this argument Lombard contrasts the "loftiness" of the spirit with the "lowliness" of the flesh,[19] and it was perhaps this spatial metaphor which, to the *sententiarius* Bonaventure, made the passage an appropriate occasion for speaking of the "distance" between soul and body and introducing a discussion of "intermediaries."

The phrase *maxime distant* in the objection presented by Aquinas, then, apparently alludes to the thirteenth-century tradition of a doctrine of intermediaries, and more particularly to the mid-century presentation of this doctrine as a feature of commentary on *Sentences* 2 d. 1 c. 6. Although the objection does not mention the doctrine itself, Aquinas' reply to it pointedly does.

The opening section of the reply hints at great antiquity in the objection, noting that, because of it, Plato (as Gregory of Nyssa, i. e., Nemesius, relates) held that the soul is present in a body as a mover is present in what it moves, or as a sailor is present in a ship, and *not* as form is present in matter; moreover, Plato said, "man" is not something composed of soul and body, but rather a soul making use of a body. Furthermore, the reply continues, it was because of this Platonic position that "certain ones" (*quidam*) looked for *media* between soul and body, such as a bodily "spirit," or the vegetative and sensitive souls, or light, by whose mediation the rational soul might be united

to a body.[20]   Aquinas thus intimately associates three
philosophical opinions regarding the union of soul and
body in human nature: the objector's view that soul
and body *maxime distant*; the Platonic definitions of
the soul as a mere "mover" of the body and of man as
"a soul making use of a body," and the doctrine of *media* uniting soul and body.

The four hypothetical *media* mentioned by
Aquinas correspond closely to the intermediaries
proposed by the thirteenth-century authors mentioned
above, all of whom suggest that there are two
intermediaries on the side of the soul, such as the
vegetative and sensitive "souls" or "powers, and two
on the side of the body, such as bodily "spirit," light,
or heat.   These hypotheses had originated in
suggestions by such authors as St. Augustine and Al-
Farabi, and their combination in a single theory of
intermediaries had begun in the twelfth century, so that
the *quidam* referred to by Aquinas thus constitute a
long and venerable tradition.[21]   Nevertheless, he goes
on bluntly to state that these proposals of intermediaries are all, from the point of view of philosophy,
"absurd" and have been refuted in the eighth book of
Aristotle's *Metaphysics*. ("quae omnia absurda sunt
secundum philosophiam, et improbata a Philosopho in
VIII *Metaph.*").

Aquinas here refers to the last chapter of
Metaphysics 8, where, at the end of a discussion of
matter and form, the principles of sensible substances,
Aristotle turns to the way in which these principles are
united.   What, he begins by asking, is the cause of
something's being one (*causaessendi unum*) when that
something is made up of parts but is more than the

sum of its parts? What, for instance, is it that makes "man" one thing and not merely the sum of "animal" and "biped"? If the question is put this way, Aristotle thinks, the difficulty cannot be resolved; on the other hand, if the parts are regarded as matter and form, that is, as potentiality and actuality, there is no difficulty at all: for there is no other cause of a thing's being one than of its being a being. The usual understanding of the question leads people to speak of "participation," or to say that knowledge is a "co-existence" of the act of knowing and the soul, or to say that life is a "composition" or "colligation" of soul with body. The reason why they are driven to these expressions, Aristotle indicates, is that they are seeking both something which makes potentiality and actuality one thing, and a difference between the two: NO English translation is needed, for it has just been given in the text (*potentiae et actus quaerunt unum faciens et differentiam*). But the principles which are united in a sensible thing are matter and form, which are related as potentiality and actuality respectively, and hence are one of themselves. The ultimate matter and the form are the *same* thing, the matter being the thing in potentiality and the form the thing in actuality; hence there is no *other* cause of unity in things generated, except whatever moves them from potentiality to actuality.[22] This chapter is certainly concerned to refute the hypothesis of a *tertium quid* added to form and matter, that is, of a "further cause" which would explain their union. On the other hand, the instances of this hypothesis which Aristotle mentions-- *coexistentia* (*synousia*), *compositio* (*synthesis*), and *colligatio* or *coniunctio* (*syndesmos*)--are processes or activities, and thus very unlike the "spirit," "souls," and "light" mentioned as hypothetical *media* between a rational soul and a body by Aquinas. Furthermore, the chapter is more concerned with the genus and difference of definition, regarded *as* matter and form respectively, than with "first" matter and "substantial" form, and touches only in passing on the union of soul and body. Again, the very notion of *medium*, with its overtone of spatial "betweenness," is absent from Aristotle's chapter.[23] Why, then, is Aquinas so confidently able to claim, without explanation, that this chapter refutes in advance the various hypotheses of *media* between soul and body current in the thirteenth century?

One reason seems to be that an opposition between *Metaphysics* 8.6 and the theory of intermediaries had already been identified by partisans of the theory, as certain remarks imply in Philip the Chancellor's *queastio* on the theme of intermediaries. In the first article of this *quaestio,* Philip, apparently borrowing from *Metaphysics* 8.6 the vocabulary of Aristotle's opponent, argues that substances which are "opposites," such as soul and body, can have a *coexistentia* with one another.[24] Again, the first objection in the following article recapitulates Aristotle's own position in *Metaphysics* 8.6, according to which there *is* no third thing uniting form and matter, since form, the cause of the being and of the oneness of a composite, is of itself united to matter.[25] In the first article, then, Philip adopts the terminology of Aristotle's adversary, and in the second he presents Aristotle's own view as that of an opponent. Aquinas' opposition of the Aristotelian text to the theory of intermediaries thus appears to be based on the presentation of this opposition within the theory. He need not demonstrate that the two are opposed; all he need do is remind his theological audience that the theory of intermediaries is "absurd according to philosophy," that is, according to an Aristotelian text, and refer it to that text. It can be left to the audience to determine whether "philosophy" has sufficient authority in this case, as Aquinas clearly thinks it does, or whether it may itself be opposed, as Philip seems to do in the passages to which I have just referred.

Still, this does not show how both Aquinas and his adversaries were able to find the theme of "intermediaries between soul and body" so evidently present in and rejected by the text of *Metaphysics* 8.6. I should like to suggest the hypothesis that a passage in Averroes' commentary on this chapter played an important role in this construal of the text. In introducing Aristotle's survey of the technical terms used to account for the unity of things--*participatio, coexistentia, compositio, colligatio*--Averroes allows himself a comparatively long prefatory comment. He begins by connecting what is to follow with the question, raised by Aristotle at the beginning of the chapter, of the unity of man. How, Averroes suggests Aristotle is about to ask, is man one and yet composed of a soul and a body *both existing in actuality?* Averroes then distinguishes two types of philosopher:

> To everyone who holds that soul and body are two diverse things, it fails to say what is the cause of the link of soul with body. But according to him who says that the soul is the perfection of the body, and

that the body does not exist without the soul, they are *not* two diverse things, and for him the question just mentioned will not arise.[26]

This text would have provided the young Aquinas with a startlingly clear key to understanding *media,* that is, to diagnosing what was going on in, for example, Bonaventure's discussion of the question of intermediaries. Proceeding from the opposition between soul and body--that is, regarding soul and body as "both existing in actuality" and as "two different things"--it fell to Bonaventure to explain "the cause of the link" (*causa ligamenti*) between soul and body. Indeed, Aquinas' presentation of the theory of intermediaries as a consequence of the Platonic definition of the soul as mover of the body seems deliberately to echo Averroes' suggestion that the need for a theory of intermediaries is a direct consequence of regarding soul and body as two different things. But Averroes' text would also make plain to Aquinas how utterly un-Aristotelian is the philosophical foundation of the theory of intermediaries. For if one regards the soul as the perfection or actuality of the body, as do Aristotle, Averroes, and Aquinas himself, then, as Averroes makes clear, soul and body cannot be regarded as two different things, and the question of intermediaries will not even arise.

Aquinas' brief reference to *Metaphysics* 8, then, which presents itself as nothing more than a sort of *sed contra* intended to dismiss all doctrines of intermediaries on the basis of Aristotle, seems to depend on Averroes' commentary at least as much as on Aristotle's text. This reference occurs precisely at the midpoint of Aquinas' reply, cutting it into two halves which correspond to the two types of philosopher distinguished by Averroes. Aquinas begins the second half of his reply, as if in response to Averroes' drastic alternative, by speaking in the first person.

"*We* say, therefore"--that is, because all hypotheses of intermediaries are absurd--"that the essence of the rational soul is *immediately* united to a body as form is to matter, and as an imprint is to wax, as is said in *De anima* 2."[27]   The reference is to the first chapter of *De anima* 2, in which, after proposing a universal description of the soul as "the first actuality of a natural organic body," Aristotle goes on to add that, accordingly, one should not ask whether soul and body are one, since the principal meaning of "one" (and of "being") is "actuality" (412b6-9). This passage, whose doctrine of the unity of matter and form coincides with that of *Metaphysics* 8, does not, as Aquinas suggests it does, contain the crucial word "immediately," so that once again he appears to be forcing Aristotle to address the thirteenth-century discussion of intermediaries. We shall return to this point when we come to consider Aquinas' *De anima* commentary.

The remainder of Aquinas' reply to objection 3 turns on a distinction between two senses of the term *convenientia,* a word sometimes translated into English as "agreement" or "befittingness." Here, however, its literal sense of "coming together" is evidently meant to counterbalance the "standing apart" (*distant*) of the objection, and the *distantia-convenientia* opposition has a precedent in Philip's discussion of intermediaries.[28]

The distinction which Aquinas presents allows him first
to make a preliminary concession to the objection and
then to establish his own fundamental point: "according
to the properties of nature" (*secundum proprietates
naturae*), he concedes, soul and body "stand far apart"
(*multum distant*); but "according to the proportion of
potency to act" (*secundum proportionem potentiae ad
actum*), soul and body "come together most closely"
(*maxime conveniunt*) in the *convenientia* which is
required in order that one thing be united to another
immediately as its form.[29]

From the foregoing it is clear that the structure of
Aquinas' reply to objection 3 is based on two
distinctions. First, there is a distinction between (1) the
view that soul and body *maxime distant,* with all the
consequences that such a view entails, and (2)
Aquinas' own view that soul and body are *immediately*
united as form and matter. Within the latter view is a
further distinction, between (a) the concession that,
with respect to *convenientia* according to properties of
nature, soul and body *multum distant,* and (b) the
insistence that, with respect to *convenientia* according
to the proportion of potentiality to actuality, soul and
body *maxime conveniunt.* This can be illustrated in
outline form:

(1) . . . propter hanc objectionem Plato posuit . . . et
     propter hoc etiamquidam quaesierunt . . . .
(2) Et ideo dicimus quod . . .
     (a) . . . secundum proprietates naturae . . .
     (b) . . . secundum proportionem potentiae ad actum.

This pattern--a polemical presentation of alternative

positions, the first of which is refuted, followed by a precision allowing a concession to the refuted position--will gradually be transformed in Aquinas' subsequent arguments for the immediacy of the rational soul's union to a body.

2. *Summa contra Gentiles* 2.71

The passage from Aquinas' *Sentences* commentary which we have just examined asserts the immediacy of the union of soul and body at the same time that it affirms the formal character of the union: "the essence of the rational soul is immediately united to a body as form is to matter" (*essentia animae rationalis immediate unitur corpori sicut forma materiae*). In the somewhat later *Summa contra Gentiles,* the immediacy of the union emerges, for the first time in Aquinas' writings, as a distinct point, and it does so as the first of a series of corollaries to the conclusion that the soul is united to a body as the form of the latter.

SCG 2.71 begins by stating that it can be concluded from what has preceded (*ex praemissis*) that the soul is immediately united to a body.[30] Aquinas is referring to the foregoing investigation of the question whether an intellectual substance can be united to a body. After formulating in chapter 56 the problem and posing objections to such a union-- objections reminiscent of the suggestion that soul and body *maxime distant*--he had gone on to consider and reject explanations of the union offered by Plato (chapters 57-58) and Averroes (59-61), as well as various materialistic accounts of the union (62-67), before concluding that certain intellectual substances are, as

Aristotle held, united to bodies as their substantial forms (68-70). As in *In Sent.*, then, but at much greater length, he proceeds from the Platonic error to the Aristotelian truth concerning the human composite.

It is from the positive conclusion of chapters 68-70, then, that, according to the opening remark of chapter 71, one can further conclude that the soul is immediately united to a body, and, Aquinas goes on to add, that it is not necessary to posit some *medium* which would unite soul to body, such as Averroes' "phantasms," other authors' "powers of the soul," or still others' bodily "spirit." This list of three candidates for the role of intermediary resembles that of *In 2 Sent.* 1.2.4 *ad* 3, but with some notable differences: apart from the fact that the bodily "spirit" has been moved to the end of the list, the vegetative and sensitive "souls" have been replaced by "powers" of soul, and, still more strikingly, the hypothesis of light as an intermediary has been replaced by the Averroistic phantasm.[31]

Chapter 71 now turns from (1) presentation of the opposition to (2) a demonstration of its own conclusion. The minor premise, which has itself been demonstrated in chapter 68, is that the soul is united to a body as form of the latter. The major premise, that form is united to matter without any intermediary, is established as follows. It belongs to form *per se*, and not through something else, that it be the act of a certain kind of body. Hence, as Aristotle proves in *Metaphysics* 8.6, there is not, apart from the agent which brings potency to actuality, "a something which makes one thing" (*aliquid unum faciens*) out of matter and form, since matter and form are related as potency and act. In short, because a form is *per se* the act of a certain kind of body, it is also *per se* united to the potency of matter, and hence requires nothing else to serve as a cause of the union.

Aquinas thus has recourse once again to *Metaphysics* 8.6 in his defense of the immediacy of the union of soul and body; though this time, not content with a mere reference to the text, he draws on it for such details as the hypothetical *unum faciens* and the agent which brings matter from potency to act. As does *In Sent.*, the present argument follows *Metaphysics* 8.6 in explaining the relation between form and matter as one between act and potency. However, whereas the earlier text had described this relationship as a *proportio,* and more generally as a *convenientia,* the present argument abandons these terms and instead focuses on the principle that form is *per se* the act of a body. The elimination of the vocabulary of *convenientia* and *proportio* and its replacement by *actus* as the focus of the argument against intermediaries constitute a conceptual simplification, a break with standard thirteenth-century terminology characterizing the union of soul and body, and a step in the direction of greater fidelity to Aristotle.

This change also helps to account for the fact that, whereas in *In Sent.* Aquinas had prefaced his discussion of the act-potency *proportio* with a concession to the objection that soul and body *maxime distant*--namely that this is true with respect to *convenientia secundum proprietates naturae*--a corresponding concession made in *SCG* 2.71 *follows* on the central point that a form is *per se* the act of a body.

The terminology of *convenientia* and *proportio,* it seems, makes the "distance" between soul and body appear more prominently than their union, while greater emphasis on the soul as *actus* brings this union into prominence as the philosophical starting point, to which any qualifications must be subsequent.

Here the concession is not to the point that soul and body "stand far apart," but rather to the theory of intermediaries itself. It can be said (*potest dici*), Aquinas grants, that there is a *medium* between soul and body, if not in being (*in essendo*), yet at least in movement (*in movendo*) and in the process of generation (*in via generationis*). He thus implies that the argument has so far been concerned with the relation of soul and body "in being"; he also evinces a concern, not present in *In Sent.,* with the ways in which intermediaries may or may not be *spoken* of. This new "distinction involving a concession" is recognizably a descendant of the former one, although the order in which it is presented is reversed and its vocabulary is completely different.

In 2 Sent. 1.2.4 *ad* 3

(a) . . . secundum proprietates naturae . . . anima et corpus multum distant . . .
(b) secundum proportionem potentiae ad actum . . . anima etcorpus maxime conveniunt . . .

SCG 2.71

(a) Potest tamen dici aliquid esse medium inter animam et corpus, etsi non in essendo,
(b) tamen in movendo et in via generationis . . .

The replacement of "proportion of potency to act" by "being" establishes a simpler and metaphysically deeper perspective within which to affirm the immediacy of the union. The replacement of unspecified "properties of nature" by "movement and process of generation" is a gain in concreteness as well as simplicity, but also indicates that even the concession to the doctrine of intermediaries must regard soul and body not as "standing apart" with opposed natures, but as somehow united. The replacement of the *distant-conveniunt* opposition by the issue of whether or not *media* may be spoken of shows Aquinas abandoning Neoplatonic metaphor for a direct addressing of the question. And the reversal in the order of presentation of concession and fundamental affirmation represents a diminishing concern with the partial truth of the doctrine of intermediaries and a greater emphasis on the more basic truth of the immediacy of the union.

There may be said to be intermediaries in the movement by which the soul moves the body because in this movement there is a certain order of movers and things moved: because the soul effects all its operations through its powers, it moves the body through the intermediary of a power. In addition, it moves the bodily members through the intermediary of a "bodily spirit." Furthermore, it moves one organ through the intermediary of another. Aquinas thus puts the hypotheses that the soul's powers or the bodily "spirit" are intermediaries in their proper place by indicating that they are intermediaries, not "in being," as the radical doctrine of intermediaries would imply, but rather "in movement."

As concerns the other way in which intermediaries

may be spoken of, Aquinas remarks that the "dispositions to a form" (*dispositiones ad formam*) precede the form itself in matter in the process of generation, although they are posterior to the form in being (*in essendo*). Hence, with respect to this temporal precedence, the dispositions of a body by which it is made the "proper perfectible" of a certain kind of form can be called "intermediary" (*possunt dici mediae*) between soul and body.

After its introductory statement of the conclusion to be proved, the argument of *SCG* 2.71 presents an argument built around two distinctions which are revisions of the two distinctions in *In Sent.* The first is a distinction between (1) the doctrine of intermediaries as presented by Averroes, *quidam,* and *alii*, and (2) an opposing argument that soul and body are immediately united. And the second is a distinction between (a) the precision that soul and body are immediately united in being, and (b) the concession that intermediaries between them may be spoken of in movement and in the process of generation. This too can be presented in outline form:

> Ex praemissis autem concludi potest . . .
> (1) . . . nec oportet ponere aliquod medium . . .
> (2) Ostensum est enim quod . . .
>   (a) . . . etsi non in essendo,
>   (b) tamen in movendo et in via generationis.

Thus *SCG* 2.71 clearly represents a "development" of the argument in *In Sent.* Two notable features of this development, namely the reversal of the order of presentation of concession to and basic disagreement with the opposing view, and the emergence of the distinction between *esse* and "movement and generation," set the stage for further developments in Aquinas' later treatments of the question.

3. *Questio disputata de spiritualibus creaturis* 3

As indicated above, four of Aquinas' treatments of the question of intermediaries between soul and body occur in works composed after September 1265. These are *QDSC* 3, *QDA* 9, *ST* 1.76.6-7, and *SLA* 2.1.366-392. In the case of the first three of these, all of which have the *quaestio* format, we shall primarily be concerned with the central and sustained arguments of the *responsiones,* rather than with the *sed contras,* or the counter-arguments and replies to them. On the basis of an initial similarity between *SCG* 2.71 and the *responsio* of *QDSC* 3--both of which begin by relating the question of intermediaries to "what has gone before"--we shall proceed by examining the latter text more closely, noting any further similarities to, as well as differences from, *SCG* 2.71.[32]

The *responsio* of *QDSC* 3 consists of two sections, namely, a direct and relatively brief answer to the question "whether the spiritual substance which is the human soul is immediately united to a body," and a much longer, supplementary discussion (starting at *Sed tunc dubium restat*) concerning a difficulty arising from this answer. A comparison of the preliminary response with *SCG* 2.71 reveals that, like the latter, it begins with a reference to *praemissa* and then proceeds through a twofold distinction: one between two philosophical positions (1 and 2) on the nature of the union of soul and body, and one between two perspectives (a and b) within which the second (correct) position may regard the union. However, just as *SCG* altered the vocabulary and ordering of *In Sent.*, so the preliminary response of *QDSC* 3 seems to be a reworking of *SCG* 2.71, one largely accomplished through a formulaic terminology which brings the pattern of argument into stark relief.

As noted, both texts begin with a reference to what has gone before:

SCG 2.71

Ex praemissis autem concludi potest quod anima immediate corpori unitur.

QDSC 3

Dicendum quod huius quaestionis veritas aliqualiterde-pendet ex praemissa . . .

Whereas *SCG* proceeds at once from its backward reference to the conclusion to be proved, *QDSC* makes the link between the foregoing and the present discussion in a more leisurely and qualified way. Nevertheless, both texts make it clear from the outset that the question of intermediaries is a subordinate one.

(1) Next, both texts consider the doctrine of intermediaries, though somewhat differently.

SCG 2.71

Nec oportet ponere aliquod medium quasi animam corpori uniens: vel phantasmata, sicut dicit Averroes; vel potentias ipsius, sicut quidam dicunt; vel etiam spiritum corporalem, sicut alii dixerunt.

QDSC 3

Si enim anima rationalis unitur corpori solum per
contactum virtualem ut motor, ut aliqui posuerunt,
nihil prohibebat dicere quod sunt multa media inter
animam et corpus, et magis inter animam et materiam
primam.

Where *SCG,* completing its statement of the conclusion
to be proved, both rejects and specifies three versions
of the doctrine of intermediaries, *QDSC,* here stating
the first member of an alternative (*si enim*), entertains
the hypothesis that the rational soul is joined to a body
merely by way of virtual contact as a mover, from
which it follows that one could "speak of" many *media*
between soul and body, and, even more, between the
soul and first matter. In contrast to *SCG, QDSC* is at
this point concerned with the philosophical basis of the
doctrine of intermediaries rather than with the different
versions of the doctrine. Note that this basis is the
Platonic view of the soul as merely the mover of a
body, a view mentioned in *In Sent.* as itself a
consequence of the opinion that soul and body *maxime
distant*; the elimination of the *distantia-convenientia*
motif leaves the Platonic view as the ultimate basis of
the theory of intermediaries.

(2) Both texts have now reached the heart of the
matter, which is in each case introduced with a
statement of the previously demonstrated premise that
a soul is joined to a body as a form.

SCG 2.71

Ostensum est enim quod anima unitur corpori ut
forma eius. Forma autem unitur materiae absque
omne medio.

QDSC 3
Si vero ponatur anima uniri corpori ut forma, necesse
est dicere quod uniatur ei immediate.

Both complete the backward reference with which they
began, recalling directly preceding arguments that an
"intellectual substance" (*SCG* 2.68-70) or a "spiritual
substance" (*QDSC* 2) is united to a body as the form
of the latter. At the same time, *QDSC* 3 completes the
presentation of its alternative between taking the soul
as a mere mover of a body (*si enim*) and regarding it
as the form of a body (*Si vero*), the latter of which requires one to speak of an immediate union. Now both
texts go on to demonstrate that the immediacy of the
union indeed follows from the established conclusion
that the soul is united as form to a body.

SCG 2.71
Per se enim competit formae quod sit actus talis
corporis, et non per aliquid aliud. Unde nec est
aliquid unumfaciens ex materia et forma nisi agens,
quod potentiam reducit ad actum, ut probat Aristotiles,
in VIII *Metaphysicae*: nam materia et forma habent se
ut potentia et actus.

QDSC 3
Omnis enim forma, sive substantialis sive accidentalis,
unitur materiae vel subiecto: unumquodque enim
secundum hoc est unum secundum quod est ens. Est
autem unumquodque ens actu per formam, sive
secundum esse substantiale sive secundum esse
accidentale: unde omnis forma est actus, et per consequens est ratio unitatis qua aliquid est unum. Sicut
igitur non est dicere quod sit aliquod aliud medium
quo materia habeat esse per suam formam, ita non potest dici quod sit aliquod aliud medium uniens

formam materiae vel subiecto.

As we saw earlier, *SCG* here first quotes the principle that it belongs to form of itself (*per se*), and not through anything else, to be the act of a certain kind of body; and then at once it draws the conclusion, a paraphrase of the end of *Metaphysics* 8.6. By contrast, *QDSC*, which makes no use of the principle mentioned in *SCG*, of the expression *per se,* of the term "body," or of any explicit reference to the *Metaphysics,* offers a more carefully reasoned argument. It begins by observing that every form, whether substantial or accidental, is united to a "matter or subject." This premise is more precise, as well as more comprehensive, than that of *SCG* on two counts, since it extends the notion of "form" to both substantial and accidental instances, and since it replaces "body" by the wider notion "matter or subject." Instead of, like *SCG,* at once fixing on the role of form as actuality, it proceeds by degrees from a more basic reality, namely, the "any one thing" (*unumquodque*) of which form is the actuality. Accordingly, between *SCG* and *QDSC* there is a shift of focus of attention from the human soul to the whole individual human being. Now *QDSC* observes, echoing Aristotle, that "any one thing" *is* one (*unum*) according as it is a being (*ens*). But, "any one thing" is an *ens actu,* a being in actuality (whether it be substantial or accidental being [*esse*]) through a form (*per formam*). Hence, every form is an actuality (*actus*), and consequently it is itself the very *ratio* ("essence" or "nature") of the unity by which anything is one. Therefore, just as one cannot say that there is some other thing which is an intermediary by which matter has being (*esse*) through its form, so one cannot say that there is some other thing which is a *medium* uniting a form to a "matter or subject".

Having in somewhat different ways established the immediacy of the union, both texts conclude by distinguishing, again in different ways, between (a) the respect in which this conclusion is to be maintained and (b) the respect or respects in which a concession can be made to the doctrine of intermediaries.

SCG 2.71

(a) Potest tamen dici aliquid esse medium inter animam et corpus etsi non in essendo...

QDSC 3

(a) Secundum igitur quod anima est forma corporis non potest esse aliquid medium inter animam et corpus.

SCG 2.71

(b) . . . Tamen in movendo et in via generationis. In movendo quidem, quia in motu quo anima movet corpus, estquidem ordo mobilium et motorum. Anima enim omnes operationes suasefficit per suas potentias: unde mediante potentia movet coprus; et adhuc membra mediante spiritu; et ulterius unum organum mediante alio organo. In via autem generationis . . . .

QDSC 3

Secundum vero quod est motor sic nichil prohibet ponere ibi multa media: manifeste enim anima per cor movet alia membra, et per spiritum etiam movet corpus.

Where *SCG* distinguishes between an immediate union

in essendo and the possibility of speaking of intermediaries *in movendo* and *in via generationis*,[33] *QDSC* contrasts two aspects of the soul itself, which *secundum quod est forma corporis* is immediately united to a body, but which *secundum quod est motor* allows the positing of *media*. A second notable change between *SCG* and *QDSC* here is that the latter does not at all consider the union of soul and body from the point of view of generation, reserving this point for the second part of its *responsio*. Finally, the hierarchy of intermediaries--powers, spirit, and bodily organs-- which, according to *SCG,* mediates the soul's movement of the body, is somewhat simplified in *QDSC,* which makes no mention of "powers" but simply states that the soul "clearly" moves the other members through the heart and the body as a whole through the "spirit."

The foregoing comparison shows *QDSC* 3 bringing the structure of *SCG* 2.71 into sharp focus. Both the distinction between two philosophical understandings of the union of soul and body and the distinction between two ways of regarding the union within the second understanding are emphasized with a spare technical terminology.

> (1)   *Si* enim anima rationalis uniatur corpori *solum* per contactum uirtualem *ut motor*, ut aliqui posuerunt, nichil prohibebat dicere quod sunt multa media inter animam et corpus, et magis inter animam et materiam primam.
>
> (2)   *Si* vero ponatur anima uniri corpori *ut forma*, necesse est dicere quod uniatur ei immediate . . .
>
> > (a)   *secundum* igitur *quod anima est*

> *forma corporis* non potest esse aliquod medium
> inter anima et corpus,
>   (b) *secundum* vero *quod est motor* sic
> nichil prohibet ponere ibi multa media.

The argument has clearly gained in simplicity and directness. *If* the soul were united to a body *merely* as a mover, one could speak of intermediaries; but *if,* as has been shown, it is united as form, it must be immediately so united. Thus, inasmuch as the soul is a form, there are no intermediaries, although inasmuch as it is a mover, intermediaries can be posited. These formulaic and balanced distinctions recur, in nearly identical terms, in other of Aquinas' later texts on the question of intermediaries: in particular, the first distinction (between 1 and 2) also establishes the foundation for each of the *responsiones* in *ST* 1.76.6-7, while the second (between a and b) also occurs at the conclusion to the first chapter of the commentary on the second book of the *De anima*. We shall turn to these texts in a moment.

The question which the long second section of the *responsio* in *QDSC* 3 addresses is, "What *is* the proper subject of the soul, related to it as matter to form?" In response to this question, Aquinas presents two positions: that of the Platonists, who, proceeding from the multiform "intelligible essences" (*ex rationibus intelligibilibus*) present in human nature, held that there are, between the rational soul and first matter, numerous intermediary substantial forms; and his own Aristotelian position, according to which there is only one substantial form in man, namely the rational soul, which gives to matter being (*dat materiae esse*) and all

further perfections pertaining to human nature. By
establishing the latter position, this supplementary
discussion shows that the immediate union demonstrated in the first section of the *responsio* is a union of
the rational soul to first matter and not to a body
already constituted by some intermediate substantial
form. The length of this second section, especially in
proportion to the comparatively brief discussion of
intermediaries in the first section, might suggest that
QDSC is more concerned with the theory of a plurality
of substantial forms than with the theory of
intermediaries as such. In any case, the hypothesis of
a plurality of substantial forms is the only version of
the theory of intermediaries specified by the *responsio*
of *QDSC* 3.

4. *Summa theologiae* 1.76.6-7

The treatment of the question of intermediaries in
ST 1.76.6-7 is divided into two parts. Article 6 asks
whether the soul is united to a body "with any
accidental dispositions mediating" (*mediantibus
dispositionibus accidentalibus*), and article 7 asks
whether the soul is united to a body "with any body
mediating" (*mediante aliquo corpore*). As mentioned
above, both *responsiones* are based on the distinction,
expressed in terms nearly identical to those of *QDSC*
3, between two philosophical understandings of the
union of soul and body.

> We must say that *if* the soul were united to a body
> *merely as a mover*, nothing would prevent there being,
> rather, it would be necessary for there to be certain

intermediate dispositions between soul and body,
namely: on the side of the soul, a power by means of
which it would move the body; and on the side of the
body, a certain aptitude by means of which it would
be able to be moved by the soul . . . . But *if* the
intellective soul is united to a body *as a* substantial
form, as has already been said above, it is impossible
that any accidental disposition fall as an intermediary
between body and soul, or between any substantial
form whatsoever and its matter.[34]

We must say that *if* the soul were united to a body
merely as a mover, as the Platonists say, it would be
proper to say that between the soul of man, or of any
animal whatsoever, and the body, certain other bodies
intervene as intermediaries; for it is proper to a mover
to move something distant by means of intermediaries
which are nearer . . . . If, however, the soul is united
to a body *as a form*, as has already been said, it is
impossible for it to be united to it with any body
mediating between them.[35]

The formula *si solum ut motor/si ut forma*--which also
patterns the *responsiones* of articles 3, 4, and 8--thus
becomes something of a refrain in *ST* 1.76, structuring
the arguments, like that of *QDSC* 3, by the alternative
between the Platonic error that soul and body are
united as two things in actuality (mover and moved)
and the Aristotelian truth that they are united in a single actuality (of informed matter).

The argument of article 6 against any mediating
accidental dispositions between soul and body is as
follows. Since matter is in potency to all actualities in
a certain order, what is first simply speaking among
actualities must be understood first within matter.
Because being is the first of all actualities, matter

cannot be understood to be, for instance, hot or quantified before it is understood to *be* in actuality; but it has being in actuality through a substantial form, which causes being simply speaking. Hence, no accidental dispositions can exist in matter before a substantial form; consequently, none can exist before the soul.[36] Note that this argument has a double focus: the order of actualities of matter, among which *esse,* the first actuality simply speaking, is first and the one which matter receives from a substantial form; and a corresponding order of understanding which reflects the absolute priority of being among actualities and hence the priority of substantial form within matter.

The argument of article 7 against a mediating body between soul and body closely parallels the corresponding section of the preliminary argument in *QDSC* 3. A thing is one thing in the way that it is a being; but form of itself makes a thing to be in actuality, since form is of its very essence an actuality. Correspondingly, form does not "give being" (*dat esse*) through any *medium*; hence the unity of a composite of matter and form comes through the form, which of itself is united to matter as matter's actuality. And thus there is no other uniter of form and matter, except the agent which causes matter to be in actuality, as is said in *Metaphysics* 8.[37]

After presenting this argument, the *responsio* of article 7 gives a carefully itemized catalog of the opinions holding that some body mediates between soul and body. "Certain Platonists," Aquinas states, said that soul and body are united through the mediation of an "incorrruptible body" inseparably united to the intellective soul. (*ST* 1.76.7 is the only one of the texts we are considering to mention this hypothetical intermediary.) Others said that soul and body are united through the mediation of a "bodily spirit." Still others said that soul and body are united through the mediation of light, which they took to be a body and to share in the nature of the quintessence, holding that the vegetative soul is united to a body by means of the light of the "sidereal" heaven, the sensitive soul by means of the light of the "crystalline" heaven, and the intellectual soul by means of the light of the "empyrean" heaven. Aquinas reserves a particular scorn for the opinion that light is an intermediary, calling it "fanciful and laughable" (*fictitium et derisibile*) for three reasons: because light is not a body; because the unalterable quintessence does not enter into the composition of mixed bodies materially, but only "virtually" (*virtualiter*); and because the soul is immediately united to a body as form to matter.[38]

5. *Sentencia libri de anima* 2.1.366-392

We next turn to Aquinas' *De anima* commentary, in particular to its explanation of the passage referred to in *In 2 Sent.* 1.2.4 *ad* 3. The passage occurs early in *De anima* 2, where, having defined the soul as the "form" or "first actuality" of a natural body which "has life in potentiality" or is "organic," Aristotle touches on the theme of the oneness of soul and body. Aquinas introduces this passage by saying that in it Aristotle resolves a difficulty (*dubitatio*) on the basis of the definition just given.

> Hence one should not ask whether soul and body are
> one, just as one does not ask whether wax and
> imprint, or, in general, whether matter and that of
> which it is matter, are one. For although "one" and
> "to be" are said in many senses, what they properly
> are is "actuality".[39]

Aquinas proceeds to explain the two statements of
this passage, in each case using the technique, not
uncommon in his Aristotelian commentaries, of introducing his exegesis of Aristotle's words with a remark
of his own. Many have asked, he says, how one thing
could be made out of soul and body, and some have
posited certain *media* by which the soul might be
united and somehow "bound" (*quodam modo colligaretur*) to a body. But this question has no place at
this point, since it has been shown that the soul is the
form of a body, which is just what Aristotle says here:
namely, that one should not ask whether one thing is
made out of soul and body, just as the question is not
raised about wax and an imprint in it, or in general
about "matter" and its "form."[40] Aquinas' smooth
transition from introductory remarks to paraphrase here
nearly succeeds in concealing the fact that he is
importing something into Aristotle's meaning by
transforming the question "whether soul and body
become one" into the question of "how" they become
one and whether they might be "bound together" by
"intermediaries."

By way of introducing the second statement made
by Aristotle in this passage, Aquinas next refers to
Metaphysics 8.6, where, he says, it has been shown that
form is per se united to matter as actuality and that it
is the same thing for matter to be united to form and

for it to be in actuality. This, Aquinas says, is just what Aristotle says here: although "one thing" (unum) and "a being" are said in many ways (for, Aquinas adds, "a being" is said both of a being in potentiality and of a being in actuality), nevertheless what is properly "a being" and "one thing" is an actuality. Because a thing is said to be "one thing" in the way that it is said to be "a being," just as a being in potentiality is "a being" not simply speaking but in a certain respect, so a thing is "one thing" not simply speaking but in a certain respect.[41]   Aquinas' concluding comment makes explicit the "immediacy" of the union of soul and body.

> And hence, just as the body has being through the soul as through its form, so, too, it is immediately united to the soul *inasmuch as the soul is the form of the body*; but *inasmuch as the soul is a mover*, nothing prevents there being some intermediary, according as one part of the body is moved by the soul with another part mediating between them.[42]

Since the body "has being" through the soul as through its form, (1) it is *immediately* united to the soul as to its form inasmuch as the soul is the form of the body; but (2) inasmuch as the soul is a mover, nothing prevents there being an intermediary between soul and body, since one part of the body is moved by the soul through the intermediary of another part. Aside from the slight change of *secundum quod* to *in quantum*, this is exactly the distinction made by *QDSC* 3 between two ways of considering the soul's relation to the body on the basis of the conclusion that the soul is a substantial form.[43]

6. *Questio disputata de anima* 9

The deepening of an ancient author's thought always
proceeds, in my view, in the direction of a deepening
of the language which he uses and of the technical
vocabulary which he constructs.[44]

Having reviewed Aquinas' treatments of the
question of intermediaries in *In 2 Sent*. 1.2.4 *ad* 3, *SCG*
2.71, *QDSC* 3, *ST* 1.76.6-7, and *SLA* 2.1.366-392, we
now proceed to his remaining text on the point,
namely, *QDA* 9, which asks "whether the soul is united
to corporeal matter through an intermediary." Our
primary purpose, as stated at the outset, is to demonstrate the uniqueness of *QDA* 9 among this group of
parallel texts.

Because of its presence in a *quaestio disputata*, its
length, and its concern with the theory of a plurality of
substantial forms in the human composite as a special
case of the theory of intermediaries, the *responsio* of
QDA 9 bears, at first sight, a particular resemblance to
QDSC 3. Furthermore, both *responsiones* fall into two
main sections, one dealing directly with the question of
intermediaries between soul and body and the other
dealing with the theory of a plurality of substantial
forms. But there are significant differences between
these two two-part structures. First, there is a shift in
· order of presentation between them: *QDSC* 3 proceeds
from the special case of the human composite to a
general discussion of the union of substantial form and
matter, while *QDA* 9 does just the reverse. There is
also between these texts of approximately equal size a

striking difference in the proportions of the parts: whereas the appended discussion in *QDSC* 3 is nearly eight times as long as the preliminary response, the two sections of the *responsio* in *QDA* 9 are of *exactly* equal length. Finally, the two texts link their respective parts in notably different ways: *QDSC* 3 abruptly announces a "remaining difficulty" (*Sed tunc dubium restat*), but *QDA* 9 has smooth continuity (*Sic igitur cum anima*). The orderly procedure from general to particular, the balance, and the continuity of *QDA* 9 suggest that it is the more unified and more carefully composed of the two.[45] Moreover, its careful setting of the question of intermediaries in the context of general considerations separates *QDA* 9 from *all* of Aquinas' other discussions of the question, each of which *begins* by speaking of the soul; here he suppresses every consideration of the soul in particular until he has established the relevant general point. The term *Anima* does not occur in the first half of the *responsio*; even the generic term *forma* does not occur in the *responsio's* opening remark; the starting point is rather the fundamental metaphysical consideration, *esse*.

The movement of *QDA* 9 from general to particular is founded on a device which constitutes the most salient difference between this text and the others, its use of an introductory and authoritative axiom. The argument does not begin, like the *SCG* and *QDSC* parallels, with a reference to "the foregoing"; nor does it begin, like the *In Sent.* and *ST* parallels, by presenting the Platonic member of the alternative between two ways of considering the union of soul and body. Rather, it begins with a statement of principle providing a starting point which not only is proper to the question itself but also sets it in the widest context: "We must say that being (*esse*) is that which most immediately and intimately (*immediatius et intimius*) comes together with (*convenit*) things, as is said in *The Book of Causes*."[46] To borrow a happy phrase coined by Lawrence Dewan in discussing a different Thomistic text,[47] Aquinas has clearly found an "adequate premise" for an argument that soul and body are immediately united. There is nothing like it in any of the other texts we have examined, each of which suggests or states that the question of intermediaries must be approached as a subordinate one. The introductory premise here, by contrast, serves notice that the question will be treated on its own terms.

Aquinas appears to have been reflecting on the adverb *immediate,* which, throughout his career, remains so crucial to his responses to the doctrine of intermediaries. In the texts we have considered previously, the term always has a polemical force, appearing as it does at the conclusion of each argument in order to negate the doctrine of intermediaries. Here, not only does it appear at the very outset, but it takes on a positive sense suggested by the explanatory gloss *et intimius*: "immediacy" here does not signify a mere negation of intermediaries, but a positive "intimacy" or "interiority." Furthermore, the term is first applied to the most basic of all unions, which is not that of soul and body or of form and matter, but that of things and their being. Note, however, that the notion of "union" does not even appear as yet: in terminology reminiscent of the *convenientia* of *In Sent.,* this introductory remark speaks rather of the being which "comes together with" (*convenit*) things. The opening gambit here thus eschews every term of the question's title--"soul," "matter," "union," "intermediary"--in order to focus on the adverb which will characterize the conclusion. Aquinas' reflection on this adverb leads him to the most immediate or intimate of comings-together, that of *esse* and things, a coming-together which, as he no doubt expects his audience will recognize, is the event of creation itself. None of his other texts on the immediacy of the union of soul and body has a starting point so significant, or so remote from its conclusion.

Slowly approaching its goal, the argument proceeds from being and things to form and matter, inferring from the opening remark that, since matter has being in actuality through form, "the form which gives being to matter" is "understood" to come to (*advenire*) matter before, and to be more immediately present in matter than, all else.[48] This remark introduces two expressions which are characteristic of the terminology of *QDA* 9 and, as we shall see, crucial to its explanation of the immediate union of soul and body: one is contained in the phrase *forma dans esse materie,*[49] and the other is the verb *intelligere* as referring to the way in which the union of form and matter is to be understood.

Proceeding from "form" to "substantial form," Aquinas next argues that, since only substantial form gives being simply speaking, any form which does not give being simply speaking will not be substantial.[50]

Of all the other texts of Aquinas on the question of intermediaries, it is the *responsio* of *ST* 1.76.6 which most closely resembles these fundamental metaphysical considerations from *QDA* 9. However, whereas the article in *ST* sets the consideration of *esse* within the alternative between Platonic and Aristotelian positions, *QDA* 9 gives it more prominence and importance, placing it at the very outset of the discussion.

Aquinas next proceeds to the central theme of the *responsio's* first half, which is developed in three steps: a statement and rejection of the theory of a plurality of substantial forms in a single composite (*Ex quo patet quod*); an account, based on Aristotle's comparison between forms and numbers, of how a single form is "understood" to constitute (*constituere*another term characteristic of this text) matter in different degrees of perfection (*Relinquitur igitur dicendum quod*); and an explanation of the ways in which intermediaries between form and matter may be "understood" (*Oportet igitur intelligere quod*). (Note that the divisions of the argument are frequently made with unobtrusive formulas leading up to a *quod*.) The first and second of these steps more briefly state points made in the long second part of the *responsio* of *QDSC* 3. The third step, which is peculiar to *QDA* 9, calls for more detailed comment.

Since one and the same form constitutes matter in different degrees of perfection, it follows that a more perfect form, according as it constitutes matter in a lower degree of perfection, "is understood" (*intelligatur*) together with matter as material in relation to a higher perfection; for example, first matter as already constituted in bodily being is matter with respect to the further perfection of life. In a way, then, a form is intermediary between (1) matter as constituted, by the form, in the actuality of a lower degree of perfection, and (2) *itself,* as the form that constitutes matter in the actuality of a higher perfec-

tion.[51]   This is something quite unparalleled in
Aquinas' responses to the position that there are intermediary substantial forms between the ultimate form
and matter. It concedes a kind of sense to the position
by translating the distinction among forms into one
among perfections and by indicating that both the distinction and the consequent intermediaries occur in our
understanding (*intelligere*).

Turning from form to matter, the argument next
explains the sense in which "bodily dispositions" may
be understood to precede form in matter, a point which
follows directly. Note that the term "intermediary"
does not occur here. As matter is understood to be
constituted in substantial being according to a lower
degree of perfection, it can consequently be understood
as subject to accidents, for certain accidents are proper
to substance according to the lower degree of
perfection, as, for instance, dimensions follow on the
constitution of matter in bodily being. Furthermore,
matter, as understood to be constituted in a lower
degree of substantial being, can be understood as
receptive of accidents by which it is "disposed" to a
higher perfection. But a distinction must be made: as
introduced into matter by an agent, these dispositions
are understood as present in matter "before" form; but
they are caused by the form itself, so that they are not
understood as dispositions prior to the form, but rather
the form is understood as prior to them, as a cause is
to its effects.[52] This is the point made in *ST* 1.76.6.

We have reached the midpoint of the argument,
where, as we noted above, Aquinas turns to the special
case of the union of the rational soul with matter. The
remaining half of the discussion is, like all of his other

texts on the question of intermediaries, structured by an alternative between the Platonic error and the Aristotelian truth concerning this question; but here, in one of the outstanding and distinctive features of this text, he reverses the order in which this alternative is presented by the other texts. By *starting* with the Aristotelian position, to which he devotes the first-four-fifths of this second half, and only then (at *Set quidam ponentes*) turning to the opposing Platonic error, he expresses an attitude which is less polemical and more emphatically theoretical than that found in the other texts on the question; whereas the other texts seem to be primarily concerned with refuting the error concerning intermediaries, *QDA* 9 seems intent above all on establishing the truth of the immediacy of the union. This placing of truth before error is of a piece with the positive meaning given to the term *immediate* at the outset of the *responsio*. It is also--as the *SCG's* alternative title (*Liber de veritate catholicae fidei contra errores infidelium*), epigraph (Prov 8:7, *Veritatem meditabitur guttur meum, et labia mea detestabuntur impium*), and first chapter suggest--more in keeping with the business of the wise man than is the polemical approach of the other texts.

The presentation of the positive and Aristotelian point consists of a detailed account of the matter, followed (at *Et hoc est quod a multis dicitur*) by a confirmation of the conclusion. This section is structured by a precision-*cum*-concession of the kind we have seen in other texts, that is, by a distinction within the Aristotelian position between two ways of regarding a soul's union with a body. The language in which the distinction is expressed, however, is the most singular terminological peculiarity of *QDA* 9. Recall the *ut forma/ut motor* formula by which the distinction is expressed in *QDSC* and *SLA*. This formula indeed appears in *QDA* 9, but only towards the end of the section, in the recapitulation mentioned above, and as "said by many": "And this is what is said by many, that 'the soul is united to a body as a form without intermediary, but as a mover through an intermediary'". ("Et hoc est quod a multis dicitur, quod anima unitur corpori ut forma sine medio, ut motor autem per medium"). But among the "many" who speak in this way, must we not include Aquinas as he expresses himself in *QDSC* and *SLA?* In *QDA* 9, on the other hand, instead of contrasting merely "the soul as a form" and "the soul as a mover" (*anima ut forma* and *anima ut motor*), he more elaborately distinguishes between "the soul according as it is a form which gives being" (*anima secundum quod est forma dans esse* an expression prepared for by the occurrence of the phrase *forma dans esse materie* at the outset of the *responsio*) and "the soul according as it is a mover and principle of operation" (*anima secundum quod est motor et principium operationis*). That is, both members of the distinction are described more precisely and at a deeper metaphysical level: "form" is replaced by form's role as "giver of being," and "mover" is specified by an expression more aptly naming the source of human "movement", namely, "principle of operation." It is hard to believe that this formulation does not reflect a dissatisfaction with the use of the simpler one in *QDSC* and *SLA*.

The consideration of the soul's first aspect, although it contains the central conclusion of *QDA* 9, is brief. It follows from what has been said that, since the soul is a substantial form because it constitutes man in a determinate species of substance, there cannot be any substantial form intermediary between it and first matter; instead, man is perfected in different degrees by the soul itself. Matter, according as it receives from the rational soul perfections of a lower degree, must be "understood" with the appropriate dispositions as the "proper matter" of the rational soul, according as the latter gives the ultimate perfection. Thus, the soul as *forma dans esse* has no other *medium* between itself and first matter.[53] (This last statement, the central conclusion of the *responsio*, contains the first occurrence of the term *medium* as a substantive in the *responsio*.)

Aquinas now proceeds to the second consideration of the soul, as "principle of operation." The proportional length and the detail of this section--which corresponds to brief remarks in *QDSC* and *SLA*--are remarkable. Also striking is the continuity between the foregoing consideration and this one, which opens with the remark that the *same* form which gives being to matter is *also* a principle of operation. Furthermore, this section, whose principal concern is with the bodily instruments of the soul's operations, begins, in the spirit of the *responsio* as a whole, with a consideration of the "giving of being" to these instruments, and only then (at *Sed cum oporteat ordinem*) turns to a consideration of their order.

The first of these considerations, proceeding from the abstract to the concrete, notes first the increasing number and diversity of operations in forms which are more perfect in "giving being"; it then (at *Et inde est quod*) turns to the corresponding diversity of bodily parts and to the "maximum distinction of parts" in man, whose rational soul is the most perfect of all natural forms and gives substantial being to each of the parts.[54]

The second consideration notes that, since the order of instruments must follow the order of operations, there is an order of movement among the parts of the body. Consequently, there is an intermediary between the soul as mover and principle of operation and the body as a whole in the sense that the soul through one first part, such as the heart, moves the other members to their vital operations. Nevertheless, according as the soul immediately gives being to the body, it gives substantial and specific being to all its parts.[55]

Aquinas now confirms the foregoing by noting that this is what is said "by many," that the soul is united to a body *ut forma sine medio, ut motor autem per medium,* and adds that this position is "according to the opinion of Aristotle," who held that the soul is the substantial form of a body.[56]

Finally, Aquinas proceeds to his polemical point. "Some," holding "according to Plato's opinion" that soul is united to body as one substance to another, "were compelled" to posit intermediaries by which the soul might be united to a body, because diverse and "distant" substances are not "bound together" unless there is something to unite them. And thus some held that "spirit and moisture," or "light," or the soul's powers, or something similar, are intermediaries between soul and body. But none of these is necessary if the soul is the form of the body: for any one thing is one according as it is a being; hence, since form of itself gives being to matter, it is of itself, and not through any other connecting link, united to its proper matter.[57]

The intricate but unified argument of *QDA* 9 may be outlined as follows.

1) The general case of substantial form
   a. being and form
   b. substantial form
      a) *dat esse materiae simpliciter* (*Unde oportet quod . . .*)
      b) is one in number
         1. refutation of pluralism (*Ex quo patet quod . . .*)
         2. account of how one form gives many perfections (*Relinquitur igitur dicendum quod . . .*)
         3. consequences:
            1) one and the same form is intermediary between matter and itself (*Oportet igitur intelligere quod . . .*)
            2) form "is understood" to be present in matter before bodily dispositions (*Materia autem prout . . .*)
2) The special case of the rational soul
   a. Aristotelian truth
      a) argument
         1. *anima secundum quod est forma dans esse* (*Sic igitur cum anima . . .*)
         2. *anima secundum quod est principium operationis*
            1) introduction (*Sed quia eadem forma . . .*)
            2) argument
               a. *esse* of bodily parts
                  a) operations (*Sed consider-*

andum est quod . . .)
  b) bodily parts (*Et inde est
     quod . . .*)
  b. ordo of bodily parts (*Sed cum op-
     orteat ordinem . . .*)
  b) confirmation (*Et hoc est quod a multis . . .*)
  b. Platonic error
  a) statement of doctrine of intermediaries (*Set
     quidam ponentes . . .*)
  b) refutation (*Sed nullum istorum . . .*)

This outline points to the distinctive features of *QDA* 9 among Aquinas' discussions of the question of intermediaries: its careful and balanced composition; its philosophical and orderly progression from fundamental considerations of being and form to the special case of the human soul; its argument that substantial form is intermediary between itself and matter; its reversal of the order in which truth and error are considered by all of the other texts we have considered; its more elaborate description of the soul's two aspects as *secundum quod est forma dans esse* and as *secundum quod est principium operationis*; and its detailed explanation of the intermediaries established by the body's order of parts.

These features, I suggest, combine to establish the literary, philosophical, and pedagogical superiority of *QDA* 9, not only over *In 2 Sent.* 1.2.4 *ad* 3 and *SCG* 2.71, but also over the *responsiones* of *QDSC* 3 and *ST* 1.76.6-7 and the treatment in *SLA* 2.1.366-392. This superiority in turn argues that *QDA* 9 was composed after these latter three texts: for why, after making such a relatively perfect statement of his view, would Aquinas then produce the less elegant and less profound treatments of *QDSC, ST,* and *SLA?* There may be reasonable answers to this question, such as that he composed the latter texts more hurriedly or with different ends in view; but until the chronology of these later writings is established with all possible certitude, the distinctiveness of *QDA* 9 among Aquinas' texts on the immediacy of the union between soul and body will stand as an argument for the "maturity"--i.e., the relative lateness--of this text.

Conclusion

Four aspects may be distinguished in Aquinas' doctrine of the rational soul's immediate union to a body.

One is a clear polemical intention. Apart from *QDA* 9, Aquinas' treatments of the question of intermediaries are centrally concerned with refuting the unnamed *quidam* who hold a doctrine of linking *media* between soul and body. As was pointed out above, these *quidam* represent a specifically thirteenth-century opinion apparently originating with Philip the Chancellor and still current in Aquinas' day in the writings of Bonaventure. The direct object of Aquinas' polemics, and the very occasion of his development of the opposing doctrine of the immediate union of soul and body, is certainly this thirteenth-century opinion, whose variations he brands as "absurd", "fanciful," and "laughable." However, his constant concern to reduce the doctrine of intermediaries to its basis in the Platonic understanding of the relation of soul and body as one of mover and moved, or more fundamentally still as a union of two substances, shows that he understands his opposition to the doctrine of intermediaries to be a skirmish in his battle with Platonism as such. In his view, the question of intermediaries must be resolved in terms of the opposition between Plato and Aristotle. This brings us to the second aspect of his doctrine, namely, its exegetical character.

Throughout his career, he appeals to two Aristotelian texts, *Metaphysics* 8.6 and *De anima* 2.1, in support of his contention that the rational soul is immediately united to a body. As was indicated above, neither of these texts contains any term corresponding to "intermediary" or "immediately," and neither of them deals with the question of intermediaries as it presented itself to Aquinas. They are, rather, concerned to establish that form and matter (in *Metaphysics* 8.6) or soul and body (in *De anima* 2.1) make up a perfect unity and are not a duality. But to deny a duality is not precisely to deny that two things are linked by intervening intermediaries, although it does implicitly exclude that possibility. Aquinas, then, had to construe these texts that is, bring out latent possibilities in them in order to make them address the thirteenth-century question of intermediaries; and in doing so he may have been helped, as was suggested above, by Averroes' Aristotelian commentaries.

The third aspect of Aquinas' doctrine is its metaphysical character, that is, its reference to the being (*esse*) of the human composite. This reference first emerges in *SCG* 2.71, where talk of intermediaries between soul and body "from the point of view of being" (*in essendo*) is excluded. It is elaborated in *QDSC* 3, where the argument is that anything has its being and its unity from its form, as well as in *ST*

1.76.6, where the principle that *esse* is the first of all
acts is introduced. And it becomes pronounced in
QDA 9, where the role of the soul as *forma dans esse*
becomes a central theme and the question is set in the
context of the most immediate or intimate of all
"comings-together," that of things and their being. It
is also in this last text, as we have seen, that the term
"immediately," in being moved from the end to the
beginning of the argument, transcends its normal
polemical connotation,   and   even   its   privative
denotation, in order to designate the positive intimacy
of the manner in which things and their being, and
hence matter and substantial form, and hence matter
and the rational soul, come together.

The doctrine's final aspect, which might be
characterized as "physiological," appears in what we
have described as Aquinas' "concession" to the doctrine of intermediaries, that is, his admission that, even
though the soul as "giver of being" is immediately
united to a body, the soul as "mover," or, in the words
of *QDA* 9, as "principle of operation," is mediately
united to a body in the sense that it moves one part of
the body through another in a hierarchy of bodily parts
which corresponds to the order of the soul's operations.

As the foregoing discussion shows, it is the third
and positive aspect of the doctrine, the central point
that soul and body are immediately united in being,
which is most significant to Aquinas himself. But
what meaning can this point have for his modern
reader, to whom the very notion of a "distance"
between soul and body, and hence the hypothesis of
"intermediaries" between them, are probably so
unintelligible as to be not worth refuting? Some re-

covery of the Platonic sense of a "gap" in human nature between two "opposing" elements would seem to be a condition of understanding the force which the doctrine of the rational soul as a substantial form immediately united to matter is meant to have. In most of the texts we have examined, the polemical presentation of the immediacy of the union seems designed to maintain the consistency of the conclusion that the soul is a substantial form. The positive and relatively independent presentation of *QDA* 9, however, rather puts the finishing touch on this conclusion by pointing out what, to Christian Neoplatonism at least, is its most disturbing implication: that spirit or intellect is immediately, that is, intimately or inwardly, present to matter in human nature.

NOTES

1.   I am grateful to Lawrence Dewan, O. P., and to Edward M. Macierowski for their comments on an earlier draft of this paper.

2.   *Les doublets de saint Thomas d'Aquin: Leur étude méthodique: Quelques réflexions, quelques exemples* (Paris: Gabriel Beauchesne, 1926).

3.   John Henry Cardinal Newman, *An Essay on the Development of Christian Doctrine* (Notre Dame, IN: University of Notre Dame, 1989), 169ff. (part 2, chapter 5).

4.   In *St. Thomas Aquinas, 1274-1974: Commemorative Studies,* ed. Armand Maurer (Toronto: Pontifical Institute of Mediaeval Studies, 1974), 1.131-158.

5.   Pegis was concerned with Aquinas' texts on the knowledge of the separated soul (131): "The difference of *ST* I, q. 89, a. 1 from *SCG* II, c. 81 has three aspects, namely, a change in doctrine, a change in St. Thomas' view of the state of the question before him, and the entry of the Aristotelian notion of *nature* into the discussion of the knowledge of the separated soul." The following comparison of Aquinas' texts on the question of intermediaries between soul and body concerns not a change in doctrine but a change in the doctrine's presentation, as well as a deepening of doctrine.

6.   See James A. Weisheipl, *Friar Thomas d'Aquino: His Life, Thought and Works* (Washington, DC: Catholic University of America, 1983), 358-360.

7. The discussion in this article will be based on the following editions:

(1) the Mandonnet edition of books 1-2 of *In Sent.* (Paris: P. Lethielleux, 1929);

(2) the Leonine edition of *SCG* (Rome: Cura et studio Fratrum Praedicatorum, 1918) vol. 14;

(3) the Leonine edition of *SLA,* in *Opera Omnia* 45 no. 1 (Rome: Commissio Leonina; Paris: Librairie Philosophique J. Vrin, 1984);

(4) the Ottawa edition of *ST* (Ottawa: Commissio Piana, 1943);

(5) the yet unpublished Leonine text of *QDSC,* ed. Joseph Cos, O. P.;

(6) and the yet unpublished Leonine text of *QDA,* ed. Bernardo Carlos Bazán. I would like to thank Fr. Cos and Dr. Bazán for allowing me to use their editions in the present study. The spelling of Latin words has been standardized throughout the texts quoted below.

Another text, *Quaestio de quodlibet* 12.7.1, dated Christmas 1270 by Weisheipl (*Friar Thomas* 367), might be counted as a seventh text on the question of intermediaries. However, because of its extreme brevity, its special status as both a *quodlibet* and a *reportatio,* and its exclusive concern with *forma corporeitas* as a hypothetical intermediary, I have not considered it in the following discussion.

8. *QDSC* 3 quotes William of Moerbeke's translation of Simplicius' commentary on the *Categories,* which was completed in March 1266 (see Weisheipl, *Friar Thomas* 364).

On the start of the composition of the *prima pars* during 1266-1267, see Leonard E. Boyle, O. P., "The Setting of the *Summa theologiae* of Saint Thomas," Etienne Gilson Series 5 (Toronto: Pontifical Institute of Mediaeval Studies, 1982) 14. Aquinas composed the 119 *quaestiones* of the *prima pars,* and at least a few *quaestiones* of the *prima secundae,* during the two academic years 1266-1267 and 1267-1268; 1.79.4 was completed after November 22, 1267 (Weisheipl, *Friar Thomas* 361). Assuming that the rate of composition of the *Summa* was fairly constant during this period, the question which which will concern us, Q. 76, must have been written sometime in the middle of the second of these academic years, late 1267 or early 1268.

On the dating of the *De anima* commentary in 1267-1268, see *SLA* 288[*].

9. "Quelques questions à propos du commentaire de S. Thomas sur le De anima," *Angelicum* 51 (1974):419-472.

10. Ibid. 453-454 n. 44bis: "La 'question disputée' *De anima* (sans doute trop longue pour avoit été réelement disputée) ne pourrait-elle pas être considérée comme un exercice préparatoire à la rédaction de ces questions de la Iª Pars? Les historiens qui placent cette 'question disputée' à Paris en 1269 invoquent deux témoignages . . . . or, il semble que les deux mss . . . soient des médiocres témoins de la famille parisien: la leçon 'parisius' ne peut donc être considérée comme un leçon autorisée, puisqu'elle manquait certainement dans l'*exemplar* universitaire parisien,

archétype de la famille . . . . On remarquera que S. Thomas, s'il connaît certainement la *Noua* du *De anima* au moment où il rédige la question *De anima* . . . ne s'en tient pas moins ordinairement au texte de la *Vetus* . . . . Sans doute est-ce l'habitude de S. Thomas de tirer de sa mémoire les vieux textes qu'il sait par coeur plutôt que de recourir aux nouveaux; la négligence cependant serait trop forte (et le contraste avec le *De unitate intellectus* trop violent) s'il s'agissait d'une question disputée à Paris à un moment et dans un milieu où une utilisation rigoreuse du texte d'Aristote s'imposait; elle s'explique si la question *De anima* a été écrite à Rome, avant même que S. Thomas ne se soit imprégné de la *Noua* en écrivant son commentaire au *De anima* (la question *De spiritualibus creaturis* est nettement plus attentive à une utilisation exacte de la *Nova*)."

11. "Le commentaire de S. Thomas d'Aquin sur le *Traité de l'âme*. Un événement: l'édition critique de la commission léonine," *Revue des Sciences Philosophiques et Théologiques* 69 (1985): 532.

12. *In 2 Sent.* 1.2.4 *ad* 3: "Praeterea, ea quae maxime distant, non uniuntur nisi minima conjunctione. Sed anima et corpus maxime distant, ut in Littera dicitur. Ergo cum conjunctio formae ad materiam sit secundum maximam unionem, videtur quod anima non sit corpori unibilis, sicut forma materiae."

13. *Philippi Cancelarii Parisiensis Summa de bono,* ed. N. Wicki (Bern: Éditions Francke, 1985),

Pars Prior, "De bono nature intellectualis creaturae con-
iuncte corporali," q. 8, 285-286.

14.   Ibid.: "Deinde   quaeritur   cuius   modi
dispositiones exigantur ad hoc ut coniungantur huiusmodi perfectiones aliis perfectibilibus. Ad quod intelli-
gendum est distantia primae animae rationalis ad corpus.   Et est multimoda distantia.   Anima enim
rationalis tres habet oppositiones ad corpus ipsum; est
enim simplex, incorporea et incorruptibilis, corpus vero
compositum, corporeum et corruptibile. Propter igitur
nimiam sui distantiam a corpore non posset anima
rationalis corpori coniungi, nisi advenirent dispositiones
sive adaptationes aliquae, quae essent media coniungendi haec ad invicem."

15.   La "Summa Duacensis" (Douai 434),
Textes Philosophiques du Moyen Age 2, ed. P.
Glorieux (Paris: Librairie Philosophique J. Vrin, 1955),
60-61.

16.   La Summa de anima di Fratre Giovanni
della Rochelle dell'Ordine de'Minori, ed. T.
Domenichelli (Prato: Typographia Giachetti, 1882),
166; St. Bonaventure, Commentaria in quatuor libros
sententiarum (Quaracchi: Studio et cura PP. Collegii a
S. Bonaventura, 1882-1889), lib. 2, dist. 1, p. 2, art. 1,
q. 2, 41-43.

17.   Magistri Petri Lombardi, Sententiae in IV
Libris Distinctae (Grottaferrata: Editiones Collegii
S. Bonaventurae ad Claras Aquas, 1971), 1.334-335.

18.   Ibid. 335: "Pro exemplo igitur futurae societatis quae inter Deum et spiritum rationalem in glorificatione eiusdem perficienda erat, animam corporeis indumentis et terrenis mansionibus copulavit.   . . . Fecit itaquehominem ex duplici substantia, corpus de terra fingens, animam vero de nihilo faciens."

19.   Ibid.: "Putaret enim creatura se non posse uniri Creatori suo tanta propinquitate ut eum tota mente diligeret et cognosceret, nisi videret spiritum, qui est *excellentissima* creatura, tam *infimae,* id est carni, quae de terra est, in tanta dilectione uniri ut non valeat arctari ad hoc ut velit eam relinquere . . . [emphasis added]." This opposition between "elevation" of the spirit and "lowliness" of the flesh gives a metaphorical "direction" to the "distance" between soul and body. For the background of this cluster of spatial metaphors, see Edward P. Mahoney's extremely erudite and philosophically suggestive article, "Metaphysical Foundations of the Hierarchy of Being According to Some Late-Medieval and Renaissance Philosophers," in *Philosophies of Existence Ancient and Medieval,* ed. Parviz Morewedge (New York: Fordham University, 1982), 165-257, particularly 209-212.

20.   *In 2 Sent.* 1.2.4 *ad* 3: Ad tertium dicendum, quod propter hanc objectionem Plato posuit, ut Gregorius Nyssenus, in *Hom. de anima* . . . narrat quod anima est in corpore sicut motor in mobili, ut nauta in navi, et non sicut forma in materia; unde dicebat quod homo non est aliquid ex anima et corpore, sed quod homo est anima utens corpore; et propter hoc

etiam quidam quaesierunt quaedam media inter animam et corpus, ut spiritum corporalem, animam vegetabilem et sensibilem, et lucem quibus mediantibus anima rationalis uniretur . . . ."

21.　　The hypothesis of a corporeal bond uniting soul and body may be traced from Plato's *Timaeus* (73b) through the Stoic doctrine of *pneuma* (see G. Verbeke, *L'Evolution de la doctrine du pneuma du stoicisme à S. Augustin* [Paris: Desclée de Brouwer; Louvain: Institut superieur de Philosophie, 1945]) to Augustine's suggestion (in *De Genesi ad litteram* 7.19.25) that the soul "administers" the body through light and air (for Aquinas' response to this suggestion, see *QDSC* 3 *ad* 7 and *ST* 1.76.7 *ad* 1); see also the references given in the Ottawa edition of *ST* 1.460. The suggestion that the soul's powers mediate between it and the body was apparently first made by Al-Farabi (see R. Zavalloni, *Richard de Mediavilla et la controverse sur la pluralité des formes* [Louvain: Éditions de l'Institut superieur de Philosophie, 1951], 428).

22.　　*Metaphysics* 8.6 (1045a7-b23) (reference is to the Latin text in *S. Thomae Aquinatis, In duodecim Metaphysicorum Aristotelis Expositio,* ed. Cathala-Spiazzi [Torino-Rome: Marietti, 1950], 419).

23.　　Note, however, that the term *medium* occurs repeatedly in Aquinas' commentary on this passage (*In duodecim Metaphysicorum* 8.5 nos. 1765-1766): "Sicut Lycophron dixit, quod scientia est *medium* inter animam et scire. Alii autem dixerunt quod ipsum vivere est *medium,* per quod coniungitur anima corpori . . . . Excludit dictas positiones; dicens, quod si hoc bene dicitur de anima et corpore, quod sit aliquod *medium* uniens, eadem ratio erit in omnibus, quae se habent ut forma et materia; quia secundum hoc, convalescere erit *medium* quasi quaedam con-substantialitas, aut quaedam coniunctio sive vinculum inter animam, per quam subsistit animal, et sanitatem. Et esse trigonum erit quoddam *medium* componens figuram trigoni. Et esse album erit quoddam *medium,* quo componitur albedo superficiei. Quod est manifeste falsum. Unde falsum est, quod vivere sit *medium,* quo componitur anima corpori; cum vivere nihil aliud sit quam esse animatum [emphasis added]."

24.   *Philippi Cancelarii Parisiensis Summa de bono* 282: "Bene ergo concedimus quod primo obiectum est quod duo opposita non sunt in eodem, multo magis nec oppositum in opposito per modum informationis. Sed duo opposita nihil impedit habere *coexistentiam,* quorum unum sit simplex, alterum compositum, quae non sunt opposita sicut oppositae qualitates cum sint substantiae. Secundum ergo quod anima est substantia habet *coexistentiam,* quia quemadmodum corpus, immo etiam verius existit nec applicatur corpori, ut per ipsum fulciatur in esse, cum per se possit existere [emphasis added]."

25.   Ibid. 283: "Sequitur quaestio utrum per medium vel sine medio uniantur. Quod autem non per medium ostenditur. Aut enim unitur ut substantia aut ut forma. Ut forma non, quia forma se ipsa unitur cum

materia et non alio principio extrinseco, quia unum et ens idem dicunt. Ergo idem est quo ens et quo est unum. Sed omne ens compositum ex materia et forma est ens per formam; ergo per eam est unum, essentialiter dico." At this point in the text, the modern editor of the *Summa de bono,* in connection with the remark *forma se ipsa unitur cum materia,* refers to Aristotle, *Metaphysics* 8.6 (1045b7-12).

26.   *Aristotelis Metaphysicorum Libri XIIII cum Averrois Cordvbensis in eosdem Commentariis* . . . (Venice: Juntas, 1562), 225rA-B: "Omnis enim qui ponit quod anima et corpus sunt duo diversa, contingit ei dicere quid sit *causa ligamenti* animae cum corpore. Qui autem dicit, quod anima est perfectio corporis, et quod corpus non existit sine anima, non sunt apud ipsum duo diversa, nec accidet ei quaestio haec."

27.   *In 2 Sent.* 1.2.4 *ad* 3: "Et ideo dicimus quod essentia animae rationalis immediate unitur corpori sicut forma materiae, et figura cerae, ut in II De anima . . . dicitur."

28.   *Philippi Cancelarii Parisiensis Summa de bono* 285-286: "Propter igitur nimiam sui *distantiam* a corpore non posset anima rationalis corpori coniungi, nisi advenirent dispositiones sive adaptationes alique, que essent media coniungendi haec ad invicem. . . . Sunt ergo adaptationes per quas anima rationalis corpori coniungitur habentes *convenientiam* cum utroque, videlicet cum corpore et anima rationali [emphasis added]."

29.   *In 2 Sent.* 1.2.4 *ad* 3: "Sciendum ergo quod
convenientia potest attendi dupliciter: aut secundum
proprietates naturae, et sic anima et corpus multumdis-
tant: aut secundum proportionem potentiae ad actum, et
sic anima et corpus maxime conveniunt. Et ista
convenientia exigitur ad hoc ut aliquid uniatur alteri
immediate ut forma; alias nec accidens subjecto nec
aliqua forma materiae uniretur; cum accidens et
subjectum etiam sint in diversis generibus, et materia
sit potentia, et forma sit actus."

30.   The text of *SCG* 2.71 will be quoted in the
following section.

31.   The reason why Aquinas does not propose
the hypothesis of intermediate *souls* in *SCG* 2.71
appears to be that he has already dealt with this
hypothesis in 2.58. As for the Averroistic phantasm,
which Aquinas treats in 2.59-61, it is an intermediary
between individual human beings and the separate
possible intellect, not between soul and body; and it
therefore is somewhat out of place as a version of the
theory of intermediaries attacked in 2.71. Chapter 71
seems to be the only place in Aquinas' writings where
it is associated with the question of intermediaries.

32.   The fourth *sed contra* of *QDSC* 3 concerns
the very passage of the *Book of Sentences* which had
occasioned Aquinas' text, *In 2 Sent.* 1.2.4 *ad* 3:
"Praeterea.   Magister dicit in I dist. II libri
Sententiarum quod unio animae ad corpus est
exemplum illius beatae unionis quae anima beata coniungitur Deo; set illa coniunctio fit sine medio; ergo et

ista unio." But whereas in *In Sent.* Aquinas seems to
have found Lombard's argument somewhat embarass-
ing because of the support it apparently lent to the objector's emphasis on the "distance" between soul and
body (his reply to objection 3 never addresses the
objector's appeal to Lombard), here, in a surprising development, he finds in Lombard's argument *confirmation* of the opinion that soul and body are immediately
united: just as the union between God and the soul
occurs without intermediary, he now reasons, so too
does the union between soul and body. Might this
rethinking of a passage of Lombard's *Sentences* be
connected with the second *Sentences* commentary
which, as Leonard Boyle has shown ("Setting of the
Summa" 14), Aquinas began during the academic year
1265-1266 and then abandoned in 1266-1267 in order
to begin composition of the *ST?* This in turn might
suggest that *QDSC* 3, which, as we have noted, was
certainly composed after March 1266, originated either
in the latter part of the first of these academic years or
in the early part of the second, that is, sometime in or
around April-December 1266.

33. *SCG* 2.71 continues: ". . . Dispositiones ad
formam praecedunt formam in materia, quamvis sint
posteriores in essendo. Unde et dispositiones corporis
quibus fit proprium perfectibile talis formae, hoc modo
possunt dici mediae inter animam et corpus."

34. *ST* 1.76.6: "Dicendum quod, *si* anima uniretur corpori *solum ut motor,* nihil prohiberet, immo
magis necessarium esset esse aliquas dispositiones
medias inter animam et corpus; potentiam scilicet ex

parte animae, per quam moveret corpus; et aliquam habilitatem ex parte corporis, per quam corpus esset ab anima mobile. . . . Sed *si* anima intellectiva unitur corpori *ut forma* substantialis, sicut iam supra dictum est, impossibile est quod aliqua dispositio accidentalis cadat media inter corpus et animam, vel inter quamcumque formam substantialem et materiam suam."

35. *ST* 1.76.7: "Dicendum quod *si* anima, secundum Platonicos, corpori uniretur *solum ut motor,* conveniens esset dicere quod inter animam hominis vel cuiuscumque animalis, et corpus, aliqua alia corpora media intervenirent; convenit enim motori aliquid distans per media magis propinqua movere--*Si* vero anima unitur corpori *ut forma,* sicut iam dictum est, impossibile est quod uniatur ei aliquo corpore mediante."

36. *ST* 1.76.6: "Et huius ratio est quia, cum materia sit in potentia ad omnes actus ordine quodam, oportet quod id quod est primum simpliciter in actibus, primo in materia intelligatur. Primum autem inter omnes actus est esse. Impossibile est ergo intelligere materiam prius esse calidam vel quantam, quam esse in actu. Esse autem in actu habet per formam substantialem, quae facit esse simpliciter, ut iam dictum est. Unde impossibile est quod quaecumque dispositiones accidentales praeexistant in materia ante formam substantialem; et per consequens neque ante animam."

37. *ST* 1.76.7: "Cuius ratio est, quia sic dicitur aliquid unum, quomodo et ens. Forma autem per seipsum facit rem esse in actu, cum per essentiam suam sit actus; nec dat esse per aliquod medium. Unde unitas rei compositae ex materia et forma est per ipsam formam, quae secundum seipsam unitur materiae ut actus eius. Nec est aliquid aliud uniens nisi agens, quod facit materiam esse in actu, ut dicitur in VIII *Metaph.*"

38. Ibid.: "Unde patet esse falsas opiniones eorum qui posuerunt aliqua corpora esse media inter animam et corpus hominis. Quorum quidam Platonici dixerunt quod anima intellectiva habet corpus incorruptibile sibi naturaliter unitum, a quo nunquam separatur, et eo mediante unitur corpori hominis corruptibili. . . . Quidam vero dixerunt quod unitur corpori mediante luce, quam dicunt esse corpus, et de natura quintae essentiae, ita quod anima vegetabilis unitur corpori mediante luce caeli siderei; anima vero sensibilis, mediante luce caeli crystallini; anima vero intellectualis, mediante luce caeli empyrei. Quod fictitium et derisibile apparet: tum quia lux non est corpus; tum quia quinta essentia non venit materialiter in compositionem corporis mixti, cum sit inalterabilis, sed virtualiter tantum; tum etiam quia anima immediate corpori unitur ut forma materiae."

39. *De anima* 412b6-9: "Unde non oportet quaerere si unum est anima et corpus, sicut neque ceram et figuram neque omnino uniuscuiusque materiam et id cuius est materia. Unum enim et esse cum multipliciter dicatur, quod proprie est, actus est."

40.   *SLA* 2.1.366-377: "Deinde cum dicit: *Unde non oportet quaerere* etc., ex diffinitione data solvit quandam dubitationem. Fuit enim a multis dubitatum quomodo ex anima et corpore fieret unum et quidam ponebant aliqua media esse quibus anima corpori uniretur et quodam modo colligaretur, sed haec dubitatio iam locum non habet, cum ostensum sit quod anima sit forma corporis. Et hoc est quod dicit quod *non oportet quaerere si* ex anima et corpore fit unum, *sicut* nec dubitatur hoc circa *ceram et figuram neque omnino* circa aliquam materiam et formam cuius est materia."

41.   *SLA* 2.1.377-387: "Ostensum est enim in VIII Methaphisice quod forma per se unitur materiae sicut actus eius, et idem est materiam uniri forme quam materiam esse in actu. Et hoc est etiam quod hic dicit quod, cum unum et ens *multipliciter dicatur,* scilicet de ente in potencia et de ente in actu, id *quod proprie est* ens et unum, est actus: nam sicut ens in potencia non est ens simpliciter sed secundum quid; sic enim dicitur aliquid unum sicut et ens."

42.   *SLA* 2.1.387-392: "Et ideo sicut corpus habet esse per animam sicut per formam, ita et unitur animae inmediate *in quantum anima est forma corporis*; *sed in quantum est motor,* nihil prohibet aliquid esse medium, prout una pars mouetur ab anima mediante alia [emphasis added]."

43.   Aquinas' introduction of the question of intermediaries in the midst of his exposition of *De anima* 412b6-9 may owe something to Averroes'

commentary on this passage (*Averrois Cordubensis Commentarium magnum in Aristotelis De anima libros,* ed. F. Stuart Crawford, Corpus Commentariorum Auerrois in Aristotelem . . . Versionum Latinarum 5.6, 1 [Cambridge, MA: Mediaeval Academy of America, 1953], 139.39-45): "And if matter and form were present in the composite as things existent in actuality, then the composite would not be said to be 'one' except in the way in which this term is used in the case of things which are one by contact and *linkage.* In fact, however, because matter in a composite differs from form only in potentiality, and the composite is a being in actuality only through the form, the composite is said to be "one" only because its form is one. ["Et si materia et forma essent in composito existentes in actu, tunc compositum non diceretur unum nisi sicut dicitur in rebus que sunt unum secundum contactum et *ligamentum.* Modo autem, quia materia non differt a forma in composito nisi potentia, et compositum non est ens in actu nisi per formam, tunc compositum non dicitur unum nisi quia sua forma est una [emphasis added]."] This restates the alternative presented by Averroes in his *Metaphysics* commentary (see n. 70 above). For the relation of Aquinas' *De anima* commentary to that of Averroes, see the introduction to the Leonine edition of Aquinas' commentary, 218*-235*.

44. Yvon Lafrance, *Méthode et exégèse en histoire de la philosophie* (Montreal-Paris: Bellarmin-Belles Lettres, 1983), 32: "L'approfondissement de la pensée d'un auteur ancien va toujours, à notre avis, dans le sens d'un

approfondissement de la langue qu'il utilise et du vocabulaire technique qu'il construit."

45. The superior unity and continuity of the *responsio* in *QDA* 9 as compared with the *responsio* in *QDSC* 3 is matched by the corresponding superiority of the *proemium* of Aquinas' commentary on the *De sensu et sensato* as compared with the *proemium* of his commentary on the *Physics*. The *responsio* of *QDA* 9 is characterized by what A. J. Festugière has called, in speaking of the *proemium* of the *De sensu* commentary, "a fixed plan to order everything under a single principle" ("le ferme dessein de tout ordonner sous un principe unique"--"La place du "De anima" dans le système aristotélicien d'après S. Thomas," *Archives d'histoire doctrinale et littéraire du moyen âge* 6 [1931]: 44). For a comparison between the two *proemia* mentioned, see Kevin White, "St. Thomas Aquinas and the Prologue to Peter of Auvergne's *Quaestiones super De sensu et sensato*," *Documenti e Studi sulla Tradizione Filosofica Medievale* 1 (1990): 434-444.

46. "Dicendum quod inter omnia esse est illud quod immediatius et intimius convenit rebus, ut dicitur in Libro de causis." This seems to be a very loose paraphrasing of the statement in *Liber De causis*: "Prima rerum creatarum est esse, et non est ante ipsum creatum aliud" (prop. 4, ed. Bardenhewer, 166.19-20) O. Bardenhewer, ed., *Die pseudo-aristotelische Schrift uber das reine Gute bekannt unter dem Namen Liber de Causis*, Freiburg im Breisgau, 1882. Compare the discussion of Aquinas' use of axioms in general in

M.-D. Chenu, *Introduction a l'Etude de Saint Thomas d'Aquin* (Montreal: Institut d'Études Médiévales; Paris: Librairie Philosophique J. Vrin, 1954) 158-160.

47. "Saint Thomas, Form, and Incorporeity," in *Etre et Savoir. Mélanges offerts au Professeur Jacques Croteau,* ed. Jean-Louis Allard (Ottawa: Presses de l'Université d'Ottowa, 1989) 85.

48. *QDA* 9: "Unde oportet quod, cum materia habeat esse actu per formam, quod forma dans esse materiae ante omnia intelligatur advenire materiae, et immediatius ceteris sibi inesse."

49. *Forma dans esse materie* is a slight modification of the axiomatic formula *forma dat esse materiae*; on the origin of this formula in Avicebron's *Fons Vitae,* see Dewan, 83-84. Variations of the expression *dare esse,* which occurs once in *QDSC* 3 and once in *ST* 1.76.7, show up ten times in *QDA* 9.

50. *QDA* 9: "Est autem hoc proprium formae substantialis quod det materiae esse simpliciter: ipsa enim est per quam res est hoc ipsum quod est. Non autem per formas accidentales habet esse simpliciter, sed esse secundum quid, puta esse magnum vel coloratum vel aliquid tale. Si qua igitur forma est que non det materiae esse simpliciter, sed adveniat materiae iam existenti in actu per aliam formam, non erit forma substantialis."

51. *QDA* 9: "Oportet igitur intelligere quod forma perfectior, secundum quod constituit materiam in

perfectione inferioris gradus, simul cum materia
composita intelligatur ut materiale respectu ulterioris
perfectionis, et sic ulterius procedendo: utpote materia
prima, secundum quod iam constituta est in esse
corporeo, est materia respectu ulterioris perfectionis
que est vita. Et exinde est quod corpus est genus
corporis viventis, et animatum, siue vivens, est
differentia, nam genus sumitur a materia et differentia
a forma. Et sic quodammodo una et eadem forma, secundum quod constituit materiam in actu inferioris
gradus, est media inter materiam et se ipsam, secundum
quod constituit eam in actu superioris gradus."

52. *QDA* 9: "Materia autem, prout intelligitur
constituta in esse substantiali secundum perfectionem
inferioris gradus, per consequens intelligi potest ut
accidentibus subiecta, nam substantia, secundum illum
inferiorem gradum perfectionis, necesse est quod
habeat quaedam accidentia propria, quae necesse est ei
inesse. Sicut ex hoc quod materia constituitur in esse
corporeo per formam, statim consequitur ut sint in ea
dimensiones per quas intelligitur materia divisibilis per
diversas partes, ut sic secundum diversas sui partes
possit esse susceptiva diversarum formarum. Et
ulterius, ex quo materia intelligitur constituta in esse
quodam substantiali, intelligi potest ut susceptiva accidentium quibus disponitur ad ulteriorem perfectionem,
secundum quam materia fit propria ad altiorem
perfectionem suscipiendam. Huiusmodi autem
dispositiones praeintelliguntur formae ut inductae ab
agente in materiam, licet sint quaedam accidentia ita
propria formae quod non nisi ex ipsa forma causentur
in materia. Vnde non praeintelliguntur in materia

forme quasi dispositiones, sed magis forma praeintelligitur eis sicut causa effectui."

53. *QDA* 9: "Sic igitur, cum anima sit forma substantialis quia constituit hominem in determinata specie substantiae, non est aliqua alia forma substantialis media inter animam et materiam primam; sed homo ab ipsa anima rationali perficitur secundum diversos gradus perfectionum, ut scilicet sit corpus, et animatum corpus, et animal rationale. Sed oportet quod materia, secundum quod intelligitur ut recipiens ab ipsa anima rationali perfectiones inferioris gradus, puta quod sit corpus et animatum corpus et animal, intelligitur simul cum dispositionibus convenientibus quod sit materia propria ad animam rationalem secundum quod dat ultimam perfectionem. Sic igitur anima, secundum quod est forma dans esse, non habet aliquid aliud medium inter se et materiam primam."

54. *QDA* 9: "Sed quia eadem forma que dat esse materiae est etiam operationis principium, eo quod unumquodque agit secundum quod est actu, necesse est quod anima, sicut et quaelibet alia forma, sit etiam operationis principium. Sed considerandum est quod secundum gradum formarum in perfectione essendi est etiam gradus earum in virtute operandi, cum operatio sit existentis in actu. Et ideo quanto aliqua forma est maioris perfectionis in dando esse, tanto etiam est maioris virtutis in operando. Unde formae perfectiores habent plures operationes et magis diversas quam formae minus perfecte. Et inde est quod ad diversitatem operationum in rebus minus perfectis sufficit diversitas accidentium; in rebus autem magis perfectis

requiritur ulterius diversitas partium, et tanto magis quanto forma fuerit perfectior. Videmus enim quod igni conveniunt diverse operationes secundum diversa accidentia, ut ferri sursum secundum levitatem, calefacere secundum calorem, et sic de aliis; set tamen quaelibet harum operationum competit igni secundum quamlibet partem eius. In corporibus vero animatis, quae nobiliores formae habent, diversis operationibus deputantur diuerse partes: sicut in plantis alia est operatio radicis, et stipitis et ramorum. Et quanto corpora animata fuerint perfectiora, tanto propter maiorem perfectionem necesse est inveniri maioremdiversitatem in partibus. Unde, cum anima rationalis sit perfectissima formarum materialium, in homine invenitur maxima distinctio partium propter diversas operationes; et anima singulis earum dat esse substantiale secundum illum modum qui competit operationi ipsarum; cuius signum est quod, remota anima, non remanet neque caro neque oculus nisi equivoce."

55. *QDA* 9: "Sed cum oporteat ordinem instrumentorum esse secundum ordinem operationum, diversarum autem operationum quae sunt ab anima una naturaliter praecedit aliam, necessarium est quod una pars corporis moveatur per aliam ad suam operationem. Sic igitur inter animam, secundum quod est motor et principium operationum, et totum corpus cadit aliquid medium, quia mediante aliqua prima parte movet alias partes ad suas operationes: sicut mediante corde mouet alia membra ad vitales operationes. Sed secundum quod dat esse corpori, immediate dat esse substantiale et specificum omnibus partibus corporis."

There appears to be a progressive simplification in Aquinas' accounts of the *media* between soul-as-mover and body from *SCG* 2.71, which mentions three such *media* (powers, spirit, and organs), to *QDSC* 3, which mentions only two (spirit and heart), to the present text, which mentions only the "one first part."

56. *QDA* 9: "Et hec opinio procedit secundum sententiam Aristotilis, qui posuit animam esse formam substantialem corporis."

57. *QDA* 9: "Sed quidam ponentes, secundum opinionem Platonis, animam uniri corpori sicut unam substantiam alii, necesse habuerunt ponere media quibus anima uniretur corpori, quia diverse substantiae et distantes non colligantur nisi sit aliquid quod uniat eas. Et sic posuerunt quidam spiritum et humorem esse medium inter animam et corpus, et quidam lucem, et quidam potentias animae uel aliquid huiusmodi. Set nullum istorum est necessarium si anima est forma corporis, quia unumquodque secundum quod est ens est unum: unde cum forma secundum se ipsam det esse materie, secundum se ipsam unitur materie proprie, et non per aliquod aliud ligamentum."

ESCHATOLOGY

EXPLORING A METAPHOR THEOLOGICALLY: THOMAS AQUINAS ON THE BEATIFIC VISION

Pamela J. Reeve
St. Augustine's Seminary
Toronto School of Theology

My purpose in this essay is to examine some of the main terms and concepts used by Thomas Aquinas in his formulation of the beatific vision. The importance of this doctrine, as the ultimate end not only of human beings but of all created intellects, is indicated in a general way in Thomas' view that the end is the highest aspect of the divine providential plan: "The first principle . . . in the disposition of providence is the end; the second, the form of the agent; the third, the disposition itself of the order of effects."[1] In an important article on the development of the doctrine of the beatific vision in the first half of the thirteenth century, H. F. Dondaine observes that in the articles on our knowledge of God in the first part of Thomas' *Summa,* "the beatific vision . . . assumes the value of a central mystery, which is at once the key to the destiny of the spirit and the basis of morality and the entire supernatural order."[2]

Although Aquinas writes primarily as a theologian, he uses reason and argument to make revealed truth accessible to human understanding while never compromising its essential mystery. In all the writings where he discusses the beatific vision, from Scripture commentaries to disputed questions, Thomas explains the vision primarily as an intellectual act. In conceptualizing it as a mode of "knowing," Thomas goes beyond the language of sense perception and specifically that of seeing, which is frequently used in Scripture. Two representative scriptural passages are "Blessed are the pure in heart, for they shall see God" (Matt 5:8) and "Now we see in a mirror dimly, but then face to face" (1 Cor 13:12).

This visual way of speaking of final beatitude has also passed into the official teaching of the Church. Less than a hundred years after Thomas' death, Benedict XII gave the following statement of the doctrine of the beatific vision in his constitution, *Benedictus Deus* (29 January 1336): The blessed "have seen and do see the divine essence by a vision that is intuitive and even face to face, with no creature functioning as a medium that would itself have the character of an object seen; rather, the divine essence shows itself to [the blessed] immediately--plainly, clearly, and openly . . . ."[3]

While the metaphor of sight has the advantage of conveying the directness and immediacy of the relation of the mind to God in the beatific vision, it is inevitably burdened with the externality and multiplicity that characterize sense perception. In its essential reality, the beatific vision is, and must be, to the highest degree, an interior, unitive act. Although

Thomas does continue to use the locution "to see God,"
his conception of the vision in terms of knowing goes
beyond the language of sensation and brings us closer
to understanding its reality.

1. Scriptural Metaphor

Since the beatific vision is a fulfillment promised
by a personal God in a revelation to a chosen people,
the primary Thomistic texts that need to be examined
are his Scripture commentaries. In his commentary on
1 Cor 13:12 ("Now we see in a mirror dimly, but then
face to face"), Thomas points out that "face to face" is
metaphorical--God, being incorporeal, does not have a
face.[4]   What Paul means here is that we shall no
longer be limited to knowing God (the first cause)
through creatures (God's effects) as in a mirror, but
shall be able to see God as he is. In his reply to an
argument citing this passage in his commentary on the
Sentences of Peter Lombard, Thomas elaborates more
fully the meaning of this metaphor in terms of
knowing. To be seen "face to face" is to be seen
immediately, not by means of something else as a
reflection is seen in a mirror. The noetic structure of
a vision in which knower and known are joined in a
relation of cognitive immediacy requires that the
"essence" of what is known, rather than a mere
likeness, be joined to the intellect. Because the essence
of a sensible, corporeal thing includes materiality, the
thing, in its existing reality, cannot be "seen"
immediately because it cannot be joined to the intellect
as it exists in itself.[5] Since God in his essential reality
is wholly immaterial, it is possible in principle for God
to be joined *immediately* to the human intellect. Such

union is a necessary and constitutive noetic condition for "seeing" God "face to face."

Here Thomas probes beyond the metaphorical language of sight to elaborate the conditions of the possibility of the beatific vision. Complementary to these conditions is the impossibility in principle of seeing God with the bodily eyes. The explicit recognition of this impossibility virtually compels the re-expression of the beatific vision in terms other than those by which it is presented in Scripture. But Thomas is also faced with Augustine's tentative speculation, in the final book of the *De civitate Dei* (22.29), that the eyes of the resurrected body may have some extraordinary new power that allows them to see immaterial things. Thomas has this speculation in mind in his scriptural commentary on the passage in Matthew, "Blessed are the pure in heart, for they shall see God" (Matt 5:8), but it will be more helpful to examine his fuller response to this idea as it is found in the commentary on Peter Lombard's *Sentences*.[6]

The demonstration of the impossibility of a corporeal vision of God is based on an analysis of the senses. Since the senses are united to corporeal organs, they are unable to sense something except by way of a physical impression--witness the axiom, "everything that is received in something, is in it according to the mode of the recipient."[7] The senses are determined by their very sensitivity to certain kinds of objects. Something can affect a sense only insofar as it has a sensible magnitude. Further, the eyes, being sensitive to visual magnitude, perceive color. It is impossible, therefore, that the eyes should perceive something having neither magnitude nor color, unless "sense" is used equivocally (*nisi sensus diceretur aequivoce*).

God cannot, therefore, be seen with the bodily eyes--at least, not as he is in himself.

The last qualification is important, since Thomas, following Augustine, recognizes an accidental mode that occurs after the resurrection and concurrently with the beatific vision, in which the senses may perceive God. In his commentary on Matt 5:8, Thomas uses an example from the *De civitate Dei* to illustrate this accidental perception:

> . . . When I see something living, we may say that I see life, insofar as I see certain indications by which its life is made known to me; this is how it will be in the divine vision, because there will be such a refulgence in the new heaven and the new earth and in our glorified bodies that through them we may be said to see God, as it were, with [our] bodily eyes.[8]

Similarly, Thomas states elsewhere in his *Sentences* commentary, "our intellect . . . will see [God] in creatures corporeally seen."[9] For Thomas, sad to say, these creatures will only be other human beings, since he maintains that there will be no plants or animals in the new heaven and the new earth.[10]

2. Philosophical Theory

In going beyond the language of sense perception in his conception of the beatific vision in terms of intellectual activity, Thomas inevitably draws on the theory of human knowledge that he adopted from Aristotle. A key element in this theory is the intermediary form by which the intellect understands the intelligible species. In an article on human

knowledge in the *Summa theologiae,* Thomas describes
the intelligible species as "the likeness of the thing
understood, which is . . . a form according to which the
intellect understands."[11]   In an earlier question on
knowledge of God in the same work, Thomas incorpo-
rates this element in explaining the noetic structure of
the beatific vision: "When any created intellect sees
God through his essence, the essence of God itself
becomes the intelligible form of the intellect."[12]
Thomas emphasizes (*ST* 1.85.2) that the intelligible
species or form is not, directly, that which is
understood (*id quod intelligitur*), but that by which the
intellect understands (*quo intelligit intellectus*).   In
specifying that it is a likeness (*similitudo*) of the thing
understood, Thomas thereby gives an explanation as to
how the thing understood is in the understanding or
mind of the knower.

The idea of an intelligible species, as that by
which the intellect understands, was developed by
Aristotle partly in response to problems encountered in
the theories of his predecessors. A view proposed by
some of the ancient natural philosophers was that
external things, in being known, were united with the
soul materially. The concise formulation of this view
is that "like is known by like." For the Presocratic
philosopher Empedocles, things existing outside the
mind are known by corresponding elements within the
soul--earth by the earthy element in the soul, fire by
the fiery element, and so on.[13]

Empedocles may have developed his theory in
response to the problem of explaining how the
separation between the knower and the known is
bridged in the act of knowing. Aristotle refined and
developed this early account in his view that the soul

knows through an intelligible rather than a material or elemental likeness. The intelligible species corresponds, in its immateriality, to the nature of the intellect; but in its form, it corresponds to the nature of the thing known. This nature is not, as Plato thought, a separately subsisting idea, but is a form existing in matter. The intelligible species is abstracted from mental images ("phantasms," as Thomas calls them) that ultimately derive from sense perception.

To better distinguish between ordinary human knowledge according to Thomas' epistemology and of the mode of human knowledge in the beatific vision, a few words regarding Thomas' understanding of ordinary human knowledge might be in order at this point. The seminals of universal concepts are innate to the intellect. These seminals are a sign of the divine light implanted by God in the human mind as a part of its created nature. Through its initial sensible experiences, the possible intellect is informed by means of the activity of the agent intellect. The agent intellect acts upon the *species sensibilis*, abstracting from them the *species intelligiblis*, the universalized species, for the possible intellect. The sensible individualized species are temporarily present, while the immaterial universalized species are not restricted by time and space.

The two-fold operation of the agent intellect, abstracting from the *species sensibilis* and informing the possible intellect of the universal, is possible because the agent intellect is the immediate principle which actually makes sensible things intelligible to the potency of the possible intellect. The possible intellect is able to be actualized by the agent intellect (as it abstracts from matter in the phantasms and acts upon the possible intellect) because of the movement of an illuminated power, a power which is connatural to the human condition and is always in act.

Thus, the soul is able to know *via* the possible intellect because the possible intellect is informed by the continual light that is diffused by the agent intellect, a light which does not enlighten the soul directly but which is naturally constituent to humans through the activity of the agent intellect. According to Thomas, the natural illuminative activity of the agent intellect is a sign by God of the continual light in humans necessary for intellectual understanding; it is not a supernatural illumination.

The beatific vision, on the other hand, differs from ordinary modes of human knowledge. Indeed, the beatific vision is beyond anything a human person can ordinarily experience, because in this life humans know God primarily through mediated experiences and modes of knowing, whereas in the beatific vision, humans will know God directly, as he is (*sicut est*). In the beatific vision, knowledge of God is not through a likeness but by his own essence (*per essentiam suam*).

One of the main difficulties that must be addressed in using terms drawn from a theory of natural knowledge is "how" God can be known, if not by an intermediate form or intelligible species derived from sense perception. No created or natural form could so represent God that God would be known directly and immediately as he is in himself through such a form. Thomas' conclusion is that the only intellectual form by which the mind could come to know God as he is in himself is God himself: the noetic demand is for a "real union" between the intellect and what it knows. As Thomas states this in the *Compendium theologiae,*

> In order that God himself [*ipse Deus*] may be
> known through his essence, God himself [*ipse Deus*]
> must become the form of the intellect knowing him,
> and must be joined to [the intellect], not so as to
> constitute a single nature, but as an intelligible
> species [is joined] to one who understands.[14]

In this quotation, the intellectual form referred to
as that by which the mind knows God differs in
meaning from the "form according to which the
intellect understands" in natural knowledge. A likeness
according to which or by which God is known as he is
in himself must be a real likeness "in" the knower and
"of" the knower to the known. In the beatific vision,
this "likeness" by which the knower knows the divine
essence is not an intelligible form abstracted from
images but is a *divinely caused mode of the intellect
itself* by which the rational creature is made "deiform."[15] The advantage of this term over the locution
in the *Compendium,* which states that "God himself
must become the form of the intellect knowing him,"
is that it expresses an "explicitly unitive" modification
in the cognitivity of the knower.

As we noted above, Thomas, maintains that the
person knows by what has come to be known as the
process of abstraction. In the case of our knowledge of
God, the divine nature cannot be received as an
abstracted substance, because of the nature of God as
non-material, but must be received as an accidental
form given by God according to supernatural
illimunation.

Thomas' explanation of the real union of the

intellect with God is especially to be found in the doctrine presented in article 5 of question 12 of the *Prima pars*. There Thomas explains how the beatific vision comes about in terms of natural change. There is, in nature, an order and hierarchy of forms such that a natural thing may receive a new form only if it first undergoes a change in its present condition. The example is given of air receiving the form of fire. Although modern chemistry might not approve of this particular example, we can think of many natural processes where this kind of change occurs. Before wood can receive the form of fire--understanding by this the undergoing of combustion--it must be sufficiently dry. Before water can go through the change of form called "freezing" and become ice, it must be sufficiently cold. Before it can receive the form of vapor or be vaporized, it must be heated to a sufficiently high temperature.

These examples are only relevant to the conception of how the human intellect can acquire a form that is proper to a higher nature, insofar as they do not suggest that the substance undergoing the change goes through such a radical transformation as to become a different kind of thing. An example of this kind of change would be radioactive decay. The decay of uranium involves an actual modification of the atomic structure of the substance such that it becomes in the end a different kind of thing--namely, lead.

Thomas describes the modification produced in the intellect that enables it to see the essence of God as a "supernatural disposition" by which the intellect is "elevated."[16] If this change is to be a true "elevation" rather than an actual change in the nature of the intellect, then human nature must remain intact even while the intellect acquires a divine form. As Thomas states in a later question examining whether natural knowledge and love remain in the beatified angels, "beatitude does not destroy nature, since it is its perfection."[17] He emphasizes that nature maintains its integrity in beatitude, since nature is related to beatitude as first to second, because beatitude is added to nature. But the first must always be preserved in the second. Therefore nature must be preserved in beatitude. And, similarly, the act of nature must be preserved in the act of beatitude.[18] As wood is dried and thereby prepared to receive the form of fire, or be inflamed, and yet is not changed in its essential nature as wood, so the human intellect is prepared to "see" God through an empowerment of the intellect (*augmentum virtutis intellectivae*).[19] This is the substance of the idea that is traditionally described in the language of light as the reception of the "light of glory" (*lumen gloriae*).

A potential difficulty with the metaphor of light is that it tends to suggest something coming between the one who sees and the one seen. Light ordinarily functions as a physical medium for visual perception, enabling the "seer" to see the "thing" seen, while being different from both. If this aspect of the metaphor, which suggests something intermediary, were not explicitly negated, the "light" of glory might be imagined to be a real medium in which God is seen. Thomas addresses the possibility of this misunderstanding in his reply to one of the arguments (*ST* 1.12.5 arg. and *ad* 2.). The second argument assumes that to see God through a medium and through God's essence are mutually exclusive. If this were the case, and if to see God through a created light is to see God through a medium, it would not be possible through such a light to see God through his essence.[20]

The clarification made by Thomas in his reply involves the explicit negation of the sensible implications of the metaphor of light. The light of glory does not function as a likeness "in" which God is seen, but is a certain perfection of the intellect, "strengthening" it to see God.[21] Light is not therefore a "medium" in which God is seen, but rather an "enhancement" of the power of the intellect "by" which God is seen.[22] Understood in the first way, the light of glory would be a third thing interposing itself between "seer" and "seen," removing the immediacy of the contact between the two. Understood in the second way, the immediacy of the union of the intellect with God is preserved, since the only effect of the "light" is to increase the power of the intellect.

The end of revelation is the manifestation of divine truth. Since divine truth is something purely intelligible and spiritual, it might be thought that the presentation of the revealed datum in sensible images would distort or even destroy its content. Thomas addresses this doubt in his reply to an argument in one of the opening articles of the *Summa,* which examines whether metaphor should be used in Scripture.[23] He replies that revealed truth is not so obscured by the sensible figures in which it is presented as to be actually nullified. The truth remains--albeit in an incomplete form, this incompleteness being an inevitable by-product of the materiality in which the revealed content is presented.

Thomas finds the use of metaphor in Scripture to be appropriate for several reasons. But, there is never a suggestion that the mind must remain satisfied with the imperfection of the sensible vehicle in which the truth is expressed. On the contrary, he states in his reply to the above argument that the very imperfection of these sensible images draws the mind to know the truth more fully and perfectly:

> . . . The ray of divine revelation is not destroyed because of the sensible forms in which it is veiled . . . but remains in its truth in such a way that it does not allow the minds to which the revelation is made to dwell on the likenesses but raises them to the knowledge of intelligible truths . . . . Also, this very concealment is useful for exercising the minds of those seeking the truth . . . .[24]

The partial concealment of divine truths in sensible images is, then, "intended" to provoke the learned to probe more deeply into the truths' inner and intelligible meanings. Even now a "hint" of how Thomas is doing precisely this in his conception of the beatific vision.

NOTES

1. *SCG* 3.80 [4] (Leonine ed., Rome: Desclée & C. Herder, 1934): "Primum . . . principium in dispositione providentiae est finis; secundum, forma agentis; tertium, ipsa dispositio ordinis effectuum."

2. H. F. Dondaine, "L'objet et le 'medium' de la vision béatifique chez les théologiens du XIIIe siècle," *Recherches de Théologie ancienne et médiévale* 19 (1952): 60: "La vision béatifique . . . prend la valeur d'un mystère central, qui est à la fois clef de la destinée de l'esprit, base de la morale et de tout l'ordre surnaturel."

3. Henry Denzinger, ed., *Enchiridion Symbolorum: Definitionum et Declarationeum de Rebus Fidei et Morum,* 32d ed. (Freiburg im Breisgau: Herder, 1963), 297 (no. 1000): "Viderunt et vident divinam essentiam visione intuitiva et etiam faciali, nulla mediante creatura in ratione objecti visi se habente, sed divina essentia immediate se nude, clare et aperte eis ostendente . . . ."

4. In R. Cai, ed., *Super epistolas S. Pauli lectura* 1 (Rome-Turin: Marietti, 1953), 387 (no. 802): "Videmus nunc per speculum in aenigmate, tunc autem facie ad faciem." He comments: "Deus, secundum quod Deus, non habet faciem, et ideo hoc, quod dicit, 'facie ad faciem,' metaphorice dicitur."

5. *IV Sent.* 49.2.1 ad 16, in *Commentum in quatuor libros Sententiarum Magistri Petri Lombardi,* vol. 2, *Opera Omnia,* vol. 7 (Parma & New York: Musurgia, 1948), 1201. *IV Sent.* 49.2.1 arg. 16 (*IV Sent.*, 1197) proposes that "God is seen face to face in

heaven, as stated in 1 Cor 13:12. But someone whom
we see face to face is seen through a likeness.
Therefore God will be seen in heaven through a
likeness, and not through his essence [. . . Deus in
patria videtur facie ad faciem, ut dicitur 1 Corinth. 13.
Sed hominem quem videmus faciem ad faciem,
videmus per similitudinem. Ergo Deus in patria
videbitur per similitudinem, et sic non per essentiam]."
In his reply (*IV Sent.* 49.2.1 ad 16--*IV Sent.* 1201),
Thomas points out that "corporeal creatures are not
said to be seen immediately, except when that which in
them can be joined to vision is joined to it: [corporeal
things,] however, cannot be joined [to vision] through
their essence by reason of [their] materiality; and
therefore they are seen immediately when their likeness
is joined to the intellect; but God can be joined to the
intellect through his essence. Hence, he would not be
seen immediately unless his essence were joined to the
intellect; and this immediate vision is called the vision
of his face [. . . Creaturae corporales non dicuntur
immediate videri, nisi quando id quod in eis est
conjungible visui, ei conjungitur: non sunt autem
conjungibiles per essentiam suam ratione materialitatis;
et ideo tunc immediate videntur quando eorum
similitudo intellectui conjungitur; sed Deus per
essentiam conjungibilis est intellectui; unde non
immediate videretur, nisi essentia sua conjungeretur
intellectui; et haec visio immediata dicitur visio
faciei]."

6. In *IV Sent.* 49.2.2, which asks, "Utrum
sancti post resurrectionem Deum corporalibus oculis
videbunt," Thomas discusses Augustine's speculation in
the corpus of the article.

7.　Lombard, *Sentences*: "Omne quod recipitur in aliquo, sit in eo per modum recipientis . . . ."

8.　*Super Evangelium S. Matthaei lectura*, ed. R. Cai, 5th ed. (Rome-Turin: Marietti, 1951), 70 (no. 434): "Cum video vivens, possumus dicere quod video vitam, inquantum video quaedam indicia quibus indicatur mihi vita sua; ita erit in visione divina, quia tanta erit refulgentia in caelo novo, et terra nova, et corporibus glorificatis, quod per ista dicemur videre Deum quasi oculis corporalibus."

9.　*IV Sent.* 49.2.2: "Quamvis enim tunc intellectus noster non videat Deum ex creaturis, tamen videbit eum in creaturis corporaliter visis.　Et hunc modum quo Deus corporaliter possit videri . . . ."

10.　*IV Sent.* 48.2.5; cf. *SCG* 4.97, *De potentia* 5.9, *Compendium theologiae* 2.170.

11.　*ST* 1.85.2: "Similitudo rei intellectae, quae est species intelligibilis, est forma secundum quam intellectus intelligit."

12.　*ST* 1.12.5: "Cum autem aliquis intellectus creatus videt Deum per essentiam, ipsa essentia Dei fit forma intelligibilis intellectus."

13.　In G. S. Kirk, J. E. Raven, and M. Schofield, *The Presocratic Philosophers,* 2d ed. (Cambridge: Cambridge University Press, 1983), 311 (no. 393): "For with earth do we see earth, with water water, with air bright air, with fire consuming fire; with Love do we see Love, Strife with dread Strife."

14. *Compendium theologiae* 105, in R. A. Verardo, ed., *Opuscula theologica* I (Rome-Turin: Marietti, 1954), 52 (no. 211): "Ad hoc quod ipse Deus per essentiam cognoscatur, oportet ipse Deus fiat forma intellectus ipsum cognoscentis, et conjungatur ei non ad unum naturam constituendam, sed sicut species intelligibilis intelligenti."

15. *ST* 1.12.5: "Secundum hoc lumen efficiuntur [societas beatorum] deiformes, idest similes Deo . . . ."

16. *ST* 1.12.5: "Cum . . . aliquis intellectus creatus videt Deum per essentiam, ipsa essentia Dei fit forma intelligibilis intellectus. Unde oportet quod aliqua dispositio supernaturalis ei superaddatur ad hoc quod elevetur in tantam sublimitatem."

17. *ST* 1.62.7 *contra:* "Beatitudo non tollit naturam; cum sit perfectio eius."

18. *ST* 1.62.7: "Natura ad beatitudinem comparatur sicut primum ad secundum; quia beatitudo naturae additur. Semper autem oportet salvari primum in secundo. Unde oportet quod natura salvetur in beatitudine. Et similiter oportet quod in actu beatitudinis salvetur actus naturae." Certain human operations that pertain only to the imperfection of this life are not preserved in beatitude, however.

19. *ST* 1.12.5: "Cum igitur virtus naturalis intellectus creati non sufficiat ad Dei essentiam videndam, . . . oportet quod ex divina gratia superaccrescat ei virtus intelligendi. Et hoc

augmentum virtutis intellectivae illuminationem intellectus vocamus; sicut et ipsum intelligibile vocatur lumen vel lux."

20.   *ST* 1.12.5 arg. 2: "Cum Deus videtur per medium, non videtur per suam essentiam. Sed cum videtur per aliquod lumen creatum, videtur per medium. Ergo non videtur per suam essentiam."

21.   *ST* 1.12.5 *ad* 2: "Lumen istud non requiritur ad videndum Dei essentiam quasi similitudo in qua Deus videatur, sed quasi perfectio quaedam intellectus, confortans ipsum ad videndum Deum."

22.   *ST* 1.12.5 *ad* 2: "Et ideo potest dici quod non est medium in quo Deus videatur, sed sub quo videtur."

23.   *ST* 1.1.9 arg. and *ad* 2.

24.   *ST* 1.1.9 *ad* 2: ". . . Radius divinae revelationis non destruitur propter figuras sensibiles quibus circumvelatur, ut dicit Dionysius, sed remanet in sua veritate; ut mentes quibus fit revelatio, non permittat in similitudinibus permanere, sed elevet eas ad cognitionem intelligibilium . . . . Et ipsa etiam occultatio figuram utilis est ad exercitium studiosorum . . . ."

MAIMONIDES AND AQUINAS ON FAITH, REASON, AND BEATITUDE

William Dunphy
University of Toronto

Introduction

A more complete title would be: "A Comparison of the Views of Rabbi Moses Maimonides and St. Thomas Aquinas on the Roles Played by Religious Faith and Philosophical Reason in the Attainment of Man's Ultimate Perfection, Happiness, or Beatitude." For some historians and interpreters of the thought of either Maimonides or of Aquinas, the very idea of such a comprison would seem pointless at best. One view of Maimonides, at least as represented in his *The Guide for the Perplexed*, portrays the medieval rabbi as cleverly hiding his own rationalistic philosophical views behind a smokescreen of traditional religious orthodoxy. Indeed, since you cannot love what you do not know, and the Torah commands the love of God, the better you know God the more you can love Him. In short, Maimonides is an elitist for whom philosophical proficiency is the *sine qua non* for the complete love of God which is the ultimate happiness for man.

Aquinas, on the other hand, despite all his philosophical and theological erudition, must hold a more populist view since, as a Christian, he would believe that man's ultimate happiness comes only through divine grace bestowed by a loving God on the proverbial "little old woman of faith" as well as on the most learned philosopher.

But how accurate are these characterizations of Maimonides and Aquinas; are they mere caricatures of their actual views? I propose to answer this question by analyzing a coherent block of texts from each thinker. To make this comparison, I propose to analyze a coherent block of texts from each thinker. For Maimonides, this will be the last four chapters, fifty-one to fifty-four, of part three of his *Guide for the Perplexed*. For Aquinas, it will be chapters twenty-five to fifty-eight of book three of his *Summa contra Gentiles*.[1]

Maimonides

Maimondes tells us that he intends chapter fifty-one of part three of the *Guide* to serve as a kind of conclusion to the entire work (*Guide*, 3.51). In it, he seeks to describe a special way of worshiping God, which he identifies with the perfection or goal of human life. He introduces that description by means of a parable about a ruler and his subjects. The subjects are divided into those who reside within the ruler's city and all the rest who are outside it. The latter group comprises all those "who have no doctrinal belief" (*qui non credunt Deum*).

Those within the city are further divided into those who are turned toward the ruler's palace and those who are facing away from it. These latter find themselves in the unfortunate position of actually distancing themselves further from the ruler the more they strive to move. Erroneous views, due either to their own speculation or to their accepting them from others, are the cause of their condition.

Among those turned toward the ruler, some are never able to see his dwelling place. These adhere to the Law but solely by means of observing all of its commandments. There are others who actually arrive at the palace but are forced to circle about its walls because they cannot find the gate through which to enter. These have achieved true beliefs by means of accepting traditional authorities and have carefully studied what these authorities have said about the pre-scribed religious practices, but they have never undertaken personal speculation regarding the very roots of their beliefs. Also circling the walls are those who have not passed beyond logic and the mathematical sciences.

The only subjects to pass through the gate into the antechambers of the palace are those who, having mastered natural science, plunge "into speculation concerning the fundamental principles of religion." The depth of their penetration into the palace is according to the depth of their speculative efforts. It remains, however, to achieve mastery of divine science or metaphysics in order to enter the inner court of the ruler.

The Latin translation of the *Guide* adds an interesting qualifier at this point. Those who have mastered the *spiritualia* are indeed "with the king in the same dwelling, but have not yet actually seen Him." Maimonides speaks of this group as "the men of science" (*sapientes*). These are the philosophers: they have attained the highest level of theoretical--that is, demonstrative--knowledge of their Creator. There are rankings even within this select group.

Finally, at the pinnacle, is the rank of the prophets; they alone reach "the ruler's council." (The Latin translation says of this group that they are "always with the king and see His face.") The prophets also are ranked hierarchically according as their viewing positions range from up close to far away.

A prophet, says Maimonides, is one who, having achieved perfection in the divine science, turns both his thoughts and his actions wholly to God, renouncing everything that is other than God and focusing his entire intellectual effort on examining the whole of creation with a view to discovering in it God's governance. (The Latin has *ad sciendum . . . creatoris essentiam quo est,* "to discover the Creator's very essence by which He exists.") Maimonides calls this life of the prophets a worshiping of God, indeed the supreme form of worship. In the next dozen or so sentences, Maimonides insisted no less than four times that this kind of worship of God can begin "only after" the intellectual apprehension of God has been achieved. Therefore, it might be inferred that for Maimonides philosophical knowledge is a necessary but not a sufficient condition for our attainment of the fullness of human perfection.

We should not be surprised that the rest of chapter fifty-one and the remaining three chapters of the *Guide*, fifty-two through fifty-four, are devoted to an examination of this perfecting sort of worship, with full attention paid to scriptural texts and to what the sages have said in the Talmud. For example, earlier in the *Guide* (3.29), Maimonides had stated that, properly understood, love and fear of God, and nothing else, constitute the fullness and perfection of divine worship. Now, in 3.52 he adds:

> You know to what extent the *Torah* lays stress upon *love: with all thy heart, and with all thy soul, and with all thy might* (Deut 6:5). For these two ends, namely, *love* and *fear*, are achieved through two things: *love* through the opinions taught by the Law, which include the apprehension of His being as He, may He be exalted, is in truth; while *fear* is achieved by means of all actions prescribed by the Law, as we have explained. Understand this summary.

Similarly, in the final chapter of the *Guide*, Maimonides ties together all of the various threads and themes of the entire work with an exposition of a scriptural text, Jeremiah 9:22-23: "Thus saith the Lord: Let not the wise man glory in his wisdom, neither let the mighty man glory in his might; let not the rich man glory in his riches, but let him that glorieth glory in this, that he understandeth and knoweth Me." As background for his exegesis of this key text, Maimonides lists the senses of the Hebrew word for wisdom (*hokhmah*), paying special attention to the wisdoms acquired through the rational and moral virtues. Thus, one who knows the whole of the Law in its true reality is called wise in these two respects. However, as he explains, the rational matter of the Law is received through tradition and is not demonstrated; and therefore we have two species of this one sense of wisdom (that is, the rational apprehension of true realities): a restricted sense, meaning the true opinions received from the Law through the books of the prophets and the sayings of the wisdom writers; and an unrestricted sense, through which the opinions of Torah are demonstrated. The sages of the Talmud are cited to indicate the proper sequence in acquiring perfection. First, learn the true opinions of the Torah as received through tradition; then, learn their demonstrations; finally, learn what actions ought to be done in the order of moral wisdom.

Maimonides goes on to show that philosophers and prophets agree both in their classification of human perfections and in their ranking of them. The perfection of external possessions (e.g., riches) is accorded the lowest rank. The perfection of a harmonious bodily temperament (e.g., strength) comes next in rank, but is still at an animal level. The acquisition of moral virtue, the third species of human perfection, is the highest of the three listed thus far, but it does not have the character of a final end or goal, but rather that of a means to something else--namely, being useful to other people. The fourth and highest species of human perfection for both philosophers and prophets is the knowledge of the divine through the rational virtues. Through this uniquely human perfection, man is man. "Let him that glorieth glory in this, that he understandeth and knoweth Me" (Jeremiah 9:23).

However, Maimonides notes, the text of Jeremiah does not stop here, but continues: "I am the Lord who exercises loving kindness, judgment, and righteousness in the earth. For in these things I delight, saith the Lord." Maimonides has just devoted chapter fifty-three to an interpretation of the meanings of loving kindness (*hesed*), judgment (*mishpat*), and righteousness (*seda-qah*). As applied to God, these terms refer to his actions. He is described as *hasid* because of the utter gratuitousness of creation, as Judge because of occur-rences in the world that result from his judgments grounded in wisdom, and finally, as *saddiq* because of his governance of the living.

Now Maimonides completes his exegesis of this wondrous verse that has "left out nothing of all that we have mentioned and that we have interpreted and led up to at length" (3.54). God is telling us, he concludes, that a man should glory in the apprehension of Himself and in the knowledge *and imitation* of his actions, especially lovingkindness, judgment, and righteousness. In other words, a person should imitate God's actions toward the world. Maimonides concludes the entire work of the *Guide* with this summary of his exegesis of the Jeremiah text:

> It is clear that the perfection of man that may truly be gloried in is the one acquired by him who has achieved, in a measure corresponding to his capacity, apprehension of Him, may He be exalted, and who knows His providence extending over His creatures as manifested in the act of bringing them into being and in their governance as it is. The way of life of such an individual, after he has achieved this apprehension, will always have in view *loving-kindness, righteousness,* and *judgement,* through assimilation to His actions, may He be exalted, just as we have explained several times in this Treatise.

Thomas Aquinas

There are many places in his writings where Aquinas deals with the question of the ultimate fulfillment and perfection of human life. For the sake of convenience, however, I will concentrate on a series of chapters in book three of his *Summa contra Gentiles* where he deals comprehensively with our question.

In this work of Christian apologetics, Aquinas sets out to propound the truths of his Catholic faith. These truths about God are divisible into two classes: those that can be investigated by human reason (e.g., that God exists and is one) and those that surpass its grasp (e.g., that God is triune and incarnate).

Aquinas maintains that it is eminently reasonable that both classes of divine truth be included within divine revelation. If those truths about God that human reason can attain, and indeed already has attained, were not included in revelation, three harmful consequences would ensue: only a few men would get to know these truths, and only after a lifetime of arduous study, and with a knowledge flawed by many errors and doubts. Since God calls all men to salvation and perfect happiness, and not just philosophers, it is most fitting that these truths also be proposed for all men to believe.

To propound to nonbelievers the truths which faith professes and reason investigates, Aquinas tells us that his manner of procedure will be "bringing forward both demonstrative and probable arguments, some of which were drawn from the books of the philosophers and of the saints, through which truth is strengthened and its adversary overcome" (*SCG* 1.9).

Book one of the *SCG* considers what belongs to

God considered in himself; book two concerns the coming forth of all creatures from God; and book three treats the ordering of creatures back to God as their ultimate end. By chapter twenty-five of the third book, Aquinas is ready to argue that the perfection or end of every intellectual substance, which constitutes its happiness or beatitude, is to know God, because the perfection of its proper operation--to know--is reached by attaining the most intelligible object--God, however little that knowledge may be. Subsequent chapters, echoing a long philosophical tradition from Aristotle through Augustine, argue against other contenders as constitutive of human happiness: carnal pleasures, honors, glory, wealth, worldly power, health, beauty, and strength. Even acts of the moral virtues are ruled out because all moral activities can be directed to something else as to a further end, while that activity which constitutes human happiness must be ultimate. In chapter thirty-seven, Aquinas concludes that the fulfillment or perfection of human life, man's ultimate happiness, consists in the contemplation of truth: an intellectual apprehension of God.

We will pay closer attention to the following three chapters, in which Aquinas distinguishes that knowledge of God (a) from the confused and general knowledge of God which is in almost all humans, (b) from the highly specialized knowledge of God obtained by a very few philosophers through demonstration, and (c) from the knowledge of God had by humans of religion through faith.

The arguments against (a) are rather obvious. Such a knowledge is inchoate and confused and, since general in nature, imperfect; these are characteristics incompatible with the perfection associated with happiness.

Aquinas proposes several arguments which prove that (b), demonstrative knowledge of God, is not the same as an intellectual apprehension of God, though demonstrative knowledge "approaches nearer to a proper knowledge of God" than our general and confused knowledge. His first argument is this: by demonstration, we can prove that God exists, is immovable, eternal, incorporeal, utterly simple, one, and the like. However, this knowledge is negative in character. We do indeed know of God how he is distinct from other beings that are moveable, temporal, corporeal, composite, many, and so on; but these demonstrations leave us ignorant of what God is in his very essence. (In a later work, the *Summa theologiae,* Aquinas reflects further on his demonstration that God exists. Through it, he says, we neither know "what" God is, nor what it is for him "to exist.") Second, Aquinas contrasts the Aristotelian position (with which he agrees), that the perfection or end of a species (in this case, beatitude) is attained always or for the most part by individuals belonging to that species, with the fact that very few men ever attain such demonstrative knowledge of God. Third, there is a contrast between the completeness of happiness and the incompleteness of demonstrative knowledge of God, between the absence of error and doubt in perfect knowledge and the admixture of error and uncertainty in the philosophers' knowledge. Fourth, since the ultimate end of all human knowledge is happiness, which is essentially that knowledge of God the possession of which leaves no further knowledge to be desired, and the philosophers' demonstrative knowledge of God is not of this sort, it therefore follows that happiness is not achieved by way of philosophy.

By what way then? Is it perhaps by way of religious faith (c)? Aquinas notes that the knowledge whereby God is known by men through faith "surpasses the knowledge of God through demonstration in this respect, namely, that by faith we know certain things about God which are so sublime that reason cannot reach them by means of demonstration."

Aquinas, however, mounts several arguments to show that "not even in this knowledge of God can man's ultimate happiness consist." They draw upon various elements of an act of faith to make that point. For example, "the intellect assents by faith to things proposed to it, because it so wills, and not through being constrained by the evidence of their truth." Again, the intellect in believing does not grasp the object of its assent and is thus imperfect in its operation *qua* intellect. Furthermore, the knowledge of faith does not set our desire at rest, for we desire to see what we believe. And finally, since faith is of absent and not present things, it cannot be man's ultimate happiness.

It seems, then, that only a knowledge of God going beyond these partial, imperfect kinds of knowledge will suffice to constitute the perfection and fulfillment of that kind of intellectual being that is man. In fact, says Aquinas, "an intellectual substance has yet another knowledge of God." Earlier in the *SCG*, in 2.96 and following, Thomas established that a separate intellectual substance (an angel), by knowing its own essence, knows something of God, its cause-- for "likeness to the cause must be found in its effect." Therefore, he concludes (now in 3.41), any intellect that apprehends a separate substance by knowing its essence would see God in a higher way than he is known by men in general, philosophers, or men of faith. Some philosophers, in fact, including Alexander of Aphrodisias, Avenpace (Ibn Bajja), and Averroes, claim that human intelligence is capable of knowing separate substances in this life and that such knowledge constitutes man's ultimate happiness; but Thomas, after examining these claims, rejects them.

Aquinas displays a sympathetic understanding of the plight of the philosophers in this matter and points to a position which will resolve their difficulties, namely, the position "that man is able to reach perfect happiness 'after' this life, since man has an immortal soul." This perfect happiness, which is "an immediate vision of God . . . promised to us in Holy Scripture," is not, however, in our power to attain, since to see God through his essence is proper only to the divine nature. "The created intellect needs to be raised to so sublime a vision by some kind of outpouring of the divine goodness," in short, by a divine gift or grace, which Aquinas thinks is most appropriately referred to as a "light," the "light of glory."

But can every human being receive this "illumination," and if so, do all see God equally? A look at Aquinas' answers to these questions will enable us to compare him better with Maimonides on the respective roles of philosophy and religion in the attainment of human happiness.

In chapter fifty-seven Aquinas seeks to prove that "there is no created intellect of so low a degree in its nature that it cannot be raised to this vision." Among created intellects, however high or low, he argues, there can be only a finite distance in perfection, while between the entire range of created intellects and the divine intellect the distance in perfection is infinite. (Aquinas uses an interesting example, drawn from the astronomy of his day: because the distance between the eye of the astronomical observer and the center of the earth is as nothing compared with the distance from the observer to, say, the eighth sphere, no appreciable distortion arises from the astronomer taking his observation point as though it were the center of the earth.)

This position, if it entailed that all human beings receiving the "light of glory" saw God equally, would obviously distance Aquinas from the hierarchial position contained in Maimonides' parable of the ruler and his subjects. There are indeed points of difference between the two thinkers, but this is not one of them.

In chapter fifty-eight, Aquinas sets out to prove that is possible for one person to see God more perfectly than another, although both see him in his essence. The reason for this difference lies in their preparation for sharing in that vision; for, Aquinas notes, "some are more virtuous, some less; and virtue is the way to happiness." The virtues Aquinas has in mind here are especially the intellectual virtues of *wisdom, science,* and *understanding.* All other things being equal, the person whose life has been devoted to pursuing a contemplative life will enjoy a qualitatively superior form of beatific vision to another recipient of the "light of glory" with little or no intellectual training. Aquinas concludes that:

> There must be diversity in the divine vision, in that some see the divine substance more perfectly, some less perfectly. Hence, in order to indicate this difference in happiness, our Lord says (John 14:2):

"In my Father's house there are many mansions."

Conclusion

At first glance, as we saw above, there seem to be vast differences separating the views of Maimonides and Aquinas on the respective roles of philosophy and religion in the attainment of human perfection. Maimonides seems elitist, with only those who have mastered the highest philosophical sciences gaining entry to the inner court of the ruler. Those religious persons who faithfully follow the 613 commandments all their lives must cool their heels on the outside. Aquinas, on the other hand, is a populist in that "the light of glory" can be given by God to whomever he chooses, from the wisest of wise men down to the proverbial "peasant-woman of faith."

Some might interpret this difference as showing that Maimonides would assign philosophy a higher role than religion in the perfecting of man, while Aquinas would be, at best, indifferent to the role of philosophy. Let us, however, make several points, so that we do not fall for that simplistic interpretation of a very real difference between our thinkers.

First of all, let us be sure what is meant by the "role of philosophy" in this question. For Aquinas, philosophy was developed by men we call "philosophers," who were, almost without exception, pagans, who lived long ago without the benefit of divine revelation and thus adopted a purely rational methodology. It would be unthinkable to Aquinas (and to most of his Christian contemporaries) that anyone who knew of the Bible would deliberately set it aside in order to pursue a purely rational approach to wisdom. It would be equally unthinkable to Aquinas, however, that anyone who knew the Bible would deliberately renounce reason and the philosophical sciences in the quest for wisdom. In this, Aquinas is following in the centuries-old footsteps of the great Augustine, who saw true philosophy and true religion as one--that is, as a love of wisdom in which faith seeks to understand what it believes.

What for Maimonides was the role of philosophy in the attainment of human perfection? In his *Guide,* at least, Maimonides does not place that philosopher whose life is totally without reference to the Law in as high a rank of perfection as the man of religion who understands the Law by the way of truth through mastery of the philosophical sciences. However, as we have seen in the parable of Maimonides, the religious man who simply accepts the truths of the Law on the authority of others is left out in the cold respecting the ruler's palace, although (and we should not forget this) he is still within the divine city limits. Apparently, then, Maimonides, like Aquinas, does not hold out much hope for achieving human perfection by imitating the great philosophers who were not aware of divine revelation. Look at the "most vicious beliefs concerning the deity" that flow from the great Aristotle's view of providence. Look at the same philosopher's error concerning God's necessary causation of the world, which "destroys the Law in its principle, necessarily gives the lie to every miracle, and reduces to inanity all the hopes and threats that the Law had held out" (*Guide* II c. 25). The man who strives for the fullness of human perfection, then, should not ignore the philosophical sciences, but rather build upon them and use them within the pathway of Torah towards achieving that apprehension of God which is the necessary foundation for that superior form of divine worship sketched out for us in the concluding chapters of *The Guide*.

In short, it makes sense to me to understand Aquinas and Maimonides as kindred spirits in their respect for and acknowledged necessity of the fruits of rational speculation functioning within the ambience of a religious faith for achieving the fullness of human perfection. Therefore, I would use the term "Christian philosophy" for what Aquinas attempts to do and, in the same sense, use the term "Jewish philosophy" for what Maimonides attempts to do in *The Guide*.

NOTES

1.   All quotations from Maimonides are taken from the excellent English translation by S. Pines, *The Guide for the Perplexed* (Chicago: University of Chicago, 1963), as is the present one, pp. 619-619 and following. The parenthetical texts in Latin are from the 1520 edition of a translation from one of the Hebrew translations of the Arabic original. This Latin version, published in Paris by A. Giustiniani, is now available in a facsimile edition by Minerva Press (Frankfurt a. M., 1964). My quotations from the *Summa contra Gentiles* are from the manual edition published by the Leonine Commission at Rome in 1934. The translations are my own.

MORALITY

AQUINAS, ABELARD, AND THE ETHICS OF INTENTION

David M. Gallagher
The Catholic University of America

Introduction

While the label, "ethics of intention," might be susceptible to several interpretations, it does seem to denote a discernable theory of moral action, a theory justifiably attributed to Peter Abelard. We find in Abelard's moral teaching two theses that constitute the core of any ethics of intention: 1) the locus of moral action is not any external deed which an agent performs but only the will's act; 2) the moral goodness and badness found in the will's act are determined solely by the will's "intention" as distinct from the will's ordination to the external act. The Abelardian understanding, however, is not an isolated view in the history of moral thought. The appearance of an almost identical understanding in the philosophy of Immanuel Kant and the persistent attractiveness of that view even in our own day are ample evidence that the ethics of intention represents a perennial philosophical and theological possibility. The reasons for holding such a view are not to be found only in the special circumstances of one era or another; rather, they are to be sought in the phenomenon of moral action itself. Hence any other doctrine of the determination of moral goodness and badness must come to terms with the ethics of intention and the reasons given to justify it.

The goal of this essay is to sketch how the moral thought of Thomas Aquinas differs from an ethics of intention and why it does so. To that end Abelardian teaching is contrasted with the Thomistic teaching on a theme common to both: the relation between "internal" acts such as intention, consent, and choice and the "external" performance of an action or deed. An analysis of this theme in both authors allows us to see how Thomas avoids subscribing to the Abelardian view and how he would respond to the arguments put forth in its favor.

It is not the point here to trace the historical development of this theme from Abelard to Aquinas but rather to concentrate on their respective theories.[1] To compare the two positions, we shall first consider Abelard's distinctions among what he calls will, sin, and deed and outline how he understands their interrelationships. Second, we shall analyze a series of distinctions which Thomas employs in his discussion of the same issues, showing how each of these distinctions allows Thomas either to formulate more precisely Abelard's view or to disagree with Abelard. Finally, we can ask what are the fundamental differences between Abelard and Aquinas which underlie more apparent differences and what are some of Thomas' views which pull him away from an ethics of intention.

In analyzing the position of Abelard, I shall rely

almost exclusively on his *Ethics* or *Scito teipsum*, his only expressly moral treatise and certainly the clearest and fullest statement of his moral teachings.[2] For Aquinas, I shall refer chiefly to his 1-2 (ad 1268-1270) and the disputed questions *De malo* (ad 1266-1267); these texts represent his most mature moral doctrine.[3]

1. Abelard

Abelard devotes the first half of his *Ethics* to explaining the precise nature of sin (*peccatum*). Having done so, he proceeds to discuss its major divisions (grievous and venial), its sources, what kind of repentance removes it from the soul, and finally the efficacy of confessing it. Within the first part of the treatise, Abelard clarifies the nature of sin through a method of distinction: he contrasts sin first with vice (*vitium*), then with will (*voluntas*), and lastly with the external deed (opus, operatio, etc.).[4]

Abelard easily distinguishes between vice and sin. Vice, specifically moral vice, is found in the mind (*animus*), and is that by which we are "made prone to sin." To be prone to sin is not itself sin, and herein lies the fundamental distinction: that by which we are prone to do something is simply different from actually doing it (*Ethics* 2-5).

But what is this sin to which vice makes us prone? For Abelard, to sin is "to consent to what is not fitting so that we either do it or forsake it" (*Ethics*, 4).[5] All sin involves a consent (*consensus*) or, better, is constituted by a consent. Insofar as this consent is a consent to do what one ought not to do, it is a fault (*culpa*) and makes the one who commits it "guilty before God." Guilt before God is an essential or constitutive element of sin; in fact, we could say that a sin is precisely that which makes us guilty. It makes us guilty before God, because at its heart there lies a contempt for God (*contemptus Dei*). We cannot harm God, but we can hold him in contempt, and this we do if we "do by no means on his account what we believe we ought to do for him," or if we do not "forsake for his account what we believe we ought to forsake" (*Ethics*, 6).[6] Here, then, are the essentials of the Abelardian concept of sin: 1) a consent (*consensus*), which is 2) a fault of the soul (*culpa animae*), the evil of which lies in expressing one's 3) contempt of God. This triad--consent, fault, and contempt of God--resurfaces again and again throughout Abelard's Ethics.

Having distinguished sin from vice, Abelard takes up its contrast with will (*voluntas*). What Abelard means by voluntas or will is quite far removed from what Aquinas or even Augustine mean by the term. For Aquinas the will is a power or faculty of the soul, the rational appetite, by which a person inclines toward a rationally perceived good, especially in an act of choice. For Augustine also, while voluntas is not a power of the soul, it is the source or locus of free activity, especially the evil activity which is sin. For both Aquinas and Augustine, will is a principle of free action, action over which an agent has control. For Abelard, in contrast, will or voluntas is any simple desire for a good, especially those desires which well up spontaneously within a person outside that person's control. The desire to preserve one's life, the lust a man experiences for a woman, the desire for eating fruit one finds on a tree; these are paradigmatic instances of Abelardian will. Clearly such desires can be directed both to good and to wicked things, and in neither case is this desire thought to be a sin. Sin only occurs when one consents to an evil desire, which is to say, when one consents to do the evil one has a will to do.

Abelard argues for this point, that will is not sin, in two ways. First he presents examples where there is evil consent without will. A servant who is pursued by his sword-brandishing master finally kills the master in order to preserve his own life. While he consented to kill his master, he never willed or desired the killing. Rather, he kills his master unwillingly (*nolens*). Of course we could point out that the servant is not without any will at all; he has a will to save his life and from this will comes his evil consent. Nevertheless, that will to save his life is in itself good; only the consent is evil, and so, clearly, the sin lies in the consent alone (*Ethics*, 6-11).

Abelard makes this point, secondly, by examining those cases in which a person does experience a will for some evil before consenting to it. Should we not say that here the evil will is sinful, along with the subsequent consent? Abelard rejects this conclusion because a person may successfully resist such desires or wills. Those who do not consent but overcome evil wills (e.g. those who resist adulterous lusts) are guilty of no sin. If fact, such evil wills provide the material for their struggle and their victory. "What great thing," asks Abelard, "do we do for God if we support nothing against our will but rather discharge what we will?" (*Ethics*, 12).[7] Hence, with respect to sin, evil desires or wills are simply a pre-condition which may or may not lead to what is truly sinful, the evil consent. Beyond this consideration is another important point of contrast between will and consent. We do not control our wills or desires. Everyone has the experience of spontaneous desires, especially evil desires, wherein one must struggle not to consent. Consent, in contrast, is always in our control. There is no sin where there is no control; for this reason will is not sinful while consent is (*Ethics*, 24-27). Indeed, Abelard says, God has not commanded us to be without lust or other evil wills--this is impossible for us--but has prohibited only our consent to them (*Ethics*, 14-15).

Sin, as we have now seen, is distinguished by Abelard from the will or desire which precedes it. More importantly for our purposes, however, is how Abelard distinguishes sin from the deed or action which follows the sinful consent. With this latter distinction we enter into the heart of his moral teaching. By "deed" Abelard designates the actual bodily performance of that to which a person consents.

Actually to eat the fruit, to engage in a sexual act, to kill someone, or to give alms to the needy, all are deeds. These and all deeds are not, according to Abelard, sins. Only the consent to do or forbear doing a deed is sin.

It seems incontrovertible that there is a real distinction between the consent and the performance of the deed. Even Aquinas, as we shall see, admits as much. But why should Abelard maintain that the sin in no way lies in the deed? A first reason is that the sin occurs in the soul while the deed occurs in the body. Not only are the body and the soul distinct, but nothing from the body alone is able to cause sin in the soul. Abelard is utterly clear on this point:

> Now we have mentioned this [that pleasure is not sinful] lest anyone, wishing perhaps every carnal

pleasure to be sin, should say that sin itself is increased by action when one carries the consent given by the mind into the commission of an act and is polluted not only by shameful consent but also by the blemishes of an action--as if an exterior and corporeal act could contaminate the soul. The doing of deeds has no bearing on an increase of sin, and nothing pollutes the soul except what is of the soul, that is, the consent which alone we have called sin, not the will which precedes it nor the doing of the deed which follows (Ethics, 22-25).[8]

A second reason is the fact that the same deed may be done with or without sin. Just as an evil will or desire is not itself sinful because it may exist without sinful consent, so too any deed, even those which usually follow from sinful consent, may be done without sin. A woman may be forced to lie with another woman's husband, while a man may be tricked into mistaking another man's wife for his own. In another example, a judge may mistakenly put the wrong man to death. Clearly such persons do not commit sins, and hence there must be nothing intrinsically sinful about these deeds, for it there were, they could never be performed without sin (Ethics, 24-25).

A third reason is to be found in the Gospel admonition that whoever looks on a woman with lust is guilty of adultery (Matt. 5:28). As we have seen, lust alone is not a sin, and so Abelard has to interpret these words "looking on a woman" to refer to "whoever shall look in such a way as to fall into consent to lust" (Matt. 5:28). So interpreted, the implication is immediate: there can be sin without an external deed. If a man should, after consenting to such lust, go on to perform the deed, the sin would have already existed before the deed and so could not be located in the deed.

While Abelard supports his position with arguments such as these, he recognizes others which might tend to undermine it. Ever the dialectician, he takes them up at some length. One argument is that sin is increased by the pleasure experienced in the act, implying that act contributes something to the sin. Here Abelard simply [points out that this view could be true only if pleasure itself were sinful. Yet many pleasures are licit and what is more, they have been attached to the acts by God himself. It does not seem that God would command us to perform actions to which he had attached sinful pleasure; pleasure then must not be sinful and so the objection fails (*Ethics*, 16-23).

A second objection comes from the various commands and prohibitions which seem, at least prima facie, to apply to deeds. Consider prohibitions such as "Thou shalt not kill," "Thou shalt not commit adultery," "Thou shalt not steal"; these are exterior actions, and, being prohibited, seem to be sins. To counter this argument, Abelard returns again to his high ground. We know that these deeds can be performed without sin. Thus, he concludes, we must interpret all such commands and prohibitions to refer to the "consent" to the deed. We are prohibited only from consenting. In fact, as Abelard argues, if it were possible to commit all the acts without consent there would be no sin, and if one could consent without doing the acts, he would be guilty of all the sins (*Ethics*, 24-27).

A third objection is more difficult, requiring a

much longer reply and forcing Abelard to develop his key notion of intention. The objection arises from the practice, both civil and ecclesiastical, of punishing crimes. Both civil judges and confessors seem to impose a larger punishment or penance on those who actually perform a sinful deed than on those who only consent to it without carrying it out. This would imply that sin is found both in the consent and in the deed, since it would be greater if the deed were performed.

Abelard responds that all these punishments are meted out by men and that men can judge only outer actions. The severity of the punishment is measured by the "practicalities of government" for the purpose of preventing public injuries. This is why, for example, fornication, a more serious sin, receives a lesser penalty than burning down a house. Only God can truly judge sins, because only God can see the soul and see the intention with which a person acts. God looks not at what is done (*quae fiunt*) but to the mind with which it is done (*quo animo fiant*), that is to say, God is the judge of intentions (*Ethics*, 42-49, especially 44).[9]

The notion of intention is obviously closely related to that of consent, since a consent will be sinful or not according to one's intention. We might describe their relation by saying that the intention is the content of the consent. When a person consents, he consents to something; there is, we might say, some proposal to which he gives his consent. A particular consent is the consent according to what is consented to, and it is precisely this that Abelard calls intentino. Thus the judge who unwittingly puts an innocent man to death, never intended to kill an innocent man. This was not his proposal, and he did not consent to this. For this reason he is guilty of no sin. Clearly then, the sinfulness of any act of consent lies in the intention with which it is made. If a proposal includes opposition to God's will, then by consenting to it one shows contempt for God, and this is to act with a sinful intention.

Implied in Abelard's absolute opposition between divine and human judgments is a cleavage between the intention and the deed. God's judgment of sin is based solely on intention and not on the deed, and this can only mean that the intention is independent of the deed. Abelard gives an example of two men, who, out of devotion, intend to build poor houses. One actually builds the house, while the other cannot because his money is stolen. God will judge both equally; for how, Abelard asks, should one's worthiness of soul depend on money (*Ethics*, 48-49)? A person, he adds, can even do the same thing at different times with different intentions, so that one time it is a sin and another time it is not (*Ethics*, 52-53). Consequently, God judges by looking at the intention alone apart from the deed. Just as consent is independent of the deed, so too is the intention which informs the consent.

What does this doctrine mean for the moral worth of the deed? There are two immediate consequences, and Abelard is quick to draw them out. First, no deed is, itself, either morally good or bad, but simply indifferent:

> Works in fact, which . . . are common to the damned and the elected alike, are all indifferent in themselves and should be called good or bad only on account of the intention of the agent, not, that is, because it is good or bad for them to be done but because they are done well or badly, that is, by the intention by which it is or

is not fitting that they should be done (*Ethics*, 44-47).[10]

Second, because the deed itself is neither good nor bad, we cannot distinguish between the goodness of the intention and the goodness of the deed, as if the two together were greater than the goodness of the intention alone. If there is any goodness in the deed, that goodness can only come from the fact that the deed is being done with a good intention. For this reason the actual performance of the deed yields no additional goodness or evil; a person is neither better nor worse for having actually carried out what he or she intended.[11]

Let us now summarize the most important points of Abelard's doctrine. (1) Will, consent, and deed are distinct entities, and independent of one another. (2) Moral goodness or evil, i.e., sin is located in the consent alone. (3) The deed is morally indifferent. (4) Any goodness found in the deed comes to it from the consent (or the intention). (5) The performance of the deed adds no goodness or badness to that found in the intention.

2. Aquinas

In order to see how Thomas Aquinas both agrees and disagrees with the Abelardian positions described above, we must grasp several distinctions which he employs in his analysis of moral action and its goodness and badness. Here we will introduce five such distinctions and show how each one contributes to Thomas' solution to the problems raised by Abelard.

(a) The Interior Act vs. the Exterior Act

According to Thomas, for an act to be a moral act, the kind of act we are discussing, it must be what he calls a human act. A human act is an act which a person does in a properly human way. What is proper to human activity is that it arises from reason and will. Whatever we do knowingly or willingly, or what amount to the same, whatever we do that is in our control is a moral act. It is possible for a person to "do" things without willing them, such as reflex responses to sudden noises, distracted movements like a man scratching his beard (Thomas' example), sleepwalking, or even simply blinking. These actions are done in a mode proper to animals, outside the control of the one doing them (*ST* 1-2.1.1 *contra* and *ad* 3; *De malo* q. 2 a. 5 *contra*).

The main point here is that an act is a properly human or moral act only if one will to do it. Thus, in a normal human act we can distinguish two things: the act of the will and the action which is willed. For example, if a person chooses to eat, we can distinguish the choice itself from the actual eating. This distinction between the act of the will (including intention, consent, choice, use) and the act which the will commands is precisely Thomas' distinction between the interior act of the will and the exterior act. Obviously this corresponds to Abelard's distinction between consent and deed, although it is more technical and precise. Strictly speaking, the interior act is the act of the will; the exterior act is any act which arises from powers of the soul other than the will at the will's command. In contrast to Abelard, Thomas understands the will (*voluntas*), as a power of the soul, specifically that power by which actions are in the control of an agent. The exterior act includes bodily acts, but also acts of thinking, memory, imagination, etc., acts arising from powers other than the will at the will's command.[12]

We should note that while we distinguish interior and exterior acts, they are actually only two aspects or two faces on a single human act. Like Abelard, Thomas distinguishes them; unlike Abelard, he does not separate them or treat them as independent entities. Nevertheless, he will say that certain moral qualities belong to the complete human act by virtue of the interior act while others belong to it by virtue of the exterior act.[13] Let us, then, express Abelard's chief points in Thomistic terms: (1) The interior and exterior acts are distinct and independent; (2) moral goodness or evil, i.e., sin, is located in the interior act alone; (3) the exterior act is morally indifferent; (4) any goodness found in the exterior act comes to it from the interior act; (5) the performance of the exterior act adds no goodness or badness to that found in the interior act.

(b) The Exterior Act in Its Natural Species vs. the Exterior Act in Its Moral Species

The second of Thomas' distinctions applies to the exterior act, the act which we carry out at the will's command. This distinction is really two ways of viewing the exterior act; viewing it one way we have the act in its natural species, while viewing it another way we take the act in its moral species. To take an exterior act in its natural species is to consider the act without reference to the interior act of the will from which it comes. To take one of Abelard's examples, simply as an external performance, there is no difference between the action of a state executioner who hangs a criminal to carry out a sentence and a man who hangs the criminal out of revenge (*Ethics* 28-29). Each carries out the same bodily motions and we could say equally of both that they hanged a man. Both acts, in their natural species, are hangings. Nevertheless, if we look at these two actions, and consider them as willed acts, that is, in their moral species, then they are very different. Insofar as they come from the will, one action is the execution of a sentence, that is, an act of justice, while the other is a murder, an act of revenge. Neither man has willed simply to hang another man; one has chosen to carry out a sentence (materially a hanging), and one has chosen to murder (also materially a hanging).[14]

Hence, when we describe an exterior act, we can usually do so in two ways, both of which are true. If one day on the street we see two men and are asked what they are doing, we can say simply that one is handing the other some money. But we can also say that the man is paying back his debt, or giving alms, or giving a bribe. The difference lies in whether or not our description makes reference to the act of the will, the choice, by which the man's act is done. If we do not include this reference to the will, we are left with the act's natural species, a non-moral description: handing over money. Such a description, however, is only partial; it is an abstraction that leaves out something which belongs to the very being of the act as a human act: the fact that it is a willed act. The description of the exterior act in its moral species, in contrast, is the full description, because it describes the exterior act precisely as a human act. The man is not willing simply to hand over money; he is will to pay his debt, give alms or give a bribe. As willed by him, the act falls into one of these categories, and, as we shall see, these categories or species of actions have a moral valuation attached to them.

When we bring this second distinction to bear upon Abelard's discussion, we can make an immediate observation. In his chief examples for demonstrating that the deed is independent of the intention, Abelard does not describe the deed, the exterior act, in its moral species but rather in its natural species. Let us turn to these examples. In the case of the man who hangs a convict to serve justice as opposed to the other who hangs him out of revenge, it is clear that these acts are the same only in their natural species. Only by restricting our description of the deed to the physical performance do we have identity. If we take the deeds as they are actually willed, we have two very different acts. In another example, a woman is forced to lie with another woman's husband and so is said to have committed the same deed as an adulteress. Here again, we might say that physically her deed is like that of one who chooses adultery, but as willed it is in no way the same. In fact, in this example, there may be no moral species at all, since the woman may not even will the deed. If we ask what she does, in a properly human way, the answer is nothing at all. From the moral point of view her "deed" has nothing in it of adultery. Finally, there are several examples in which a person is ignorant of what he does: a judge erroneously killing an innocent man, a man tricked into thinking another woman is his wife and having sexual relations with her, a man in ignorance marrying his own sister. The judge's deed is then equated with a murderer's, the tricked husband's with that of an adulterer, and the ignorant brother's with that of an incestuous man.

It is true, in all these cases, that the action performed is, under a certain description, the same as that of one who truly wills such deeds. But in all cases, the act has not been willed as a sinful deed. In willing to do what they do, these agents have not willed murder, adultery, or incest, and so, properly speaking, we cannot call their acts, their exterior acts, by these names. The effect of ignorance is precisely to break the normal link between the interior and exterior acts, whereby one wills the exterior act one in fact does. Ignorance, we could say, drives a wedge between them, such that the exterior act performed is not the same as what the agent willed. Abelard capitalizes precisely on this gap to make it seem that, even in normal cases, the two are independent. Since the exterior action of the ignorant, non-sinning agent in its natural species is the same as the exterior act of a sinner in its natural species, Abelard concludes that in neither case is there sin in the exterior act. Because he takes the deed to be the exterior act primarily as it falls into a natural species, it seems to be wholly independent of the interior act and morally insignificant.

(c) The Exterior Act as Good, Bad, or Indifferent in Species

We may grant that Abelard has overlooked the distinction between the moral and natural species, and consequently, the fact that we can truly describe the exterior act or deed only by reference to the interior act from which it flows. Nevertheless, to recognize this fact only seems to confirm another of Abelard's positions, namely, that the moral goodness or badness of the exterior act depends completely on the interior act or, as he states it, upon the intention. If the exterior act has a moral species only insofar as it is willed, does it not seem that all its moral characteristics, including its moral goodness or badness, must come to it from the will? Should we not conclude that the moral goodness of the exterior act is simply an extension of that of the interior act?

Thomas does not take this position. To see why, we must introduce a third distinction, once again a distinction within the exterior act. If we take the exterior act in its moral species, that is, as that which we are choosing to do when we make a choice, this act is, in itself, even before we choose it, morally good, bad, or indifferent. How is this so? On both the natural level and the supernatural level an act is good if it tends toward human fulfillment (*beatitudo/felicitas*), bad if it is destructive of human fulfillment, and indifferent if in itself it neither promotes nor harms that fulfillment. For example, an act of almsgiving is good in itself because, as the gift of material support to a person in need, it is directly ordered to that person's fulfillment, even if only at the level of physical needs. Acts of justice are good insofar as they promote the social harmony required for human fulfillment; acts of religion such as prayer or worship are good insofar as these acts constitute part of human fulfillment, that is, one's proper relationship to the divine. In contrast, acts of injustice destroy social harmony; adultery is destructive of the material union and all the goods it provides; gluttony is destructive of bodily health and distracts a person from more fulfilling activities.[15]

If we say, then, that acts are good, bad, or indifferent, this will have an effect on the will which is directed to these acts. For Thomas we can will or choose something only if we know what we are choosing, and included in our rational grasp of an action is its moral goodness or its moral evil. Recognizing more or less clearly that a proposed act will promote or detract from our human fulfillment, we see that act as morally good or morally bad. Thus, a man does not choose simply to hand over money; he chooses to give alms and chooses it as morally good, or he chooses to give a bribe and chooses it as morally bad. Because the will is directed to the exterior act as good or as evil, the will's own act (choice) becomes thereby good or evil. Almsgiving is good and to will it is a good act of the will; likewise, bribery is bad and to will bribery is a bad act of the will. Hence, the will itself becomes good or bad because it chooses an exterior act which, in itself, is good or bad. In Thomas' technical terms, the interior act of the will receives a specification as good or bad from its object, that is, from the exterior act.[16]

Thomas appeals here to a basic principle: activities are specified by their objects. Just as an act of memory is the particular act it is because it is the act of remembering this incident, and an act of seeing is the act it is because it is directed to this visible object, so too the will's act is the act it is according to the object at which it aims. Hence, as we have said, if the will aims at a bad exterior act, that act of the will becomes thereby a bad act; if it aims at a good act it becomes, to that extent, good. The goodness or

badness of the will's choice is itself derivative from
that of the exterior act, not of course the exterior act as
actually performed, but the exterior act as it is grasped
by reason.[17]

For Aquinas, then, we have the following position:
the exterior act is what it is in its moral species
according to the sort of will with which it is carried
out, but that will itself is what it is because it is
directed to that exterior act. We might express it by
saying that while the will causes the exterior act
actually to exist as a moral act, it does not make the
exterior act to have the goodness or evil it has. Rather,
the exterior act, being the kind of act it is, has its own
intrinsic goodness or evil which the will acquires in
actually willing such an act. In technical terms, the
exterior act exercises formal causality on the interior
act, while the interior act exercises efficient causality
on the exterior act.[18]

We might note here that according to this doctrine,
in contrast to Abelard's, what happens in the body does
effect what happens in the soul. It is not that the will
can be moved, in a efficient way, by what occurs in the
body; this would destroy the free character of its act.
But, the will's act is *specified* by its object, and to the
extent that that act is bodily (e.g., adultery) we can say
that the body does, in a real way, have an effect in the
soul.

(d) The Intrinsic Goodness of the Exterior Act vs. the Goodness of the Exterior Act Deriving from Its Order to an End

The doctrine just described presents a full-scale
reversal of Abelard's view. Moral goodness and evil

are first in the exterior act, at least insofar as the act is
grasped by reason and presented to the will. But we
do not yet have the full story as Thomas tells it. He,
too, along with Abelard, recognizes that the exterior
can and often does receive a goodness or badness
which exists first in the interior act of the will. To see
how this is so, we must grasp the fourth of Thomas'
distinctions. Unlike the previous two distinctions, this
one is found within the interior act.

There are two objects to which the will's act is
directed. The first of these, as we have just seen, is
the exterior act which is chosen: almsgiving, murder,
adultery, repaying a debt, etc. Second, there is the end
or goal for which that act is chosen. Thus, a person
may give alms because he or she wants to help the
poor, that is, out of charity. Another person may do so
only for the sake of maintaining a certain reputation
among his fellows, that is, out of vainglory. In other
words, the same exterior act even in its moral species
can be chosen for different ends. Thus, Thomas
distinguishes between the willing of the end (intention
in his sense of the term) and the willing of the object
(choice). While distinct, these are not separate. It is
impossible to choose an act without also intending
some end, and likewise to intend an end is to will as
the goal of what is being chosen.[19]

Both intending the end and choosing the exterior
act (the means to the end) are parts of the interior act
of the will. They stand in different relationships,
however, to the exterior act, the act of intention being
somewhat more independent of the exterior act for its
goodness or badness. As we have just seen, the will is
specified by the exterior act. Now we are able to say
more precisely that the will's choice is specified by the

exterior act. The act of intention, in contrast, is specified by its own object, which is not the exterior act, but rather that end or good for which the agent chooses that act. The determination of the goal can depend on the agent's will alone. For example, a man chooses to give alms out of vainglory. While doing so, he recognizes that this is not a good motive or end, and thus, he rectifies his intention and now gives the alms out of charity. The exterior act is the same in this case, both in its natural species and in its moral species: all along, what the man chooses, to give alms, is the same. That the chosen act should be directed to this end and not another is determined by the will of the agent.[20] This particular point is especially important with respect to the ultimate end, that goal to which a person directs all his or her acts. Whether that goal is God or self--Thomas says these are the two ultimate possibilities--is determined by each person's will (*ST* 1-2.77.4). Hence, the intention of the end does not depend on the exterior act for its specification the way choice does.

Nevertheless, the interior act does have an effect on the exterior act. According to Thomas, the exterior act has *two* sources of goodness or badness. In addition to this intrinsic goodness or badness, it also receives a moral determination from the intention of the end. The exterior act shares in the goodness of evil of the end for which the person chooses it: if chosen for a good end, the exterior act shares in that goodness; if chosen for a bad end, it will share in that badness. Thus, an exterior act may have a two-fold goodness: if someone gives alms for love of God, the act is good because of its kind *and* because of the end the agent intends in choosing it (*ST* 1-2.20.1 *contra*). An act may have a double evil: Thomas uses Aristotle's example of a man who commits adultery in order to steal. Finally, an act may be mixed: a person chooses a good act for a bad end (almsgiving for vainglory) or a bad act for a good end (stealing to give alms). In the mixed cases, he argues, the act as a whole is evil; if any one aspect of the act is evil, the complete act is evil. This is the doctrine of *ex integra causa*: an act is good if all its significant elements are good, and bad if any one of them is bad.[21]

It is in this last position, the doctrine of *ex integra causa*, that Thomas is, we might say, most Abelardian. There are, he allows, certain cases where the goodness or badness of the exterior act depends solely upon the interior act of the will. In the first place, there are those exterior acts which in their moral species are indifferent. They do not, in and of themselves, bespeak any ordination or disordination to human fulfillment. Thomas' example is simply picking up straw. These indifferent acts, however, receive a moral determination from the end for which they are chosen. If chosen for a good end, they are good. If for a bad end they are bad. As we have said, the goodness or badness of the intention is a matter of the interior act alone, and so, in these cases, the goodness or badness of the exterior act is wholly derivative from that of the interior act (*ST* 1-2.20.2 *contra*; *De malo* q. 2 a. 3 *contra*).

In the second place, there are those exterior acts which are in themselves good but are done for a bad end. Here the exterior act is rendered bad because of the intention for which it is chosen. Although almsgiving in its kind is good, insofar as it is chosen by this person for this bad end, it is not good, but evil.

Again, the moral determination of the exterior act comes wholly from the interior act (*ST* 1.-2.20.2 *contra*).

In these two sorts of actions, Abelard's emphasis on the interior act is, for Thomas, justified. Here he can say, along with Abelard, that the goodness or badness of the exterior act is derived solely from the intention with which it is done. These, of course, are only a portion of all the moral acts committed and consequently Thomas parts company with Abelard.

(e) Willing in the Order of Intention vs. Willing in the Order of Execution

Let us turn to a final point of comparison between Abelard and Aquinas. According to Abelard, the deed does not add any further goodness to the goodness already found in the intention. A person who both intends and performs a deed is no better than a person who intends to do something but is somehow prevented--even if only for lack of occasion--from actually performing the deed. We have seen an example of this in the two men who intend to build poorhouses. The intention of him whose money is stolen is no less good because he never built the poorhouse.

Thomas in a way agrees with Abelard, but in another way, he does not. His explanation, however, requires a fifth distinction. This is the distinction, within the will's act, between the order of intention and the order of execution. The use of "intention" here is rather confusing, since it is not identical either with Abelard's use of the term or with Aquinas' use of it to refer to those acts of the will by which a person tends toward some good as something he wants. I may want to steal, and so I decide that I need to commit adultery to do so. I may even make the choice to commit the adultery and the stealing. These are true acts of willing, but they alone do not accomplish the adultery or the stealing. In addition, I have to will actually to move myself to the actions; in this case, I have to will the bodily motions necessary to achieve the adultery that I want and that I have chosen. This willing of the actual carrying out of the action is said to be in the order of execution. We might speak of the order of intentions as the order of wanting and the order of execution as the order of attaining what is wanted (*ST* 1-2.16.4 *contra*).

Aquinas says that the will, in the order of intention, is complete or perfect when one chooses an act (*ST* 1-2.16.4 *contra*). Before the choice, one only thinks about some goal and what action one might take to achieve it, having, we might say, a general sort of desire for it. In choosing it, however, a person commits himself to that action; we can say that he *now* wants it in the fullest sense, in the sense that he is now determined actually to carry out the action. While the choice is not the act, it is not a true choice unless it is such that the person will carry out the act if circumstances permit (*ST* 1-2.20.4 *contra*).

The will in the order of execution (*usus*), on the other hand, is complete or perfect only when the exterior action is complete.[22] Only when I have committed the adultery and the stealing is my willing complete in the order of execution. If for some reason, even exterior circumstances outside my control, I am unable to accomplish what I chose to do, my willing, in the order of execution is imperfect. The reason is that motion or tendency is complete or perfect if it achieves its term or goal. If the tendency or motion of the will, in the order of execution, is to carry out the exterior act, that tendency or motion will not be perfect unless the action is achieved.

If we speak of the order of intention, then Aquinas agrees with Abelard: the will in that order is completed in the act of choice, whether or not the exterior act occurs. If a person chooses a good act for a good end, that choice is good; so too, if a person chooses a bad act or even a good act for a bad end, that choice is bad, whether or not the exterior act occurs. In this sense the man who builds the poorhouse has no better an act of will than the one who is prevented from doing so. Nevertheless, if we speak of the order of execution, it is clear that the will of the one who actually carries out the exterior act is better than the will of him who is unable to do so. The willing of the first, having attained its goal, is complete or perfect, while the second is not. This, of course, is not the fault of the second man and he is not to be blamed for the failure. Nevertheless, the fact remains that in the order of execution, the will of the first man is perfected while that of the second is not. Hence, we can say that the performance of the exterior act does make even the interior act of the will better.[23] We might note that for Thomas the order of intention is far more important in terms of the moral worth of one's actions. It remains true, nonetheless, that for him an action which is carried out contains more goodness than one that is not. Thus, it is right, not only in the eyes of man, but of God also, that one who actually performs a sinful deed should receive a greater punishment than one who willed to do so but was prevented (ST 1-2.20.4).

Conclusion

Let us now summarize the contrast between the Abelardian and Thomistic positions. (1) Thomas distinguishes the interior and exterior acts, but unlike Abelard does not separate them, but rather treats them as a unity, dependent upon each other in various ways for their moral qualifications. (2) While for Abelard moral goodness and badness are found only in consent, for Thomas they are located in both the interior and exterior acts. We should recognize, however, that the most important of these is in the interior act insofar as ordination to the end is most determinative of moral goodness, and this is derived primarily from the will. (3) For Abelard the exterior act is indifferent. For Thomas the exterior act is always indifferent if taken in its natural species. In its moral species, however, it may be good or bad. As good or bad, it is an originative source of goodness or badness for the interior act of the will. (4) For Abelard any goodness or badness in the exterior act comes to it form the interior act. For Aquinas, on the other hand, only some of its goodness or badness comes to it from the interior act. As we have seen, in its moral species, the exterior act has a goodness or badness of its own. (5) For Thomas, in contrast to Abelard, the performance of the exterior act adds to the goodness of the whole human act insofar as it is the perfection of the will's act in the order of execution.

Within this contrast we can see the arguments by which one might be led to adopt an ethics of intention and how Thomas responds to them. In the first place, one can point to the fact that acts or deeds considered to be morally bad are in fact the same as some actions we take to one good or at least indifferent. Such is the example of the two hangings. To answer, Thomas can invoke his distinction between the natural and the moral species of the moral act. The two acts are the same only when considered in their natural species. But the natural species is an abstraction from precisely that aspect of human action that renders it moral action: the fact that it is willed. The full description of the exterior act or deed includes reference to the will, particularly to the choice which gives rise to the act. So understood, acts which seemed to be identical no longer are so.

In the second place, one can point to the common recognition that a person who attempts a morally good act but fails in the execution for reasons outside his or her control is morally better for having made the attempt and still worthy of praise. The opposite is true for morally bad acts. Thus, it seems that the external performance is "detachable" from the act of willing and that, consequently, moral goodness and badness must arise in the will's act separately from the external act. Thomas' distinction between the order of intention and the order of execution and his distinction between acts which are good, bad, and indifferent in kind allow him to form a reply. The morally most significant act of the will, choice (which corresponds to Abelard's consent), falls within the order of intention. That is, it does not directly command other powers to their acts; such acts of the will, especially *usus*, fall into the order of execution. The act of choice, then, is complete prior to the execution, and this explains why there can be moral goodness and badness even when circumstances prevent the execution. Nevertheless, even in the order of intention, the exterior act plays a decisive role, that of specifying the will's act of choice. Although the exterior act may not have real existence--for that execution is required--it does have an existence in the thinking of the agent, and this allows the will's act, even in the order of intention, to be directed to it.[24] Even when the exterior act is prevented, it can determine the goodness of the will's act of choice. Here the distinction of exterior acts into good, bad, or indifferent becomes crucial. This goodness, badness, or indifference of the act is grasped by reason and is an essential aspect of the object at which the will aims when choice occurs. Thus, while the will can acquire a moral determination independently of the actual execution of the exterior act, it cannot do so independently of the exterior act altogether. Thomas, then, would point to Abelard's failure to distinguish the two orders of willing and how the exterior act is found in each of them to explain why he came to his mistaken position.

In conclusion we might point to three philosophical positions with their rather obvious theological ramifications that Thomas holds, which underlie his understanding of the relation between the interior and exterior acts and which tend to pull him away from an ethics of intention like that of Abelard or Kant. In the first place, Thomas' understanding of the relationship between body and soul is unlike Abelard's; whereas Abelard considers the body and soul as different from one another, Thomas always maintains that they constitute a single thing, united as matter to form. Thus, while it may be possible to point to bodily aspects of an action and distinguish them form spiritual aspects, the two aspects are in fact united in a single human act. Mirroring the body-soul unity, the exterior and interior acts are related as matter and form (*ST* 1-1.17.4 *contra*; *De malo* q. 2 a. 2 *ad* 5). We see this unity especially when we consider that the exterior act in its moral species--taken as a human act--cannot be adequately described solely in bodily terms. Likewise the interior act is formally specified by the exterior act. The human act as a whole, including the interior act is complete and perfect only in the exterior performance.

In the second place, in Thomas' understanding of nature and its place in the moral life, the moral life consists in the perfection of nature, the achievement of the end proper to human nature. Moral goodness is found primarily in the will, but not only in the will. What is more, the will's moral goodness lies in its ordination to what fulfills the whole nature, not simply the will itself. Since human nature is complex and includes several different compositions such as that of body and soul, its fulfillment will be correspondingly complex. Within this fulfillment the spiritual excellences like that of the will are clearly paramount, yet nevertheless, fulfillment lies in more than the will, and includes even the good state of the body. As a consequence, the moral life does not have as its ultimate goal simply the good state of the will. It is not enough that the will be conformed to law (Kant) or even to the will of God (Abelard). The law itself is only a means by which the rational agent can direct itself freely to its end, and the will of God with respect to the creature is precisely that it attain its end.[25]

In the third place, Thomas denies not merely that human fulfillment lies only in an act of the will, but even that it lies principly in such an act. Rather, human fulfillment is found principally or essentially in an act of the intellect, the contemplation of God. This means that human perfection, while including the interior act of the will, lies principally in an exterior act. The will's moral rectitude, in fact, lies precisely in its proper ordering to this act of contemplation, and the whole moral life lies in the attainment of this activity and all the conditions it requires. In this context one is likely neither to see the moral goodness of the will's act as independent of the exterior act, nor to discount the exterior act as morally insignificant. Rather, one sees the will's act as a necessary condition for a higher act, the act of contemplating the divine essence in which human fulfillment lies.[26]

NOTES

1.   For some discussion of Abelard's theory of moral action see R. Blomme, *La doctrine du péché dans les écoles théologiques de la première moitié du XIIe siècle* (Louvain: Publications Universitaires; Gembloux: Éditions J. Duculot, 1958).   For the development from Abelard to Aquinas, see O. Lottin, *Psychologie et morale aux XIIe et XIIIe siècles,* 6 vol. (Louvain: Abbaye du Mont Cear; Gembloux: J. Duculot, 1942-1960), especially "Le problème de la moralité intrinsèque, d'Abélard à Saint Thomas D'Aquin" (2.421-468) and "L'intention morale de Pierre Abélard à Thomas d'Aquin" (4.307-486).   See also D. Luscombe, *The School of Peter Abelard: The Influence of Abelard's Thought in the Early Scholastic Period* (Cambridge: Cambridge University, 1969).   Two works which compare Abelard and Aquinas and to which I am indebted are T. Belmans, *Le sens objectif de l'agir humain: Pour relire la morale conjugale de Saint Thomas* (Vatican City: Libreria Editrice Vaticana, 1980), and R. Sokolowski, *Moral Action* (Bloomington, Indiana: Indiana University, 1985), especially appendix C, "Intentions and the Will: Aquinas and Abelard."

2.   All quotations and citations from the *Ethics* are from D. E. Luscombe, ed., *Peter Abelard's 'Ethics'* (Oxford: Clarendon, 1971).

3.   All quotations and citations from Aquinas' works are from the Leonine editions of *ST* 1-2 (vols. 6-7) and of *De malo* (vol. 23).

4.   Other terms used by Abelard for the external deed are *actus, actio, actio operis, operum executio, operatio peccati,* and *peccatum perficere.* For the identity of their meanings, see Blomme, *La doctrine du péché* 198 n. 1.

5.   "Vitium itaque est quo ad peccandum proni efficimur, hoc est, inclinamur ad consentiendum ei quod non conuenit, ut illud scilicet faciamus aut dimittamus."

6.   "Peccatum itaque nostrum contemptus creatoris est, et peccare est creatorem contempnere, hoc est, id nequaquam facere propter ipsum quod credimus propter ipsum a nobis esse faciendum, vel non dimittere propter ipsum quod credimus esse dimittendum."

7.   "Quid enim magnum pro Deo facimus si nichil nostrae voluntati aduersum toleramus, sed magis quod uolumus implemus?" Haec autem ad hoc induximus, ne quis volens forte omnem carnis delectationem esse peccatum, diceret operationis, ut non solummodo consensu turpitudinis, verum etiam maculis contaminaretur actionis, tamquam si animam contaminare posset quod exterius in corpore fieret. Nichil ergo ad augmentum peccati pertinet qualiscumque operum executio, et nichil animam nisi quod ipsius est coinquinat, hoc est consensus quem solummodo peccatum esse diximus, non voluntatem eum predentem vel acitonem operis subsequentem. Cf. ibid., 40: "Cum enim omnia peccata sin animae tantum, non carnis . . . ."

8.   Abelard, *Ethics.*

9. Abelard, *Ethics*: "Solum quippe animum in remuneratione boni vel mali, non effecta operum, Deus adtendit, ne quid de culpa vel do bona voluntate nostra proveniat pensat, sed ipsum animum in proposito suae intentionis, non in effectu exterioris operis, diiudicat."

10. Abelard, *Ethics*, 44-47: "Opera quippe quae, ut prediximus, eque reprobis ut electis communia sunt, omnia in se indifferentia sunt nec nisi pro intentione agentis bona vel mala dicenda sunt, non videlicet quia bonum vel malum sit ea fieri, sed quia bene vel male fiunt, hoc est, ea intentione qua convenit fieri, aut minime."

11. Abelard, *Ethics*, 46-53.

12. *ST* 1-2.18.1 *contra*: "Aliqui actus dicuntur humani, inquantum sunt voluntarii, sicut supra dictum est. In actu autem voluntario invenitur duplex actus, scilicet actus interior voluntatis et actus exterior . . . ." *ST* 1-2.6.4 *contra*: ". . . Duplex est actus voluntatis: unus quidem qui est eius immediate, velut ab ipsa elictus, scilicet velle; alius autem est actus voluntatis a voluntate imperaturs, et mediante alia potentia exercitus, ut ambulare et loqui, qui a voluntate imperantur mediante potentia motiva." See also 1-2.1.1. *ad* 2, 1-2.6.3 *contra*, 1-2.74.2 *contra*; *De malo* q. 2 a. 1 *contra*. I am here considering as essentially equivalent the distinction made between interior and exterior acts and taht made between voluntary acts elicited from the will itself and voluntary acts commanded by the will. See, e.g., *De malo* q. 2 a. 2 *ad* 1: "Voluntate producitur non solum actus interior quem voluntas elicit, set etiam actus exterior quem

voluntas imperat . . . ." On this point see S. Pinckaers, *Les actes humains* (Paris: Desclée, 1966) 184-86.

13. On the unity of the interior and exterior act, see *ST* 1-2.17.4 *contra* and 1-2.20.3 *ad* 1. Thomas discusses the goodness and badness of the interior act in q. 19 and of the exterior act in q. 20. This latter question especially treats the interrelationships of the two within a single moral act.

14. For the distinction between the natural and moral species, see *ST* 1-2.1.3 *ad* 3, 1-2.17.4 *contra*, 1-2.18.7 *ad* 1, 1-2.18.8 *ad* 3, 1-2.19.1 *ad* 3, 1.2.19.7 *ad*1, 1-2.20.3 *ad* 1, 1-2.20.6 *contra*. Especially illustrative is 1-2.18.5 *ad* 3, where Thomas answers an objection which argues that adultery and the conjugal act cannot be different in species because they can have the same effect: "Ad tertium dicendum quod actus coniugalis et adulterium, secundum quod comparantur ad rationem, differunt specie, et habent effectus specie differentes; quia unum eorum meretur laudem et praemium, aliud viturperium et poenam. Sed secundum quod comparantur ad potentiam generativam, non differunt specie. Et sic habent unum effectum secundum speciem."

15. For the doctrine of acts which are good, bad, and indifferent in kind, see *ST* 1-2.18.5-9, 1-2.20.1-3, and *De malo* q. 2 a. 4, especially *ad* 5: "Actus autem moralis, sicut dictum est, recipit speciem ab obiecto secundum quod comparatur ad rationem. Et ideo dicitur communiter quod actus quidam sunt boni vel mali ex genere, et quod actus bonus ex genere est actus

cadens supra debitam materiam, sicut pascere esurientem, actus autem malus ex genere est qui cadit supra indebitam materiam, sicut subtrahere aliena: materia enim actus dicitur obiectum ipsius.''

16. See *ST* 1-2.9.1 and 1-2.18.5 for the role of reason in the specification of acts. Also see 1-2.19.1 *ad* 3: ''Bonum per rationem repraesentatur voluntati ut obiectum; et inquantum cadit sub ordine rationis, pertinet ad genus moris, et causat bonitatem moralem in actu voluntatis. Ratio enim principium est humanorum et moralium actuum, ...'' One should also consider *De malo* q. 2 a. 3 *contra*: ''Si igitur consideretur actus secundum se malus, puta furtum vel homicidium, prout est in apprehensione secundum suam rationem, sic primordialiter in ipso inuenitur ratio mali, quia non est uestitus debitis circumstantiis; et ex hoc ipso quod est actus malus, id est priuatus debito modo, specie et ordine, habet rationem peccati: sic enim in se consideratus comparatur ad voluntatem ut obiectum prout est volitus. Sicut autem actus sunt preuii potentiis, ita et obiecta actibus; unde primordialiter inuenitur ratio mali et peccati in actu exterior sic considerato quam in actu voluntatis . . . .'' See also *De malo* q. 2 a. 3 *ad* 3 and *ad* 8.

17. *ST* 1-2.20.1 *contra*: ''Bonitas autem vel malitia quam habet actus exterior secundum se, propter debitam materioam et debitas circumstantias, non derivatur a voluntate, sed magis a ratione. Unde si consideretur bonitas exterioris actus secundum quod est in ordinatione et apprehensione rationis, prior est quam bonitas actus voluntatis: sed si consideretur secundum quod est in executione operis, sequitur bonitatem

voluntatis quae est principium eius." Some representative texts reflecting the general doctrine that the moral quality of the will comes to it from its object are *ST* 1-2.18.2 and 5, 1-2.19.1-2 and 5, 102.20.1 *ad* 1, and 1-2.20.2 *contra*.

18. An illustrative text is *ST* 1-2.20.1 *ad* 1: "Ad primum ergo dicendum quod actus exterior est obiectum voluntatis, inquantum proponitur voluntati a ratione ut quoddam bonum apprehensum et ordinatum per rationem: et sic est prius quam bonum actus voluntatis. Inquantum vero consistit in executione operis, est effectus voluntatis, et sequitur voluntatem."

19. Thomas treats the will's *intentio* for the end in *ST* 1-2.12 and the *electio* of the means in 1-2.13. For the unity of the two acts, see 1-2.8.3 and 1-2.12.4.

20. *ST* 1-2.20.2 *contra*: "In actu exterior potest considerari duplex bonitas vel malitia: una secundum debitam materiam et circumstantias; alia secundum ordinem ad finem. Et illa quidem quae est secundum ordinem ad finem, tota dependet ex voluntate. Illa autem quae est ex debita materia vel circumstantiis, dependet ex ratione: et ex hac dependet bonitas voluntatis, secundum quod in ipsam fertur."

21. *ST* 1-2.18.4 *ad* 3: "Non tamen est actio bona simpliciter, nisi omnes bonitates concurrant: quia *quilibet singularis defectus causat malum, bonum autem causatur ex integra causa*, ut Dionysius dicit, 4 cap. *De div. nom*. . . . ." See also 1-2.19.6 *ad* 1, 1-2.19.7 *ad* 3, 1-2.19.20.2 *contra*; *De malo* q. 2 a. 4 *ad* 2."

22. For use (*usus*) as the act of the will executing what is chosen, see *ST* 1-2.16.

23. *ST* 1-2.20.4: "Si autem loquamur de bonitate actus exterioris quam habet secundum materiam et debitas circumstantias, sic comparatur ad voluntatem ut terminus et finis. Et hoc modo addit ad bonitatem vel malitiam voluntatis: quia omnis inclinatio vel motus perficitur in hoc quod consequitur finem, vel attingit terminum." Cf. *De malo* 1. 2 a. 2 *ad* 8.

24. *De malo* q. 2 a. 3 *contra*: "Ideo autem diximus per prius esse malum in actu exterior quam in voluntate, si actus exteiror in apprehensione consideretur, e conuerso autem si consideretur in exequtione operis, quia actus exterior comparatur ad actum voluntatis ut obiectum quod habet rationem finis; finis autem est posterior in esse, set prior in intentione."

25. E.g., *ST* 1-2.90.2 *contra*: "Lex pertinet ad id quod est principium humanorum actuum, ex eo quod est regula et mensura . . . . Primum autem principium in operativiis, quorum est ratio practica, est finis ultimus. Est autem ultimus finis humanae vitae felicitas vel beatitudo, ut supra habitum est. Unde oportet quod lex maxime respeciat ordinem qui est in beatitudinem." Also see *SCG* 3.122: "Non enim Deus a nobis offenditur nisi ex eo quod contra nostrum bonum agimus . . . ."

26. An earlier, shorter version of this paper, entitled "Will and Deed in Abelard and Aquinas," was

presented at the Ninth International Congress of Medieval Philosophy at Ottawa, August 1992.